Shaun Rein

The War for
China's Wallet

Profiting from the New World Order

ISBN 978-1-5015-1594-1
e-ISBN (PDF) 978-1-5015-0761-8
e-ISBN (EPUB) 978-1-5015-0751-9

Library of Congress Cataloging-in-Publication Data
A CIP catalog record for this book has been applied for at the Library of Congress.

Bibliographic information published by the Deutsche Nationalbibliothek
The Deutsche Nationalbibliothek lists this publication in the Deutsche Nationalbibliografie;
detailed bibliographic data are available on the Internet at http://dnb.dnb.de.

© 2018 Shaun Rein
Published by Walter de Gruyter Inc., Boston/Berlin
Printing and binding: CPI book GmbH, Leck
♾ Printed on acid-free paper
Printed in Germany

www.degruyter.com

Shaun Rein
The War for China's Wallet

Advance Praise

The world faces no bigger geopolitical challenge than the brewing fight between China and the US. But how China deals with the rest of the world—countries and companies alike—is just as important, if not more important, than how it deals with the US directly. *The War for China's Wallet* is essential reading from one of our top rising China talents.

−Ian Bremmer,
Founder, Eurasia Group,
Author, *Us vs Them: The Failure of Globalism*

Drawing upon more than 15 years of experience as a successful businessman in Shanghai, Shaun Rein's new book offers an insider's perspective on China's sophisticated use of economic carrots and sticks for political purposes. *The War for China's Wallet* has much to say about PRC grand strategy as well as its effects on the lives of ordinary people. This is a deeply informative and yet delightfully readable account, sure to interest China specialists and the general public alike.

−Elizabeth Perry,
Henry Rosovsky Professor of Government,
Harvard University

The War for China's Wallet is the third book by the astute China observer Shaun Rein dealing with China's rapidly growing economy. In this work, he uses both analysis and his extensive personal experiences to explain how China is using its economic power to shape its relations with the rest of the world. The focus is on how Chinese is using foreign economic policies, ranging from trade restrictions and boycotts to the "one belt one road" world infrastructure development effort, to further its broader international objectives. The book is a lively read on an important subject that typically gets only brief passing treatment by both the press and the scholarly community.

−Dwight H. Perkins,
Professor of Economics, Emeritus,
Harvard University

I've always been impressed by Shaun Rein's speeches, which are insightful, well-argued, eloquently delivered and right to the point. This book bears the same characteristics as his speech.

China's mixture of a market economy with strong state regulatory power has challenged both the international order and economic disciplines. A good understanding of China's statecraft and how it punishes and rewards certain nations and companies, will certainly help the business world to gain an advantage in the fight for China's fat wallet. And Shaun, with his rare insight and his rich experience in the Chinese market and economy, is just the right person to offer such advice.

–Zhang Lijia,
Social Commentator,
Author of *Socialism is Great!* and *Lotus*

Tom Tom,

From buying lights to building them, may your future be bright and happy. I am so proud of how you follow your own path and beat your own drum.

Love,
Baba

Acknowledgments

Writing a book is never an easy endeavor. Many people over the years have given me help, support, and advice. Thank you to all who have mentored me and pushed me to my limits.

To my colleagues at the China Market Research Group (CMR), thank you for helping to build the culture that makes CMR such a fantastic place to work—I am so proud of what we have been able to accomplish since we started in 2005. I would particularly like to thank my colleague Ben Cavender who shouldered more responsibility on client projects while I was off researching and writing this book.

I also need to thank Claire Adair. Claire is an undergraduate student at Princeton University and was a summer associate consultant with my firm. More than anyone, she gave invaluable feedback on the book. She has a very bright future indeed, and I look forward to watching her career develop.

I would also like to thank Nick Wallwork. He was publisher for Asia for John Wiley when I wrote two books with them—*The End of Cheap China* and *The End of Copycat China*. When he moved to De Gruyter, I followed him along and am thankful and appreciative of the decade-long partnership we have had. I would also like to thank Jeffrey Pepper, who has been a fabulous and innovative editor at De Gruyter, Mary Sudul and Jaya Dalal for their edits, and the rest of the contributors there.

Thank you to all the people I interviewed for this book. Some names had to be changed/kept anonymous for the sensitivity of living in and dealing with China. Nothing material was changed.

I would like to thank my wife, Jessica, for dealing over the years with the ups and downs of being married to an author and entrepreneur who constantly and perhaps restlessly scans the world for new opportunities. Last, I would like to thank my son, Tom, directly. I am very proud of what he has become. He follows his own path and passions and pushes me to become a better person. What a lucky father I am!

About the Author

Shaun Rein is the Founder and Managing Director of the China Market Research Group (CMR), the world's leading strategic market intelligence firm focused on China. He works with Boards of Directors, CEOs, and senior executives of Fortune 500 and leading Chinese companies, private equity firms, SMEs, and long/hedge funds to develop their China growth and investment strategies.

Rein authored the international best-sellers *The End of Cheap China* and *The End of Copycat China*. *Publishers Weekly* named *Cheap* a top 10 business book for 2012. The *Financial Times* called *Copycat* "Intriguing."

Rein is regularly featured in the *Wall Street Journal*, *The New York Times*, and *The Financial Times*. He frequently appears on CNN, BBC, CNBC, Bloomberg, PBS, and MSNBC. Rein formerly taught executive education classes for London Business School. He received a master's degree from Harvard University, a BA with Honors from McGill University, and sits on the Asia Council for St. Paul's School.

Contents

Introduction

Shanghai, China, March 2017

The message coming into my inbox was somewhat ominous—"Can you help me? We are suffering!"

The note came from an old South Korean friend and former client, JJ. Having left the business world for politics, JJ was now an advisor to one of South Korea's leading presidential candidates. Facing national elections in just a few weeks, he frantically looked for a way to restore Sino-South Korean relations—critical for South Korea's economy. Earlier that month, South Korea had installed Terminal High Altitude Area Defense (THAAD), an anti-ballistic missile defense system developed by the Americans. China was not happy.

In the face of China's wrath, JJ wanted help in dealing with THAAD and its ramifications.

Ostensibly intended as a shield against North Korea, THAAD would enable Seoul to shoot down any short, medium and intermediate range ballistic missiles that North Korea decided to launch towards the south. Yet China took umbrage at THAAD's deployment. Enraged at the deployment, Beijing let its ire be known, both through traditional diplomatic channels, shrill op-eds, and editorials in state-owned media outlets like *Global Times* and the *People's Daily* that called for "expanding [China's] nuclear arsenal" (*Global Times*) or even offering a "military response." (*People's Daily*)

China's biggest weapon in the dispute was its state "wallet". The government instituted crippling economic punishments in the hope that South Korea would halt THAAD's deployment. As the Chinese government blocked K-Pop and South Korean movie stars from touring China, Chinese consumers redoubled the nation's efforts, boycotting Korean brands. Chinese tourists visiting South Korea dropped 40 percent year on year in March, decimating the nation's retail sector. To JJ's dismay, China's economic punishments were only just beginning.

I asked JJ what I could do to help. I thought he would ask me to brief his candidate on China's political situation. Perhaps even ask my firm that I founded in 2005, The China Market Research Group (CMR) to develop a marketing campaign to restore South Korean brands in the eyes of Chinese consumers.

JJ's immediate response took me by complete surprise. He requested that I arrange a backroom meeting between Chinese President Xi Jinping and his South Korean presidential candidate. The economic pain launched by China had cut to

DOI 10.1515/9781501507618-201

the bone of Korean society. He and his candidate were desperate to alleviate tension and restore Sino-South Korean ties. "Please," he messaged.

Intrigued to see if I could play a bridge role between the two countries to reduce tension, I contacted connections in Beijing to see whether a meeting between President Xi and JJ's South Korean presidential candidate could be arranged. The response took 24 hours, but was firm: no meetings with South Korea until THAAD was halted. No wiggle room whatsoever. China's economic punishment was not about to let up.

The Wallet as a Winning Strategy

Upon its emergence as an economic superpower, China has created and refined a new form of statecraft. Using its hefty state wallet to both punish and reward, China is able to politically maneuver countries with economic manipulation. Applying carrots to those who comply with China's political demands, and sticks to those who don't, China has increasingly relied on its financial ability to bend both countries and now companies to its shifting political will. Those who cross China politically—as South Korea did in its deployment of THAAD—will soon experience a barrage of economic losses, bolstered by government blocks and regulations, Chinese state-owned media attacks and boycotting Chinese consumers. Yet as we will see in Chapters 1 and 2, China is also generous to those who stay on Beijing's good side. Nations adhering to China's political demands and underlying motivations, as well as politically well-connected companies specifically, are lavishly compensated. Doling out long-term low interest loans and infrastructural aid, China keeps its friends close and rewards erstwhile enemies who decide to gravitate toward the eastern superpower.

Economic statecraft is a concept familiar to many. But China's sophisticated use of carrots and sticks to influence political outcomes is unprecedented on the world stage. Historically, Western countries have used a variety of tools—including economic sanctions and blockades—to punish conventional enemies. Similarly, generous economic rewards—as were witnessed under the U.S. Marshall Plan or Japan's low interest loans starting in the 1960s to Southeast Asian countries—have attracted nations reliant on Western aid. But China's coordination of carrots and sticks diverges from the West's in two critical ways.

In addition to the force of China's wallet—combining regulatory power, media and the compliance of a billion consumers, China does not discriminate between 'allies' and 'enemies.' It may economically cripple nations one day with an economic hammer, lathering them with profits and flattery the next. Depending on who obstructs and who enables China's political objectives, anyone could get a carrot and anyone a stick.

For those accustomed to the Western convention of alliances and enmity, China's indiscriminate use of economic statecraft may seem reckless, or merely baffling. Wouldn't China be throwing a wedge in diplomatic efforts every time it punished an ally, dismantling any foundation of trust? How would it go about enticing enemies to submit to its political will, even with decadent rewards?

Such questions require a deeper understanding of China's relationships abroad.

China's Hot, Medium and Cold Partners

To inform an appreciation of China's global worldview, I have developed the following framework that allows the mapping of different countries as they relate to China—both in terms of their dealings with China at the state level and with regard to how they are perceived by Chinese consumers. This framework is relevant from about 2007 onward, the period in which China became viewed by other nations as a rival with the U.S. for economic superpower status. Within the framework's classification, there are three primary categories in which countries have positioned themselves—these I have defined *Hot Partner*, *Warm Partner* and *Cold Partner*. None of these are distinctly broken down as ally or enemy. It is essential to note that China does not have true allies nor does it really have true enemies by definitions of American realist and neorealist schools of thought. In lieu of these more rigid camps, China seeks to maximize gains in each relationship as long as countries avoid threatening its notion of sovereignty and the one-China principle.

There exists much grey area when dealing with China, but countries that orbit near Category 1 *Hot Partner* have benefitted vastly from such close ties, reaping gains often unnoticed by outside observers. New Zealand, for example, falls comfortably into this category, occupying a special niche of China's affection as one of the first western nations to open up diplomatic relations and recognize the legitimacy of China's Community Party. Also, the first western nation to open a free trade zone with China in April 2008, New Zealand profits from China's economic loyalty, largely in exchange for its own perceived loyalty to the government. However, *Hot Partners* aside from New Zealand tend to be poorer nations like Pakistan, Cambodia, Laos, or Ethiopia that Chinese consumers do not trust for quality control, showing little excitement for their brands and do not particularly want to visit as tourists aside from a few exceptions like Cambodia. In these cases, most economic ties are forged by the government and driven by state-owned enterprises rather than by everyday consumers. Countries in this category also run the risk of losing independence because so much of their economies are based on political ties to China.

The second category, *Warm Partner* is where most of the political volatility takes place. Unsurprisingly, countries falling into this category are most likely to experience China's carrot and stick approach. Given the higher volatility of markets in this category, *Warm Partner* countries have the greatest appeal for hedge funds as it is much more possible to bet against prevailing wisdom that *Warn Partner* countries will remain close to or fall against China. With this in mind, companies operating in these nations must constantly be on the lookout for political changes, supplementing efforts with special, long-term attempts to show they are friends of China. If they fail to establish a sufficient reputation of loyalty, they run the risk of being singled out for protest if their home countries do something to cross China's interests, as we shall see in Chapter 2 with the effects on South Korean brands Lotte, KIA and Orion. Countries that fall into this category do benefit from China's economic rise, but also have been able to stake out relatively independent political positions unlike *Hot Partner* countries.

The third category *Cold Partner* countries still have trade with China, but relations tend not to be warm. Wary of a rising China, many countries in this category share close ties with America and/or Taiwan. Needless to say, *Cold Partner* countries like Mexico and India are not looked upon favorably either by the Chinese state or China's numerous consumers, and as a result are losing out on Chinese FDI, tourist dollars and the opportunity to sell into China. Some *Cold Partner* countries like Japan do have much trade with China and have products loved by Chinese but the amount of trade would be higher if there were better political relations.

1. *Hot Partner*: Countries in this category such as Cambodia, Laos, Ethiopia, Pakistan, Greece, Hungary, Venezuela, Iran, and New Zealand have benefited the most from close relations with China. New Zealand surprises many with its closeness to China, but it has largely maintained such close ties so as to counter-balance Australian power, adopting a Waltzian neorealist form of decision-making.

2. *Warm Partner*: countries in this category, such as Thailand, United Kingdom, Germany, Australia, Indonesia, and France waffle over the decision to remain fully neutral or to pick a side—be it Chinese or American. These nations tend to profit from Chinese consumers' view of their brands as exotic, reaping gain from Chinese tourism as well. Warm Partner countries are also strategically positioned to play off both China and America, seeking favors alternately from each camp.

3. *Cold Partner*: Taking strong positions against China, these countries have not benefited from China's rise, at least not directly or as much as they could if they had forged closer ties with China. Nations in this category include the Philippines, Vietnam, Mexico, Belize, Burkina Faso, Nicaragua and India. India's case is particular as it is neither exceedingly close to China nor does it have strong ties to the United States, meaning it receives less state support and investment from both camps. Yet given its sheer size of over 1 billion people, it is able to independently garner the attention of global business.

In assessing one's approach to China, one must take stock of countries shifting between categories. Particularly in recent years, countries have altered their dealings with China, requiring policy-makers and businesses alike to evaluate the implications of these shifts. For example, the United Kingdom—under Prime Minister Theresa May and her predecessor David Cameron—has moved up to the second category of *Warm Partner* now benefiting from London's position as a clearinghouse for RMB transactions. The same can be said of Canada, which moved from *Cold Partner* under Prime Minister Stephen Harper (2006–2015), to *Warm Partner* under Prime Minister Justin Trudeau (2015–). Wisely using his father Pierre Trudeau's strong relationship with China—a tie enjoyed during Pierre's tenure as Prime Minister from 1980–1984—the younger Prime Minister Trudeau has been successful in jumpstarting economic ties.

As we have seen already, South Korea has perhaps undergone the most dramatic shifts between *Cold Partner* and *Hot Partner* with regard to both China and America. Other nations like Japan, Singapore and the Philippines also swing from *Warm* to *Cold* and back again depending on political winds.

But perhaps the most important question we need to be answering is that of China's ambition itself. Does China *want* to become the world's principal superpower, rising to replace the American-led system that has dominated world dynamics since the end of World War II? Historically, war breaks loose when an up-and-coming power competes with the dominant hegemon for influence. This has happened from time immemorial. Demonstrated by Graham Allison with the Thucydides Trap, war is inevitable unless the two competing powers agree and act upon specific moves to alleviate tension. Nations engage in a perpetual state of mutual distrust, arming themselves often to the point at which war is inevitable. (Simply glance back at the buildup of arms that resulted in the horrors of the 20th century.) Yet despite the fear mongering by pundits, it is clear that China does not want to replace the world system, a reality we must internalize in order to avoid the deadly Thucydides Trap.

Not only does China show no interest in global hegemony and an overturn of the current system, but it also feels hesitant with regard to becoming a global superpower. Yes, China desires a more qualitative say and higher degree of clout in current institutions like the World Bank and the International Monetary Fund (IMF). But China is trying to influence and lead these organizations rather than trying to upend or stop their power. At the same time, given traditional Western powers' disproportionate influential grip on these intergovernmental organizations, China seeks the creation of new, Chinese-led institutions that will act more favorably toward countries typically regarded second class given their exclusion from an Anglo, European colonial power structure. China has thus established the One Belt One Road initiative as well as the Asian Infrastructure Investment Bank (AIIB), which we will analyze more closely in Chapters 1–3. It is important to note, however, that these new initiatives and institutions are not targeted at the displacement of the World Bank, IMF or even the Asian Development Bank, but are rather intended to supplement and cooperate with them.

In terms of China's political ties, it is also important to consider that China is not necessarily seeking allies. This notion is critical to understand given the prevailing naïveté of American foreign policy analysts whose imposition of assumptions—based on the traditional western alliance system—leads them to conclude that China cannot project power because it does not have any allies. This is a poor interpretation of the situation. Rather, China attempts to be friendly with its neighbors, concurrently acknowledging that it can never share a close alliance akin to that shared by the U.S. with Canada or by France with the United Kingdom. It instead tries to place countries in Category 1 *Hot Partner* or Category 2 *Warm Partner*.

Why can't China engage in alliances in the same way younger western countries do? One primary reason involves a linguistic and cultural divide of historically monumental dimensions between China and its neighbors—let alone the divide between China and a Western civilization with whom it came into contact after millennia of its own evolution. Apart from this gap, modern China is still operating atop thousands of years of relationships—relationships mediated for most of history by a vastly different geopolitical landscape. Most countries, tribes and kingdoms, from modern day Vietnam to Korea, were essentially vassal states functioning within distinct government systems.

Take China and Vietnam's relationship, for example. It is difficult—if not virtually impossible—for the two modern nations to ignore millennia of tension and become 'true allies' despite their physical proximity and amount of economic trade. Many street names in Vietnam's biggest cities memorialize martyrs who fought against Chinese encroachment during imperial times for example. Many Vietnamese today remain wary of Chinese intentions and do not want to lose political independence. Yet American policy-makers readily and naively group the two together as Communist states with a shared Confucian heritage, a classification oblivious to the ideology's weak link in the face of history.

China does not seek firm, conventional alliances with other nations. A civilization all its own, it can never be true friends, so it instead seeks to be friendly, using economic punishments and military threats when necessary to maintain its position.

China's *Hot*, *Warm* and *Cold* categories thus form a critical framework for understanding both China's political and economic dealings abroad. Without strict camps of allies and enemies, nations and businesses seeking to profit from the Chinese market must keep abreast of Beijing's political aims. China's underlying motivations, as well as its mid- and long-term initiatives, will be key informants as to where one must stand in order to profit from China's powerful growth engine.

Preface

Delving into the concepts illustrated above, *The War for China's Wallet* (*WCW*) explores China's finely tuned methods of punishing states and companies that cross it politically, while conversely rewarding those that comply with the government's demands. Drawing on a host of examples and their implications, this book demonstrates how China synchronizes its economic weapons and rewards, its skillfully employed control of state media, and an ability to rally Chinese consumers to its side.

The economic force behind China's State Wallet—not to mention wallets of everyday Chinese consumers—is a power no nation or individual business can easily withstand. Although China is known as the world's factory, it actually imports more from 40 countries in the world including Switzerland, Germany, Brazil, Australia than it exports to these nations. In 2016, it ran a $27.5 billion USD trade surplus with Switzerland for example, $8.9 billion USD with Germany.[i]

Policy-makers, businesspeople and investors alike have a vital stake in understanding China's long-term plans, including initiatives such as One Belt One Road (OBOR), the Asian Infrastructure Investment Bank (AIIB), as well as reclamation of islands in the South China Sea. Only in 1) understanding how these initiatives will develop and the opportunities afforded for countries and companies seeking to profit from them, 2) appreciating the reasons underlying China's pursuit of increased land and sea power, and 3) gaining an acute awareness of how Chinese consumers are evolving and operate in a low trust environment, will countries and companies know how to benefit from China's continued economic growth.

The War for China's Wallet seeks to illuminate these essential insights, granting anyone armed with them a key to the Chinese wallet.

Utilizing China's distinctive framework of *Hot*, *Warm* and *Cold Partners*, *The War for China's Wallet* will illustrate how China's government approaches nations and companies in each category. Further elaborating on the initiatives of various states and businesses, the *WCW* will demonstrate what has and has not worked. With these analyses in mind—bolstered by a deepened understanding of the above framework—businessmen, investors and policy-makers will be better prepared to determine an optimal approach to China, making sure not to alienate America in the process.

While the heady days of China's 10 percent growth may be gone, retail sales continue to grow around 10 percent annually as China sees a shift from its investment-based economy to one based on consumption, services and innovation. There are multi-billion dollar profits to be made by companies focusing not only

DOI 10.1515/9781501507618-202

on market realities but also on political ones. American companies like General Electric and Honeywell, despite America's Cold Partner status, have already expounded on the profits they expect to make from China's tremendous OBOR. Other companies will benefit from China's global acquisition spree, as Chinese companies seek to acquire brands, technology and management know-how, looking to diversify revenue streams outside of China.

The War for China's Wallet will provide case studies, personal experiences from my past two decades in China, and primary research from interviews with thousands of business executives, consumers, and government officials that my colleagues and I have conducted at the firm I started, the China Market Research Group (CMR) in 2005. Bolstered by these insights, the *WCW* will guide companies in understanding how to profit from China's outbound economic plans and a shifting consumer base that is increasingly nationalistic, making sure to minimize risks in the process. Nations and companies that get it right will reap immense benefit from China's Wallet, but those who miscalculate face the grim fate of losing out on the world's largest growth engine for the next two decades.

***

The book is divided into two parts—the first looks at the politics of China's rise in the international arena. Only by understanding how China's government views the world can nations and companies benefit from growth and mitigate risk. The second part looks more closely at China's economic rise and shift to consumption and innovation, what it means for businesses dealing with the Chinese state directly, and Chinese consumers who are disrupting global trade patterns. This part of the book will offer concrete action items for companies and governments to follow in order to attract Chinese investment and sell to Chinese companies and consumers.

On a personal basis, I am writing this book as I am about to turn 40 years old. I have lived approximately the same amount of time in my current home country of China as I have in my birth country the United States, which coincidentally fits as I am ethnically half Chinese and half Jewish American. I worry that tension will continue to rise between the two countries that I love, often made worse by a lack of understanding of the intentions and realities both countries face. Far too many analysts, pundits and government officials in the United States do not get the real situation on the ground in China, or have their own ulterior motives for misunderstanding. Ultra-nationalists in America like Steven Bannon, Former Chief Strategist to US President Donald Trump and Executive Chairman of Breitbart News; or Peter Navarro, Assistant to President Trump, Director of Trade and Industrial Policy, and the Director of the White House National Trade Council, and author of *Death by China* think America is locked in an "economic war" with China. The situation is the same with officials and media outlets in Beijing like *Global Times* who are getting paradoxically more nervous and emboldened from the chaos in the Trump administration. I hope that this book will help reduce some of the misunderstandings by bringing greater clarity to both sides and by highlighting why it is dangerous if ultra-nationalists on both sides gain too much power.

Perhaps the most dangerous flashpoint in the Asia-Pacific Region after that of the Korean Peninsula is the tension building in the South China Sea, so that is where we shall start the next chapter. It is also incidentally where I began my lifelong interest in China.

Chapter 1
China's Economic Hammer

Manila, Philippines, March 1996

U.S. First Lady Hillary Clinton readied herself to testify in Washington, D.C., amid the spreading Whitewater scandal. On the other side of the globe, I was living in Manila, capital of the Philippines and "Pearl of the Orient." In both capitals and at discos around the world blared the pop song *Macarena* by one-hit wonder Los del Río. Schoolkids and adults alike shook to the Spanish beat in synchronized dance.

It was one of those searing hot days in Manila, where you can fry an egg by cracking it open onto the scorching black tar of the street. I had just finished lecturing at Trinity College of Quezon City, where I was spending the semester, when I made my way to the Manila Hotel. Built at the behest of American President William Howard Taft (1909–1913)—soon to assume the position of the Philippines' first civilian Governor-General—the hotel was officially opened on July 4, 1912. In celebration of America's Independence Day, the hotel's inauguration underscored the Philippines' closeness to the U.S. To this day, many Filipinos call their country America's 51st state.

Two decades later, the Manila Hotel continued to serve as a site for U.S. government involvement. Holding court as Military Advisor and Field Marshal to the Commonwealth Government of the Philippines, United States Five-Star General Douglas MacArthur operated out of the Manila Hotel from 1935–1941. From his penthouse suite, MacArthur built a blueprint for the Philippines' future and laid the groundwork for American hegemony in Asia, plans that began enactment under his dominating gaze.

Awed by the hotel's history, I entered its stately lobby doors. I wondered how many military planning sessions General MacArthur must have held within these walls, strategizing with Filipino leaders such as Manuel L. Quezon[1] or House Speaker Benigno Aquino Sr., whose grandson and namesake would become the Philippines' president seven decades later. Few buildings in the world stood as a greater testament to American power abroad.

---

[1] President of the Commonwealth of the Philippines from 1935 to 1944.

DOI 10.1515/9781501507618-001

While most Americans do not think of their country as a colonial power as they would the British, Dutch, or French empires, the United States effectively colonized the Philippines during the 20th century. MacArthur, Taft, and other American officials cherry-picked families like the Aquinos to dominate generations of local politics. English became one of the nation's two official languages, right alongside Filipino.

Flooded with thoughts of the site's significance, I made my way to a table in the corner of the room where Commodore Al Santos and his wife Ester waited for me to have afternoon tea. Dressed in a simply embroidered, cream-colored *Barong*,[2] Al Santos extended his hand to welcome me in a warm embrace. Having been a key figure in the navy under Ferdinand Marcos' regime (1965–1986) in the 1960s and 70s, the now-retired Commodore Santos had notably stood out for his incorruptibility. Well-liked by both his superiors and subordinates, the Commodore had risen in the ranks despite refusing to bribe his way to the top.

The Commodore's wife, Ester—previously in charge of running Trinity College of Quezon City and St. Luke's Nursing School—had brought me to Trinity's high school division to teach 9th grade English for a semester. With a petite frame and short hair that circled her face, Ester sat next to the retired Commodore, beckoning me to sit. Exuding warmth, Mrs. Santos seemed to wear a perpetual smile that curled from one ear to the other. To this day, I do not think I have met a finer couple that did more to help people find their paths in life. Regardless of someone's affluence or upbringing, the Santos' always had a kind and encouraging word to leave.

Slated to return soon to the U.S. to pursue my own university studies, I wanted to thank Ester and Al for arranging my semester of teaching. Moved by my experience and cognizant of the population's needs, I wanted to know what I could do for the Philippines on an ongoing basis. Keen to learn from the Santos' expertise, I also sought their advice in determining the next step in my career.

"What should I study and do next?" I asked them both. The Commodore touched his perfectly coiffed, jet-black hair, and looked me directly in the eyes with an unwavering gaze. "China," he said, then took another sip of his tea. "We are all going to have to learn how to deal with China politically, economically, and militarily. They are regaining power and will become an unstoppable force, the way they were during Imperial times. The whole world will have to know about how to deal with a rising China, so that is what you should study."

---

[2] The *Barong*, or *Barong Tagalog*, is the Philippines' national dress for men.

Until then, I hadn't given much thought to the country that was home to my mother's ancestors. I only knew of China as having a crazy big population, dim sum, and those White Rabbit candies I enjoyed scarfing down when visiting my aunt's house. But that was about it. In the mid 1990s, most Americans were still talking about the rise of Japan as if it were a bogeyman whose business acumen would threaten the American way of life. Hollywood and the business papers presented Americans with a new warning—whether a book hitting the shelves, movies a la Sean Connery and Wesley Snipe's *Rising Sun*, or a red-in-the-face pundit—cautioning Americans that they might soon be slaving away for Japanese companies. Many feared the rise of a nation America had so decisively defeated at the end of World War II, a mere five decades before. Few predicted that Japan would soon embark on a multi-decade phase of sluggish growth, losing prestige in international affairs.

By contrast, whenever anyone thought of China, they thought of ping pong diplomacy, hunger, Mao Zedong, the disastrous Cultural Revolution, and the more recent Tiananmen Square Incident of 1989, in which hundreds of protesting students and military soldiers alike were killed in pitched battles on June 4th. Americans hardly thought of the Middle Kingdom as an up-and-coming nation, ready to compete for hegemony in the Asia-Pacific region, let alone in the rest of the world.

This disregard of China was not unique to the American public. Not until President Bill Clinton's second term—five years into his presidency—did Clinton finally make an official trip to China in 1998, visiting from June 24 to July 3. When hosted at Peking University, China's most famous institution of higher learning, Clinton chastised China's leadership for a lack of democracy in the country. Aside from insulting his hosts—a common, if misguided, strategy adopted by American politicians when traveling abroad—Clinton's speech neither mentioned the South China Sea nor China's relations with Southeast Asian countries like the Philippines and Indonesia. Instead, the American president focused on the Korean Peninsula and on Indian-Pakistani relations, given that the latter two countries seemed to be on the brink of war. On May 28, barely one month before Clinton's visit, Pakistan had launched Chagai-I, five simultaneous underground nuclear tests in the Ras Koh Hills of Balochistan Province's Chagai District. Atop escalating tensions, Pakistan's move struck fear throughout the world that India would seek military retaliation to counteract Pakistan's armament.[i]

Listening to the Commodore, I was struck by the weight of his forecasts, particularly regarding the potential for conflict in the strategically invaluable South China Sea. If America's leaders were not even considering China and its role in regional waters—an expanse of vital importance to China's neighbors—I had better travel throughout the region and learn as much as I could about Chinese culture and history. It was then and there that my career as a China observer was decided. After my stint in the Philippines, I lived in South Korea for a while, where I taught English. In South Korea, I also engaged with the political and business elite who echoed Commodore Santos' views about China's rise, guiding my career in a similar direction. Gaining further insight into Asia-Pacific dynamics while there, I learned that much of America's foreign policy establishment was twenty years behind in its understanding of the region, rendering its analyses woefully simplistic and naive.

★★★

2016

Twenty years later, at the edge of glistening aqua blue waters, I gazed out at the South China Sea, a shimmering 1,351,000 square-mile expanse of the Pacific Ocean. Home to some of the world's top scuba diving sites, the South China Sea has also been the scene of major disputes, the most bitter battled out between China and the Philippines. But other nations are also party to the bickering: Taiwan, Malaysia, Brunei, Indonesia, and Vietnam all vie against China and the Philippines for access to the sea's potential crude oil deposits, natural gas, and fishing zones.

Estimates of oil quantities under the South China Sea range from a mere 11 billion barrels to a whopping 213 billion. To put the size of these deposits into perspective, Saudi Arabia has confirmed reserves of 268 billion barrels, Iraq has 144 billion. Yet most of the South China Sea's potential oil is buried so deep under the ocean that even the largest oil giants like Exxon-Mobil and PetroChina still lack the necessary technology to bring this black gold to the surface. Furthermore, while involved countries certainly seek control over these potential oil fields, oil is currently neither the primary contested goal nor the biggest cause of regional friction.[ii]

Skirmishes over control of the South China Sea essentially boil down to interregional competition for the creation of buffer zones in case of war, and exertion of power over shipping zones. And these competing interests are indeed well founded. Over $5 trillion USD worth of global trade—or one-third of total global shipping—flows through the South China Sea every year. In times of war, anyone controlling these shipping lanes has the power to enact a trade blockade, swiftly starving enemies into submission. Currently, China seems most intent on controlling the shipping lanes, dedicating more efforts to asserting authority than any other nation.

Over the past decade, China's primary medium for controlling the sea has been its bolstering of the People's Liberation Army Navy (PLAN). Realizing that domination of the sea was critical to increasing China's regional power overall, President Xi Jinping accelerated the country's naval expansion in earnest after assuming power in 2012. Dovetailed with the president's anti-corruption crackdown, China's naval expansion has been a clear priority. Arresting more senior army officers for corruption than naval ones, Xi has also installed more senior naval officers that are loyal to him, confirming the Navy's position as China's premier fighting power. In its expansion, PLAN further demonstrated the nation's prowess when it elected to build its first domestically built aircraft carrier over similar models from abroad, launching the Type 001A Shandong on April 26, 2017.[iii]

Intraregional military attacks between Chinese Coast Guard ships and fishing trawlers of different nations have been fairly minor, albeit regular. Yet the risk of military engagement continues to rise as both China and America become more aggressive in asserting their control of the area. In 2012, for example, China evicted Filipino fishermen trawling near the reclaimed island Scarborough Shoal, drawing heavy protests from Manila, which threatened deployment of more Filipino naval patrols. Nations have also sent military ships to patrol the seas and anchor near reclaimed islands, further increasing tensions. On October 21, 2015, the U.S. destroyer USS Lassen (DDG-82) navigated within 12 nautical miles of the Spratly Island. Less than a year later, on April 22 2016, the Americans sent four A-10 Thunderbolts and two HH-60G Pave Hawks to fly near Scarborough Shoal. In both operations, the U.S. was essentially telling China that neither it nor other nations recognized Chinese sovereignty in these areas. Unbowed to American might, China seized an American underwater drone at the end of 2016.

Amidst this escalating tension, Chinese fighter jets have also been more frequently deployed to intercept American spy planes. On May 17, 2017, two Chinese Sukhoi Su-30 jets intercepted a U.S. WC-135 spy plane, closing to within a 150 feet (45 m) radius. The U.S. immediately lodged protests complaining that China's fighter jets flew perilously close to the American plane.[iv]

Competition for control of specific island chains, such as the Spratly and Paracel Islands, certainly accounts for much of the escalating tensions. Yet the chief cause for heated hostility lies in nations' dredging of the sea to build reclaimed islands like Scarborough Shoal. Adopting a methodical approach, China has outpaced its competition, building reclaimed islands greater in size and number than any other regional player. Having already built seven artificial islands,

China has further installed airfields, ports, and lighthouses on the reclaimed landmasses. To put these figures into perspective, Vietnam, Malaysia, the Philippines and Taiwan have reclaimed about 100 acres in the past 45 years, combined. China, on the other hand, has reclaimed a total of 3,000 acres in the Spratlys in the past three years alone.[v]

***

Commodore Santos had shown prescience that day in the Manila Hotel. Twenty years after his prophecy, China's unprecedented rise now sees the nation flexing its muscles to neighbors, particularly in its growing control of the South China Sea. Exacerbated by the proximity of China's seven reclaimed islands, neighbors worry these might readily be converted to military bases were war to break out. The disputed Scarborough Shoal, for instance, lies a mere 130 miles from the Philippines, reachable by a swift missile attack.[vi]

Aggravating regional anxiety in December of 2016, the Asia Maritime Transparency Initiative (AMTI)—part of the Center for Strategic & International Studies (CSIS)—claimed it had satellite imagery of Chinese-installed weapon systems on all seven of its artificial islands. Referencing the pictorial evidence, AMTI further claimed that China has installed antiaircraft weapons, essentially transforming the islands into "unsinkable aircraft carriers."[vii]

The sheer speed and magnitude of China's oceanic expansion produces mounting fear throughout the region. Asserting that its development is defensive in nature, China pooh-poohs the expressed concerns of neighboring countries, reminding them that China is neither alone in reclaiming islands nor in bolstering its naval capabilities. Yet no other nation has been as systematic in its buildup of reclaimed islands. Regional neighbors seem almost haphazard in their planning. Why have they not put up more of a resistance, and why has China's expansion skyrocketed so suddenly?

Previously, many nations looked to America for support, granted a bulwark against Chinese expansion by U.S. policies under Presidents Bill Clinton and George W. Bush. But this reliability began to change under President Barack Obama, as China seemed to view the U.S. as a pushover during his presidency. Apart from deploying 1,250 marines in Darwin, Australia—thousands of miles away from the main scene of tensions in the South China Sea—President Obama merely issued a few words of warning to counteract China's efforts. The president's Pivot to Asia seemed more like window dressing than an initiative with any teeth. In an opportune climate, China sped up construction of the reclaimed islands. They felt it best to move in swiftly lest a more rigid and hawkish president—as Hillary Clinton might have been—crack down on the region soon.

Fortunately for China, President Donald Trump has sought to forge strong economic relations with China, taking a low-key approach to battling China in general and in the South China Sea dispute. Chiefly seeking to extract better business deals with China, such as resuming American beef imports into the country after fears of mad cow disease halted the influx or lessening restrictions for America's banks and electric vehicle makers to expand in China, Trump has also dedicated efforts to obtaining Chinese assistance with the Korean peninsula crisis.

Yet perhaps the greatest enabler of China's long-term ambitions was the tragedy of September 11, 2001. America's operation to dismantle al-Qaeda and hunt for Osama Bin Laden diverted tremendous U.S. resources away from the Asia-Pacific region, leaving China relatively unobstructed in its expansionist efforts. The relinquishing of America's regulatory oversight left many countries in the region unsteady in the face of China's upsurge.

This newfound absence of American power leaves little clarity when determining how to mitigate China's reclamation of the sea, not to mention its growing power across the region. While the political and business elite of most regional neighbors are undoubtedly wary of China's long-term ambitions, and frightened of Chinese expansion in the sea, they need nonetheless to remain close to the neighborhood's economic superpower. Of those with whom I spoke during my travels, none dared risk all-out war, cognizant that their strength was insufficient to resist Chinese might alone. For most regional players, China had emerged as their largest or second largest trading partner.

Further complicating matters, the elite benefit most from China's rising trade with their home countries. Typically in command of the large, family-owned conglomerates that dominate local markets, these elites hold a significant proportion of their nation's wealth. They also often have ethnic Chinese ancestry and Chinese language skills which makes it easier for them to navigate both political and business circles in China. For example, Thailand's Charoen Pokphand Group (CP Group), run by Dhanin Chearavanont, Thailand's second wealthiest person with a net worth of $6.8 billion USD who traces his ancestry back to China, is the largest shareholder in China's Ping An Insurance and is a major shareholder in CITIC Group, a leading Chinese financial services conglomerate. Similarly, Henry Sy, founder of SM Investments Holding and the wealthiest person in the Philippines, traces his ancestral lineage back to China. He has also made significant investments into China in the retail space.

While Southeast Asia's middle class has experienced remarkable growth in recent years—notably in Thailand and Indonesia—there still exists an enormous wealth disparity separating many in abject poverty from a handful of affluent elites like the Chearavanonts and Sys. Experiencing the growth of personal riches, these elites have become more pro-China in recent years, especially now that Donald Trump focuses on domestic American issues at the expense of intervention in foreign lands (which are perceived as marginal in their impacts on American national interests). Without the reliability of U.S. support and mediation, the South China Sea region has now experienced a power vacuum. And in its swift occupation of this void, China is taking great strides to present itself as a friendly partner, opening up trade relations on an unprecedented scale.

To counteract criticism of its moves in the region, China doles out carrots in the form of long-term loans and infrastructure investments in regional countries, targeting specifically those regions and conglomerates that benefit the ruling elite the most, thus building critical support from domestic forces.

In light of China's takeover and America's exodus, perhaps the only institution capable of stopping Chinese ambitions is the Association of Southeast Asian Nations (ASEAN). Resistance would require the all member nations of this organization to agree to a united front. Averse to arguing against multilateral bodies, however, China prefers to divide and conquer, convincing nations of its intentions individually. In these bilateral attempts to deal with Southeast Asian nations, China has successfully used its powerful wallet to smooth out relations, thus rendering ASEAN largely ineffectual in containing Chinese expansion.

★★★

In weathering the power imbalance, countries have adopted disparate tactics to manage China's growth. *Hot Partners* like Cambodia and Laos have found that politically supporting the Chinese government by blocking critical statements on China by ASEAN serves them profitably, earning them quid pro quo long-term low interest loans and infrastructure investments. Other countries, such as the *Cold Partner* Philippines, have been punished economically for taking a more aggressive stand against China's expansion in the region, as we shall see later, by having its mango exports into China blocked.

Much of the dispute lies on China's "Nine-Dash Line," the demarcation line China uses to claim control of large swathes the South China Sea and which overlaps with competing claims by other nations. The area includes the Paracel Islands, the Spratly Islands, Scarborough Shoal, and all of the reclaimed islands in the Sea.

Cambodia, for instance, has long supported China's Nine-Dash Line in ASEAN summits, deeming China's long-term infrastructure investments a worthy reward. After preventing ASEAN from criticizing China over the South China Sea

Dispute in June 2016, Cambodia was proved right. In just a few days, China doled out another $600 million USD in low-interest loans to Cambodia.

But China not only uses its wallet to build support in Southeast Asia. It has also found takers in Europe, where Hot Partners Greece, Croatia, and Hungary have similarly done China's political bidding in return for investment. In June 2017, for example, Greece blocked a European Union Statement at the United Nations that chastised China for its human rights record, calling the attack on China "unconstructive." Like Cambodia, Greece has received massive Chinese investment in the post-Great Recession period. In 2016, for instance, China's COSCO Shipping (China Ocean Shipping Company)—owner of a giant container fleet—took a 51 percent stake in Greece's largest port.[viii] Following its divide and conquer logic, China has learned to isolate countries, benefit them economically, and thus earn their political support in intergovernmental associations—a manipulation of the multilateral system that weakens its very foundation.

In addition, China has specifically appealed to the personal ambitions of the political elite, either through direct financial support or through creation of jobs. Importantly, given the nature of its political system, China is not bound to two-year election cycles. The Chinese government can spend years, if not decades, cultivating relationships, thereby building unwavering political support abroad, especially from nations whose election cycles are similar to China's. This is one reason why China has forged closer relationships with countries in Africa and the Middle East, for example, whose leaders are also unburdened by regular election cycles.

China's long-term, continual support of Cambodian incumbent prime minister Hun Sen, for example, has gradually secured Cambodia's role as a hatchet man for China and moved the country from Cold Partner to Hot Partner and displays China's long-term strategy for building alliances. Only thirty years ago, in 1988, the long-standing Prime Minister called China "the root of everything that is evil." Yet less than a decade later, Hun Sen seemed to change his mind entirely, calling China Cambodia's "most trustworthy friend" in the 1990s. What could have possibly accounted for such a dramatic 180[ix] degree turn?

In July 1996, President of China Jiang Zemin welcomed Prime Minister Hun Sen for a state visit to China, going as far as to pick him up in a Chinese airplane and shower him with compliments. Viewing Hun Sen as a man with whom they could do business, the Chinese chose to ingratiate themselves through flattery—a more welcome tactic than that of U.S. politicians, who had lectured Cambodia and others nations to embrace American ideals of democracy for decades.

In contrast to its U.S. counterpart, the Chinese government has taken a no-lecture, stay-out-of-internal-affairs approach in dealing with other countries.

As a result, many states without democratic elections prefer working with China to powers like the United States, which consistently condemn their lack of democracy.

Unlike China's savvy business approach to building support in Cambodia, America's tactic has done the opposite, straining relations even more. In March 2017, the U.S. demanded that Cambodia, one of the world's poorest nations—with 18.9 percent of its population living under the poverty line[3]—repay $500 million USD in loans to the United States, home to the world's greatest nominal GDP. Adding insult to injury, much of what Cambodia borrowed from the U.S. during the Vietnam War was used to help feed refugees displaced precisely because of American bombing. Contrast that with China's strategy of giving out low interest loans—and often forgiving those loans—to co-opt the Cambodian elite and create general goodwill. As one Cambodian I interviewed in Siem Reap told me, "We always get support from China. We love them. The Americans on the other hand[x] always seem to be telling us what to do and telling us we are wrong."

Using a combination of its Wallet as a tool of diplomacy along with military action has become a well-worn playbook for Chinese policy makers. Target poorer nations whose strained economic circumstances make their elite more susceptible to seeking profitable business deals. Co-opt the elite of these nations for whom such deals will be personally enriching. Dole out the desired business contracts to effectively convert these nations to vassal states. Then use them in international associations like ASEAN or the UN to block criticism of China.

It is important to remember, however, that many countries gravitating toward China's orbit aren't merely attracted by the economic benefits of being a Hot Partner with China. Apart from the fiscal pull, many also feel pushed into working with China by an overly critical U.S. that condemns their political systems or human rights violations. This deterrent will become increasingly strong as much of the world rejects democracy or elects political leaders that prefer isolationism to globalism. We have even seen this latter trend in the United Kingdom where Brexit has emphasized protectionism, a gentle indication that even European nations may appreciate China's policy of non-interference.

★★★

---

[3] The Asian Development Bank (ADB) declared this figure in 2012 in its assessment of Cambodia's population. https://www.adb.org/sites/default/files/institutional-document/151706/cambodia-country-poverty-analysis-2014.pdf

Countries that antagonize China politically can quickly move from being a Hot Partner or Warm Partner to a Cold Partner. China swiftly uses its wallet to punish these countries that move from Hot or Warm Partner to Cold Partner in order to try to bring them back into line and to warn other nations thinking of becoming less supportive.

This happened in 2016 to Singapore which suddenly found itself falling into the Cold Partner category. Previously, under Prime Ministers Lee Kuan Yew (1965–1990) and Goh Chok Tong (1990–2004), Singapore managed to be friendly both to the United States and to China. Prime Minister Lee played his Chinese ethnic race card to build trust with China's leaders, starting with Mao Zedong, Zhou Enlai, and Deng Xiaoping. He showed China's leaders how a culturally Chinese-dominant nation, such as Singapore, can be controlled by a strong arm political leader, yet also use elections and capitalist ideas to become accepted by American policymakers. After all, despite elections, Singapore has been ruled by one family, the Lees, for over 35 years, longer than any Chinese figure.

But friendliness to China began wearing off under Lee's son Lee Hsien Loong, who became Prime Minister in 2004. He notably has less of a personal relationship with China's leaders.

Enraging China in 2016, Singapore under the junior Lee resolutely disputed China's moves in the South China Sea and supported the Philippines. Attempting to issue a communiqué by the Non-Aligned Movement (NAM)—a 120 member nation organization started by countries during the Cold War that wanted to align with neither the Soviet Union nor the United States—Singapore sought multilateral condemnation of Chinese initiatives to reclaim islands and dominate sea channels.

Singapore has also enraged China by attempting to buy military weapons from Taiwan. Singapore had nine armored vehicles it bought from Taiwan seized by Hong Kong customs in November 2016. By seizing the vehicles, China continued to show its displeasure with both Singapore and Taiwan and exert more pressure on them.[xi]

Relations between China and Singapore froze. In a noticeable show of the cold relations, the Singaporean Prime Minister was not invited to attend China's May 2017 kick-off summit for its One Belt One Road (OBOR) initiative. Instead of sending a presidential delegation as dozens of other countries in the region, Singapore was represented by a significantly lower ranking National Development Minister, Lawrence Wong.[xii]

As a result of its actions, Singapore has lost billions of dollars in potential deals with China, its largest trade partner.

Starkly contrasted with Singapore's moves in recent years are Malaysia, Indonesia, and Vietnam, whose delegations to the OBOR summit were led by Malaysian Prime Minister Najib Razak, Indonesian President Joko Widodo, and Vietnamese President Tran Dai Quang. Seeking closer ties with China despite escalating tensions in the South China Sea, these neighbors have tremendously profited from their support.

All three were amply rewarded for making the trek to China. Malaysian Prime Minister Najib Razak signed $7.2 billion USD worth of deals and said ties between the two nations were at their "best ever." In the same vein, Indonesia established a $5 billion USD loan facility, and Vietnam inked five agreements with China on economic and technological cooperation.[xiii]

Reiterating the power of China's carrots, Beijing has made its policy clear: bend to China's political will and the nation will dole out billions in loans to long-term friendly nations like Cambodia and Laos, vastly enriching countries that cozy up to China and concurrently reject the U.S. Yet national benefit is not the only reward China's government can grant. As demonstrated with the recent scandal surrounding Malaysia's state investment fund, getting close to China might even save presidencies. Critically under fire starting in 2015 for the 1MDB (1Malaysia Development Berhad) scandal, Malaysian Prime Minister Najib Razak has largely remained afloat at the hands of Chinese money and has weathered allegations that he siphoned off billions of dollars from a sovereign wealth fund. By continuing to attract Chinese investment, Razak has been able to build a coalition of domestic support from key figures who benefit directly from the Chinese investment as well as broad-based support from Malaysian voters who see job creation from China's investment.

***

Nations like the Philippines that do not support China, on the other hand, lose out on billions of dollars of trade, as Singapore has painfully experienced. A clear demonstration of this loss was witnessed in the Philippines' confrontational stand against China's maritime claims. Under President Benigno Aquino III (2010–2016), the Philippines took China to arbitration under Annex VII to the United Nations Convention on the Law of the Sea (UNCLOS). Vehemently protesting China's territorial claims in the South China Sea, the Philippines demanded a determination of the legality of China's "Nine-Dash Line." Indicative that China's overall threat played prominently in neighbors' retaliation, the Nine-Dash Line was initially put forth by Taiwan but elicited nowhere near the same extent of protest as when China adopted it.

China's reaction to the Philippines' legal maneuver was swift. Imports of Filipino mangoes plummeted, and Chinese tourists flocked in greater numbers to more pro-China countries like Cambodia and Thailand, halting tourism to the Philippines *en masse*. As might be expected, the *Global Times* fanned the flames. Reporting fruit sellers' boycotting of Filipino mangoes, the paper quoted one anonymous source, "our online shop will not sell Cebu mangoes from the Philippines and will not sell any snacks imported from the country any more."[xiv]

Of its Southeast Asian neighbors, the Philippines have historically stood farthest from China and closest to the United States. Now that China is forcing countries to stake out a position, nations must decide whether to orbit China *or* the U.S. While a handful of nations have managed to remain relatively neutral, as Thailand has succeeded in doing, it is increasingly difficult to remain impartial without antagonizing either side.

These decisions are not easy—siding with one nation over the other typically uproots decades of alliances, unearthing heated historical tensions. The Philippines' decision to favor China over the U.S. has been particularly vexing given its historical closeness to America. The country has never occupied a vassal state relationship with China as the Koreas or Vietnam had done in imperial times. Perhaps more importantly, Filipinos lack the same cultural and racial ties. Only 1.8 percent of the population has Chinese ancestry—similar levels to Indonesia's 1.2 percent, vastly differentiating Filipinos from Malaysians (24.6 percent Chinese) and Singaporeans (74.2 percent Chinese) that share China's same cultural and trade links. On top of this, Filipinos have long considered themselves the 51st state of America, a self-designation legitimized by America's essential colonization of the Philippines under MacArthur. Serving as a seat of various American military bases in Subic Bay and Clark Airbase in Angeles City, the Philippines only closed these in 1991 and 1992 as a result of growing local opposition in the 1990s.

In adapting his policy, Duarte has provided a guidebook for other countries to figure out how to benefit from both China and America. Considering the Philippines closeness with America, it is useful to see what Duterte has done. The warming relations between China and the Philippines also shows just how coercive China's wallet can be in the face of an American power vacuum in the region.

The post-Marcos years (1965–1986) proved fairly chaotic politically for the Philippines. Incarcerated for plundering $80 million USD from state coffers, the Philippines' 13th President, Joseph Estrada (1998–2001), was soon followed to jail by his successor. Caught in electoral fraud, former President Gloria Macapagal Arroyo (2001–2010) was also found guilty in the alleged theft of $8.8 million USD from the state lottery. In the case of Filipino presidents that haven't been arrested, including Fidel Ramos and Benigno Aquino III, these have been hampered by one-time 6-year term limits, effectively rendering them lame duck presidents.

In the early- to mid-2010s, President Benigno Aquino III (2010–2016)—son of former President Corazon Aquino and offspring of political royalty—moved the Philippines closer to America. After generations of Filipino reliance on American power, Aquino further confirmed the Philippines' pro-U.S. stance in its rejection of Chinese power—demonstrated in the president's decision to take China to arbitration at the UN. In the early 1980s, senator Benigno Aquino Jr. (Aquino III's father), was assassinated upon his return to Manila after exile in America, precipitating the downfall of Ferdinand Marcos' regime. Aquino III's grandfather, Benigno Aquino Sr., had served as speaker of the Philippine House from 1943–1944, well known also in American political circles. This also shows how America essentially cherry-picked Filipino leaders for the past century. Circumstances in the Philippines reversed dramatically when Rodrigo Duterte was elected president in 2016. The hard-charging, foul-mouthed former Mayor of Davao City called President Barack Obama "the son of a whore," and has implicitly sanctioned rape in unabashed jokes. He also said he would never visit the "lousy" U.S.[4] A stark divergence from the "American-crowned" Aquino clan, Duterte stands well apart from the political elite classes represented by these former pro-America politicians.

Taking a far more pragmatic stance in dealing with China, Duterte has been handsomely rewarded. Immediately responding to Duterte's criticism of the U.S., and of President Obama in particular, China offered the Philippines billions in low-interest loans (much as Japan had done in the decades following World War II). Duterte had even joked before he got the loans that he would get closer to China if it gave him billions in loans. He therefore has been able to signal publicly that essentially his friendship and loyalty could be bought—a viewpoint well-understood and accepted by China.

As demonstrated with the Philippines, China has refined its use of economic punishment as a method of coercing Cold Partner countries into the Warm Partner category.

The minute a country suspends its support of China, no matter how long it had been a Hot Partner, it gets banished to Cold Partner status—an experience keenly felt by Singapore. But China's newly polished statecraft has perfected the art of rewards, too. Granting carrots to newly minted Warm Partners or Hot

---

[4] http://www.reuters.com/article/us-philippines-duterte-idUSKBN1A61DX

Partners, like Duterte's Philippines or Razak's Malaysia, China knows how to keep its neighbors close.

★★★

The battle for control of the South China Sea is just beginning. Yet unless all countries in Southeast Asia somehow manage to coordinate with the United States in mounting a united front against Chinese incursion, China's victory seems relatively certain. Continuously refining its new form of statecraft, China cleverly singles out countries like Cambodia and Laos, influencing Hot Partners within multilateral systems like ASEAN or the UN.

Aside from tension in the South China Sea, perhaps the most contentious area is that on the Korean Peninsula. President Donald Trump has taken a more strident approach to cajoling China to help resolve the tensions and risks of a nuclear-capable North Korea. That is our next example to see how China operates and projects power (Chapter 2).

★★★★★

Dialogue:
Parag Khanna, Managing Partner, Hybrid Reality Pte Ltd.

I first met Parag in 2013 on one of his visits to Shanghai and enjoyed hearing his insights on a wide range of subjects, from politics, to economics, to how we view the world. He is a Senior Research Fellow at the Lee Kuan Yew School (at the National University of Singapore), CNN Contributor, and the author of several bestselling books including *Connectography: Mapping the Future of Global Civilization* and *The Second World: Empires and Influence in the New Global Order*.

Rein: It is arguably natural and in some ways necessary for superpowers to establish a military presence for the purpose of exerting power globally and safeguarding economic and security interests. As China emerges as the world's second superpower, do you think China's dominance of the South China Sea is inevitable, just given China's sheer size? Can Asian nations without U.S. backing put up an effective resistance against China's claims? If it is indeed possible for smaller Asian nations to push back against China's claims, how should they go about doing so without running the risk of being economically punished as the Philippines was after taking China to arbitration for its "Nine-Dash Line"?

Khanna: It is indeed natural for a country to follow the pattern of import substitution, mass industrialization, generating export-led growth and large surpluses, accumulating massive currency reserves, and investing those assets in national infrastructure and modernization—including of the military. That is precisely the story of America in the 19th century and China in the late 20th and early 21st centuries.

Because China is so dependent on foreign inflows of oil, gas, and food, it needs to secure these supply chains not only through overseas trade and investment—it is now the world's largest trading power and an ever larger foreign investor—but also through certain military relationships and precautions.

To "put up resistance" to what China is doing is to assume that the prior status quo of the U.S. dominating Asia's waters through its Cold War alliance system is the "natural" state of affairs. But there is no such thing in geopolitics. There is only constant adjustment based on power and ambition, diplomacy, and strategy. China's military investments from anti-ship ballistic missiles, stealth submarines, and fortifying disputed islands in the South China Sea will surely continue more or less unabated.

That said, the fate of the South China Sea is not an all-or-nothing proposition. The fact that China is making expansive claims does not mean it will achieve all of them or that they will all at once require accession, or none at all, sparking counter-balancing and conflict. There is no fixed end state to the South China Sea and different disputes will evolve at different speeds.

Some aspects of China's claims such as the Air Defense Identification Zone (ADIZ) may be ignored by neighbors, while other measures such as accepting Chinese naval ship escorts in specific territories may be accepted. The Philippines has given ground (literally) on the Scarborough Shoal but not on more minor coastal islands, while Vietnam is not giving way at all, and instead has signed oil and gas exploration agreements with Exxon in the Paracel Island cluster to make clear that it will not back down.

For its part, the U.S. is helping concerned allies strengthen their defense capabilities and better coordinate with each other. Vietnam, Indonesia, Japan, India, and Australia are all countries that—whether or not they are claimant states in the South China Sea—are expanding their naval cooperation to show some common resolve.

History shows that it is useful to take a firm line with China to "draw a line in the water" as it were. China would not want to unnecessarily engage in uncontrolled military escalation in such a situation. With such deterrence in place, it opens the door to negotiating potential energy extraction and marketization cooperation agreements, which I strongly advocate, especially since this maritime body truly is shared among nearly a dozen important powers whose thirst for energy will not be quenched through conflict that disrupts major global supply chains.

Rein: Singapore has received the cold shoulder from China after it supported claims by the Philippines against China's "Nine-Dash Line." Do you think Singapore will be able to revive ties with China? If so, how?

Khanna: Technically, Singapore's position was to support international arbitration in the name of a peaceful settlement of the dispute, not to take the Philippines side as such—though indeed this is how the move has been interpreted in China. Despite the current diplomatic tensions between the two, there is no doubt that China and Singapore have a special relationship. Many still remember Lee Kuan Yew's guidance for China, which has been utterly invaluable in making China what it is today. Furthermore, it is still a major investor in China and technology provider in key areas such as infrastructure services. The credibility of many Belt and Road Initiative (BRI) projects, for example, will surely hinge on Singaporean participation. Of course, China does not need Singapore in the coming decades the way it did in the past forty years, but there is still a very mutually beneficial symbiosis.

Rein: China has claimed that its reclamation of islands in the South China Sea is essentially defensive in nature. Yet it is installing weapon systems on these islands. How do you view this build-up of weapon systems on China's reclaimed islands? Should we trust that China's intentions are indeed defensive?

Khanna: In any situation where countries deploy weapons, they declare it to be defensive in nature. That is nothing new. Installing weapon systems on reclaimed South China Sea islands can be justified on the grounds that they are monitoring strategic yet otherwise ungoverned waters and thus providing collective benefits (public goods) against piracy, for example. In reality, such weapons can be used to attack adversaries maneuvering in the region such as Vietnamese or American warships. We cannot say how this will play out, but it is not unprecedented in the sense that this is also how the U.S. uses Pacific Islands such as Guam.

Rein: Vietnam and Taiwan have also reclaimed islands, yet China has received the brunt of America's criticism. Why do you think this is? Do you see a difference between China's reclamation of islands and that by Vietnam and Taiwan? *Is* there a legal difference?

Khanna: While many islands in the South China Sea have long been disputed, it is the changing of the status quo through China's de facto island build-up and positioning of military assets that has led to China being fingered by other claimants and the international community. It has taken "first mover advantage," so to speak. Most legal experts concur that while the Philippines has a stronger legal case, it is of course much weaker militarily than Vietnam, which is much stronger militarily but has a weaker legal case. Despite this paradox, both situations will play out very differently because of Vietnam's history of standing up to China (they fought a brief border war in 1979) versus the Philippines kowtowing approach. Taiwan's claims are the weakest because in various historical settings they have been subordinated to mainland China's, and also because Taiwan is not formally recognized as a state by many countries and is increasingly isolated diplomatically if not economically.

Rein: As referenced above, the Philippines under President Aquino took China to arbitration over China's exerted "Nine-Dash Line." By contrast, President Duterte has taken a more accommodating approach in addition to criticizing American hegemony, and in return has received billions of dollars in low-interest loans and infrastructure investments from China. Do you believe Duterte's is a wise long-term plan?

Khanna: Duterte's response to China's offers of effectively ceding islands in exchange for economic benefits is predictable, though it is too soon to tell if it will work. He has quickly followed up by ordering the military to strengthen its position and fortify residual islands, which will give the country slightly more confidence that even as it de facto abdicates the Scarborough Shoal, its territorial losses will stop at that. In the meantime, Dutuerte certainly should maximize the benefits of Chinese infrastructure loans and grants to implement his national economic modernization agenda, as other countries are also doing. This ultimately will make the Philippines a stronger nation. But around the corner may lurk scenarios where future investments are made contingent on further rejecting America's military presence in the country, and this could lead to a renewed round of escalation and threats.

Rein: After President Trump abandoned the Trans Pacific Partnership (TPP) and reiterated his commitment to an "America First" strategy, China has moved to fill the economic power vacuum by promoting free trade and expanding its One Belt One Road Initiative. How much unease do you see in the region as a result of Trump's rise, and to what degree are Asia-Pacific nations still willing to consider

America the world's policeman? Has there been a shift in political leaders' ability to rely on America? If so, do you think it likely that many would now put their lot with China, either because they are essentially forced to or seek the inherent economic rewards, or both?

Khanna: Trade is not a zero-sum game, and in truth there was no vacuum to be filled by Trump's withdrawing the U.S. from the TPP. Trade expansion has been enormous across Asia in the past two decades, and particularly the past ten years. All countries that were part of the TPP negotiations were also simultaneously negotiating the Regional Comprehensive Economic Partnership (RCEP) as well, while also participating in the One Belt One Road discussions. Most are also founding members of the Asian Infrastructure Investment Bank (AIIB). The point is that the choice is not between TPP and RCEP or OBOR, but rather that trade is expanding in all directions, the only difference being the speed and degree. For example, even without TPP, China's energy imports from America are skyrocketing.

In trade, countries are very mercurial and always playing all sides. This is, quite frankly, a very good thing. More trade and openness is better, and countries choose which agreements they participate in or don't. If America chooses not to join TPP, TPP will move forward without America—as is indeed the case. My prediction is that the U.S. will realize that it is losing Asian market share in key areas and that trade agreements are the only way to impose the kinds of standards American exporters need to penetrate markets. The only question is how much market share will America have already lost once it comes around to this realization.

Rein: How should President Trump deal with China's growing ambitions in the South China Sea? Should he send more troops to act as a deterrent, as President Obama did in sending marines to Darwin, Australia? Should he take an even stronger approach by sending American troops directly to the disputed territories, having them land on and occupy some of the disputed islands and reefs? And in either of these cases, how do you think China would react?

Khanna: Because the U.S. has expended such tremendous and irrevocable resources into military activity in Iraq and Afghanistan over the past nearly two decades, the military is stretched and there is little appetite for conflict involving further large-scale loss of American life. This is why Trump's general approach has been to combine promises of greater military funding with simultaneous demands for greater burden-sharing among allies. Placing many more Americans in Japan, South Korea, the Philippines, or elsewhere as "tripwires" to conflict would not be consistent with this approach, and there is little appetite for it.

Indeed, most American leaders and members of the public would prefer to see Asians sort out their own disputes with America playing a largely deterrent role in the background. This is the path I would like to see as well. During the Cold War, the U.S. security umbrella provided the stability for Europe to integrate its political and even military institutions such that conflict between European nations was unthinkable. Given Asia's particular history of rivalries and diversity, replicating that accomplishment will certainly be far more difficult, but it is certainly the end state that we should aspire toward.

Case Study: Appoint the Right Ambassador or Country Head

For countries seeking to benefit from trade with China, it is critical to appoint well-versed senior level envoys capable of positioning their represented nations advantageously within China's Hot, Warm, and Cold Partner framework. Opening up regular dialogue with Chinese senior officials is key, much as the U.S. did in 2006, when President George W. Bush and China's then President Hu Jintao launched the Strategic Economic Dialogue (SED). Under the SED, the U.S. and China respectively appointed U.S. Treasury Secretary Hank Paulson and Vice Premier Wu Yi to meet twice a year, offering clout to their negotiations. Trusted officials geared with experience and gravitas, Paulson and Wu Yi were equipped to handle even the toughest of issues and compromises.

By appointing such senior officials, both parties significantly lessened mutual suspicion and established major trade deals as a result. An immense success, the SED has moved America into a *warmer* subset of the *Cold Partner* category—likely as close as two superpowers can get. Facilitated by the SED and similar bilateral efforts, China-US trade has soared in the past decade. American exports to China have more than doubled from less than $50 billion USD in 2006 to $113 billion USD by 2016. Barring a radical shift in relations, growth of U.S. exports to China are expected to continue as the Chinese ease restrictions on American beef and remain interested in U.S. agricultural products.[xv]

Conducting regular senior level meetings is key to fruitful trade relations like those enjoyed by the U.S. and China. However, it is equally critical for countries to select the right ambassador to represent them adeptly on a daily basis and secure favorable trade deals. Conversely, emissaries prone to gaffes and excessive criticism of the Chinese government and its people will leave a great deal of damage in their wake—both political and economic. States must therefore strike a careful balance, appointing an ambassador qualified to represent home nation interests; able to push back against China in key areas—even in the challenging realms of border disputes, protectionism, and human rights; but all the while remaining tactful in forging friendly relations.

Although Sino-U.S. relations have undergone ups and downs in recent decades, both Republican and Democratic administrations have chosen fairly wise ambassadors, from Clark T. Randt, Jr. (2001–2009), to Jon M. Huntsman, Jr. (2009–2011), to Gary Locke (2011–2014), and finally Max Baucus (2014–2017). Each showed remarkable prowess in forging stronger economic deals for the U.S. while simultaneously pushing back against China when it threatened American interests—both economic and ideological. Ambassador Huntsman, for instance, attended[xvi]a few of the 2011 Jasmine Revolution's pro-democracy protests in support of freedom of speech and democracy, and fought resolutely for better intellectual property protection. Simultaneously, however, he was keenly able to ingratiate himself with the Chinese by speaking Mandarin and praising China's government when needed. Perhaps most importantly, he was never seen as talking down to the Chinese people or their government. As Professor Jin Canrong, associate dean of Beijing's Renmin University School of International Relations, has told the *South China Morning Post*, "Huntsman knows how to deal with China, including its people, and he has done a pretty good job."[xvii]

Contrast the outcomes of these diplomatic efforts with those experienced by Mexico after President Felipe Calderón appointed Jorge Guajardo as Mexico's ambassador to China in 2007, a position he held for six years. Guajardo's consistent animosity and criticism of China's political system have debilitated Mexican exports to China and damaged independent business relations. After leaving his post, Guajardo has heavily chastised the Communist Party and its one-party state in speeches and on Twitter. Adding insult to injury, he has compared the CCP to Mexico's Institutional Revolutionary Party (PRI)—one Guajardo's own party replaced and often vilifies[xviii]. Drawing parallels between the PRI's political dysfunction and China's governmental corruption, Guajardo has suggested that the Communist Party may be on its way to collapse, wracked with corruption and factional infighting, and having lost legitimacy among its people. Guajardo has time and again argued for Chinese political reform and even a replacement of the system. Understandably, such savage and relentless denigrations of the Chinese government have left a bad taste in the mouths of everyday Chinese, subsequently damaging the image of Mexico in the minds of Chinese consumers.[xix]

Leaving few unscathed, Guajardo's constant criticisms—during both his ambassadorship and his later work as a consultant for McLarty Associates, helping firms expand and deal with China—have indeed riled key people in China. As was expressed to me by a well-connected Beijing insider, "All he does is criticize. He has severely set back Mexico-China relations." Echoing this sentiment, one member of Mexico's Foreign Service complained, "We're always cleaning up his messes. Even now, years later."

Consequently, while Sino-Mexican trade grew under Guajardo's ambassadorship, growth was far from what it should have been considering China's booming economy at the time. If Mexico had been positioned as a Warm Partner, rather than garnering the Cold Partner status induced by Guajardo, Mexican businesses would have benefitted enormously. Instead, Mexico only exported $4.87 billion USD of products to China by 2015—a figure just slightly greater than the $3.35 billion USD of Mexican exports to a significantly smaller Spanish market. After cancelling a $3.75 billion USD train deal with China, Mexico further damaged its reputation, tarnishing its image as a trustworthy country in the eyes of everyday Chinese. One of the reasons tequila sales are so low in China is precisely this damaged image—Chinese consumers now view Mexican brands not only as cheap and untrustworthy but also as representative of a Cold Partner nation. Many have therefore flocked to French cognac or Scottish whiskey, favoring Warm Partner countries[xx] instead.

Particularly in light of America's U-turn in dealing with Mexico under the current Trump administration, Mexico would do well to increase its trade with China and thereby cease reliance on its largest trading partner to the north. Growing closer to China would additionally help offset any political and economic risks posed by a more volatile President Trump. However, Mexico has a long way to go in repairing the damage inflicted on Sino-Mexican relations, both by hurtful policies and diplomatically ruinous ambassadors such as Guajardo.

Key Action Items

1. Chinese respect strength in negotiation. It is therefore important that countries appoint ambassadors that can resist China politically, even be critical. Ambassadors should avoid projecting submissiveness by bowing down as minimally as possible.

2. Nonetheless, all ambassadors regardless of national origin must be diplomatic and avoid picking too many fights or excessively criticizing China's government—both during and after their administrations. Exemplified well by Huntsman and other American ambassadors, "respectful but critical" is always a good mantra to follow. Condescension and arrogance will achieve nothing but conflict.

3. Within the business realm, companies should similarly appoint country heads that are neither conflict-averse nor overly belligerent. They must be

able and willing to notify the Chinese government when it launches a poor policy, such as those promoting protectionism, but should avoid unproductive and unwarranted accusations both in the press and in meetings with Chinese government officials.

Chapter 2
The Hammer and the Carrot

April 2017

It was a hot spring on the Korean Peninsula.

North Korea's dictator Kim Jong-un, who American Senator John McCain has called a "crazy fat kid," was preparing more nuclear weapons tests. The rotund dictator had just finished overseeing a parade celebrating "The Day of the Sun," a holiday marking the birthday of Kim Il-sung, founder of North Korea and grandfather of Kim Jong-un.

During the parade, North Korea's military displayed missile canisters bigger and longer than ever before. The broadcast bravado left Pentagon analysts buzzing, wondering if the impressive canisters were an empty Potemkin village or if North Korea had truly made great strides in creating new solid fuel missiles like the KN-15 or a modified BM-25 Musudan to attack America. Either way, the signal was clear: North Korea under Kim sought to achieve nuclear capabilities just as his father the late Kim Jong-il had striven for when lording over the country. U.S. President Donald J. Trump's bellicose Tweets and threats of stronger economic sanctions would not force young dictator Kim to back down in his quest.

In fact, the opposite seemed to occur. In the face of President Trump and U.S. Secretary of Defense James "Mad Dog" Mattis' attacks on North Korea's maneuvers, Kim became ever more oppositional, taking a hard line on the United States. For several months, it appeared North Korea was launching a new missile test every few weeks while official media continued to attack American hegemony. North Korea's Central News Agency (KCNA) even lashed out directly at ally China for cooperating with the United States over increasing economic sanctions. Censuring North Korea's long-time ally and essential trading partner, KCNA called

DOI 10.1515/9781501507618-002

China's economic sanctions a "senseless act that axes the pillar of bilateral relations."[5i]

Rumors swirled that in February, only two months prior, Kim had ordered his older half-brother Kim Jong-nam poisoned to death at an airport in Kuala Lumpur, Malaysia. Other rumors suggested the assassination was apparently prompted by Kim Jong-nam's talks with agents of the U.S. Central Intelligence Agency (CIA) about replacing his incumbent half-brother as head of North Korea in a potential American-led coup. Gossip in spy circles suggested the elder Kim had hundreds of thousands in American cash on his body when murdered. Adding a bit of Hollywood drama to the poisoning, Siti Aisyah and Doan Thi Huong—the two young women from Indonesia and Vietnam caught swiping poison on Kim Jong-nam's face—claimed they had no idea they were handling real poison, instead under the impression it was all for a prank television show.

The questions worrying analysts: What would Kim do next, and worse, was war imminent?

★★★

Hundreds of miles to the south, tensions in Seoul were palpable. Every subsequent North Korean missile test saw the KOSPI[6] drop a few percentage points, and the clarion call by American pundits to take out Kim grow louder.

Several candidates vied for the South Korean presidency after their previous leader, Park Geun-hye, jailed for a multi-million dollar bribery scandal that shook South Korea to the core. Lee Jae-yong, the 48-year-old heir to Samsung Group—South Korea's largest conglomerate, accounting for over 17 percent of the country's gross domestic product with divisions spanning from mobile phones to real estate—was also caught up in the scandal, now hunkering in a 6.3-square-meter jail cell in Seoul Detention Center.

Perhaps the biggest issue facing the candidates was whether to continue deployment of Terminal High Altitude Area Defense (THAAD), an anti-ballistic

---

[5] Such direct criticism of China by Pyongyang is unusual and indicative of the extent to which Kim's regime is tied to North Korea's nuclear program, even at the risk of its ties with China. China's accounts for 90 percent of North Korea's trade so is an essential lifeline for the country. ("The agency made it clear that Pyongyang will never give up its nuclear program in return for maintaining relations with China, saying the nuclear program is 'as precious as' its own life, no matter how valuable the North-China friendship is.")
http://world.kbs.co.kr/english/news/news_hotissue_detail.htm?No=10070379.
[6] Korea's stock exchange, officially the Korea Composite Stock Price Index.

missile defense system developed by the Americans. Aside from using diplomatic channels and the state-owned media to criticize South Korea,[ii] the Chinese government[iii] also used extensive economic punishment, including blocking K-Pop and South Korean movie stars from touring China. By as early as March 2017, tour groups from China to South Korea had dropped 40 percent year over year, decimating retail sales and the leisure sector. But the economic punishments were only just beginning. South Korean Soprano Jo Sumi had to cancel her China tour, as did pianist Park Kun-woo.[iv] The Shanghai Ballet replaced a Korean, Kim Ji-young, as the lead role in a performance of Swan Lake. China even blocked South Korean trade minister Joo Hyung-hwan from visiting the annual Boao Forum in Hainan, China, where businessmen and government elite mingle.[v] As one senior executive of a large real estate developer told me in September 2017, "We had to cancel all performances and exhibitions by South Korean artists and musicians that we had planned for our malls."

All the while, the Chinese state-owned *Global Times* called for more economic weapons to be directed at South Korea: "We also propose that Chinese society should coordinate voluntarily in expanding restrictions on South Korean cultural goods and entertainment exports to China, and block them when necessary," reported an editorial.[vi] Chinese consumers quickly heeded the call and started buying Japanese and German auto brands like Toyota and Volkswagen over Korean brands like Hyundai and KIA. Clearly effective, these measures witnessed a year over year halving of KIA's March 2017 sales in China.[vii] The assault on Korea's economy was serious—after all, although China is known as an export machine, South Korea actually exports more to China than the other way around. In 2016, for example, South Korea ran a $72.2 billion USD surplus.

Back home in Shanghai, around the time my friend JJ contacted me (see Preface), I prepared to do an hour-long radio debate on WAMU for National Public Radio (NPR) along with Gideon Rachman, the Financial Times Chief Foreign Correspondent, and Sheila Smith, a Senior Fellow on the Council on Foreign Relations. While the debate centered around how President Trump and his Chinese counterpart, President Xi Jinping, viewed THAAD and the tensions on the Korean peninsula, I was also going to argue controversially that China does not control North Korea as many American political analysts and President Trump believe despite it being such a large trading partner. North Korea might fall into the Hot Partner category, but that did not mean China has complete sway—it still has to use carrots and sticks to keep North Korea in line. Kim Jong-un has no personal relationship with China's leadership. In fact, North Korea and China's historical closeness has been more a marriage of convenience than one due to mutual respect or Communist linkages as many American analysts believe. Kim Il Sung, Kim's grandfather, had a tense, bitter relationship with China's leaders. Peng Dehuai, a leading Chinese general, for example called Kim "extremely childish" for how he ran the Korean War (1950–1953). He also bridled when China criticized him for being "feudal" by anointing his son as successor. The following links further address the issues surrounding the China-North Korea relationship:

https://www.washingtonpost.com/opinions/why-kim-jong-un-is-alienating-china/2017/10/01/20d99adc-a541-11e7-ade1-76d061d56efa_story.html?utm_term=.23bd22dbac48

http://www.38north.org/2017/09/jperson092617/

In recent months, the South Korean economy had floundered as a result of Beijing's anger at President Park's agreement to accelerate the installation of THAAD, which occurred just months before her arrest. Her decision ended the warming of ties between South Korea and China that began in summer 2013 when President Xi hosted President Park for a state summit. It was around the same time that President Obama's ill-fated China Pivot seemed to be failing as countries gravitated more closely towards China's orbit. If even South Korea, one of America's closest allies, distanced itself from America in favor of China's warm economic embrace, other nations were soon to fall into line.

President Park's decision stunned the region in July 2016, announcing closer military cooperation with the United States and the installation of THAAD—in direct opposition to China. The Chinese[viii] felt President Park had betrayed them, slapping them in the face. As mentioned before, Chinese consumers promptly heeded calls by state media, boycotting South Korean products like KIA cars and Amore Pacific cosmetics, and elected to visit destinations such as Japan, Indonesia, and Thailand over South Korea. The boycotts devastated South Korea's economy. China was South Korea's largest trade partner, with which it shared $124.4 billion USD of trade in 2016—almost double the trade with the U.S. at $66.8 billion that same year. Even a 10 percent drop had a dramatic impact on the everyday lives of South Koreans.

In a new form of statecraft to pressure South Korea's business community, China's government even appeared to target and single out Lotte—another *chaebol*[7] conglomerate that rivals Samsung for influence and size—in its barrage

---

[7] Chaebol is a large (South Korean) business conglomerate, typically a family-owned one.

of economic punishment. China's divvying out of such pressures to different countries and sectors is not unprecedented. Having previously targeted states and sectors (such as social media where it has blocked Facebook and Twitter from being seen in China without a Virtual Private Network VPN), China has also punished companies like Google and GlaxoSmithKline (GSK) for breaking Chinese law. However, the government's targeting of Lotte was the first time China seemed to execute such an all-encompassing attack on a specific company operating in China for actions undertaken outside its borders.

In the months leading up to April 2017—after JJ had been denied a meeting between President Xi and his presidential candidate—87 of Lotte's 99 retail outlets across China were shut down by officials citing fire code infractions. Construction on its multi-billion dollar theme park, which was poised to compete with Shanghai's Disneyland and Beijing's soon-to-open Universal Studios, was halted. A joint venture between Lotte Shanghai Foods and American chocolate maker Hershey's was ordered to stop production. Local tax bureaus across the country audited Lotte's diverse operations, and online consumers started calling for the boycott of all Lotte snack products through WeChat[8] messaging groups and other media platforms. Chen Ou, the founder of Jumei Youpin, a large group-buying platform similar to Groupon, announced, "we have completely scrubbed the name of Lotte from our Web site," further expressing, "we would rather die than carry its goods in the future."

What brought about such ire from China toward Lotte specifically? Lotte had ceded the golf course that was now being used for THAAD deployment in the Seongju region, southeast of Seoul. Despite Lotte's investment of over $5 billion USD in China, not to mention its employment of tens of thousands of Chinese (rendering it a friend to China), the conglomerate bore the brunt of government and consumer anger toward THAAD. Lotte's protests, claiming it had no hand in THAAD's deployment and was merely following its home government's demands, had little effect in absolving the chaebol of public blame in China. Ultimately, Lotte announced that it was looking to sell most of its retail outlets in China as it did not expect to see a turnaround in their business anytime soon.

Even rival South Korean confectioner, Orion, saw its Choco Pie sales suffer as consumers mistook it for part of the Lotte group and boycotted the company's (formerly) popular snack cakes. Orion announced earlier in April that it was lowering production in its six China plants. Meanwhile, the company's public

---

[8] WeChat is a Chinese social media mobile app that one can also buy wealth management products through and shop online.

relations team sought to convince Chinese consumers through online messaging that Orion was not part of Lotte Group, but to no avail. While China's foreign ministry denied targeting Lotte—a move of plausible deniability—the coincidence of Lotte's fire code violations, tax troubles, and the role it played in THAAD's installation left no doubt as to the reasons for Lotte's losses.

Now understood by South Korea's business community, and global businesses by extension, Beijing's message was clear: if you want access to China's wallet, you must adhere to our political demands. If you do not, you will be punished as South Korea has been. Even more alarmingly, companies realized that they too were subject to punishment as Lotte had been. Apart from governing bodies, companies would also be required to bend to China's political will, even if that meant going against the decisions of home governments. This sent chills through the global business community. Boardrooms scrambled to develop contingency plans lest their companies unwittingly get caught up in a political fight. Relying on press releases and typical government lobbying firms would no longer suffice in crisis situations. Companies needed to install leaders and strategies more akin to those required for the title of Secretary of State than of public relations head.

It was at the height of Lotte's and South Korea's economic strain when I received JJ's inquiry to see if I could arrange a meeting with President Xi and JJ's presidential candidate.

***

An understanding of Beijing's resolute position requires consideration of its perspective in the face of THAAD and what the "defense system" represents. Many South Koreans and Americans alike underestimated the fear that THAAD has generated among Chinese. Their miscalculation results from a lack of awareness about the paradoxical role America plays in the region (and in most of the world for that matter)—both stabilizing and destabilizing. Smaller countries that do not have long-term historical ties with China, such as Australia, are comforted by a greater American presence. Yet the sentiment is less benign in countries like Cambodia or Laos, which suffered under American military aggression during the Vietnam War. Other regimes see how America helped replace Muammar Gaddafi in Libya or Saddam Hussein in Iraq and remain wary of America's long-term intentions and willingness to push for regime change.

The Chinese have a right, in truth, to be worried about THAAD and America's overall military presence in the Asia-Pacific region. China views America's presence more as an ongoing military threat than as that of a friendly police officer, despite U.S. efforts to present itself as the latter. With 35,000 American troops based in South Korea and a little over 39,000 in Japan,[ix] the invasion of China is no logistical difficulty. Were Kim's regime to topple in North Korea, American troops could drive into China in a matter of hours, relatively unhindered. To put it into perspective, imagine how Americans would feel if China had 35,000 troops in Mexico, and another 39,000 in Cuba.

Until America reduces its military presence in Asia, especially in South Korea, it will continue to be looked upon by the Chinese as a long-term threat, regardless of the short-term Sino-US warming of relations as we have seen between President Trump and President Xi. China is indeed beginning to find Kim Jong-un's regime more troublesome, recognizing its potential threat to regional stability if North Korea achieves its nuclear aspirations. Yet it is unlikely that China will take initiatives toward a regime change or look to neuter Kim unless America first reduces its military presence in the region.

Kim's father (Kim Jong-il) had been a useful buffer against the Americans for China—a role still played by the DPRK (Democratic People's Republic of Korea) to an extent—but Dictator Kim is looked upon with more scorn in China, having demonstrated unhinged volatility and over aggressiveness to seek nuclear weapon capability. No Chinese senior officials have welcomed the young dictator to China on a state visit, nor have any visited him in North Korea's capital Pyongyang after he had his uncle, Jang Song-thaek, executed in 2013.[9] President Trump and his successors thus have the potential to make a grand bargain with China to make the Peninsula safer. Yet the Chinese will not cross a certain red line in handling their unruly neighbor—such as imposing cutting-to-the-bone economic sanctions—unless they are first assured of China's long-term safety, regardless of the American administration or political party in power. A massive U.S. troop reduction is therefore necessary for China's peace of mind, enabling subsequent Beijing-led measures to put Kim's regime in a vice.

---

[9] Kim Jong-un's uncle, Jang Song-thaek, served in the role of critical intermediary between Beijing and Pyongyang. Married to Kim Il-sung's only daughter (the late Kim Jong-il's sister) and considered young Kim's mentor, he was the only primary North Korean official associated with China's more agreeably perceived Kim Jong-il. Song-thaek's support of China-endorsed economic reforms made him a diplomatic friend of Beijing, meeting with former Chinese President Hu Jintao and cooperating with the Chinese government. His execution on December 12, 2013, was therefore a blow to Sino-North Korean relations, leaving a more unmanageable leader to be dealt with by China (http://www.businessinsider.com/jang-song-thaek-execution-and-china-2013-12).

***

A result of China's need for assured regional security, THAAD's threat to China received a commensurately threatening response, as we have already seen. This response played keenly on the minds of South Korean presidential candidates as they prepared for a heated election.

In the face of South Korea's deteriorating economy, candidates used THAAD to differentiate themselves. Some like Moon Jae-in, previously a student activist and Chief of Staff to former President Roh Moo-hyun (2003–2008), promised to halt deployment of THAAD and rethink its importance. Others like Ahn Hee-jung, Governor of Chungcheongnam-do Province, advocated consideration of further deployment. All candidates, however, stated plans to renew relations with China, a goal transcending party divides.

I was therefore not really surprised after thinking about it, after initially being completely surprised, when approached by JJ to arrange a meeting between his candidate and China's top leader. Yet the rejection by the Chinese to secure a back channel—the overture met with firm refusal—shed light on South Korea's quandary. Regardless of what its government did at this point, South Korea risked infuriating China and irking America, the latter now run by a temperamental President Trump for whom military strikes against the DPRK were not out of the question.[10] Caught in the middle, South Korea was unsure of how to proceed until presidential elections were concluded. Even then, South Korea saw no way to win.

Ultimately, Moon Jae-in, generally considered South Korea's most pro-China candidate, won the presidency and assumed office on May 10, 2017. In addition to promoting diplomacy and discussion over military action against the North, President Moon's platform challenged the nation's stance on THAAD. He questioned the Ministry of Defense's decision not merely to continue THAAD's installation, but to accelerate it—a measure even more perplexing given the recent impeachment of former President Park, seen by many as THAAD's champion. Throughout his campaign, Moon seemed to focus more on South Korean relations with China than on any pure domestic issues facing the country.

Yet despite President Moon's more moderate approach to THAAD, China's media outlets showed no sign of fatigue in their barrage of South Korea. Under sustained pressure from the South Korean business community, President Moon

---

[10] Trump's decision to keep military strikes on the table in handling North Korea appears par for the course given his launch of military strikes against Syria earlier in the year.

finally surrendered to China's demands on June 7, calling for THAAD's immediate suspension.

Messages of capitulation flooded South Korea's official media. "We are not saying the two launchers and other equipment that have already been deployed should be withdrawn. But those that have yet to be deployed will have to wait," said a senior official from Moon's office, as reported by South Korea's Yonhap news agency. Left unnamed by Yonhap, Moon's senior official further stated that the assessment could take up to a year. By delaying rather than cancelling THAAD deployment completely, Moon attempted to placate China but also appease South Korean military hardliners who demanded that THAAD's installation be continued.

Meanwhile, Chinese state media predictably embraced the news. *The Global Times*, for example, expounded on the benefits President Moon could reap from a closer relationship with China, encouraging the new president to move away from America's patronage as Filipino president Rodrigo Duterte had done.[x] Again, in China's modern form of statecraft it synchronizes messaging by the state, the media, and consumers.

After a battle of wills, victory was clear—China's combination of traditional statecraft and economic punishment had caused President Moon to back down. Importantly, in getting what it wanted, China did not fire a single missile or send warships to patrol South Korean waters. Beijing had invented a new form of statecraft: instead of guns and ships, the government deployed economic carrots and cudgels, even against China's erstwhile allies. Simultaneously using state-owned media to cajole, threaten, and rally everyday Chinese consumers, Beijing was able to secure its political goals.

Traditionally, major powers such as the United States will implement economic sanctions against enemies like Iran, Cuba, or North Korea, bullying problematic nations into submission, often over decades, before resorting to military action. But China has started to use economic weapons even against friendly nations, coercively orienting their governments towards China's preferred direction. Contrary to the claims of many pundits who suggest that China prioritizes economic growth at all costs, China has demonstrated an unmistakable willingness to sacrifice short-term economic growth opportunities in order to bend other nations to its political will.

Neighboring countries are growing accustomed to China's economic weapons. In November 2016, Mongolia hosted the Dalai Lama for four days at the invitation of a Mongolian monastery. Much to China's chagrin, Mongolian senior officials welcomed the Tibetan spiritual leader, viewed by the Chinese government as a traitorous separatist rather than the peace-lover he is considered to be elsewhere. Within a month of the Dalai Lama's brief tour, China ceased imports of Mongolian commodities and canceled a visit by Mongolia's Deputy Prime Minister to Beijing. Only after Mongolia apologized a few weeks later did tensions cool and imports resume. Given that 75 percent of Mongolia's exports rely on its trade with China—contrasted with a meager 0.57 percent involved in U.S. trade—Mongolia's decision to back down and apologize was a foregone conclusion.[xi]

Similarly, the Nobel Peace Prize committee appointed by Norway's Storting[11] outraged China when it conferred the 2010 Nobel Peace Prize on Chinese dissident Liu Xiaobo. Calling for the overthrow of the Chinese Communist Party, Liu Xiaobo is looked upon dimly by most of his fellow citizens, and it therefore raised Chinese eyebrows when the Nobel committee bestowed the honorable title on Liu Xiaobo. Responsible for the Nobel committee's appointment, Norway would surely not elude Chinese retaliation. Beijing immediately ended normal relations. Norwegian salmon imports to China dropped 61.8 percent within a month.

Just as they had done with South Korean Orion Choco Pie or KIA's auto, Chinese consumers voted with their wallets, buying imports of Scottish and Tasmanian salmon and thereby indicating favor for governments in the UK and Australia that have taken a friendlier stance toward Chinese government policies. It took six years for Norway to normalize relations with China. Adding strain to patience, normalization was only complete once Norway released the following statement: "The Norwegian Government reiterates its commitment to the one China policy, fully respects China's sovereignty and territorial integrity, attaches high importance to China's core interests and major concerns, will not support actions that undermine them, and will do its best to avoid any future damage to the bilateral relations." The result? Norwegian salmon swiftly repopulated China's grocery shelves, cheered on by state-owned media and bought in droves by eager Chinese consumers.[xii]

The lesson to be learned? Nations and companies erring in the footsteps of Norway or Lotte will quickly find themselves in Beijing's crosshairs, as trespassers against Chinese security concerns increasingly get brought into line. In a classic execution of coercive diplomacy, China will apply economic pressure to transgressors while rewarding those who acquiesce, as South Korea, Norway, and Mongolia ultimately deemed best.

★★★★★

---

[11] The Storting is Norway's supreme legislature.

Dialogue:
Jacques deLisle, Stephen A. Cozen Professor of Law and Professor of Political Science, University of Pennsylvania

I first met Jacques deLisle in 2003 when he invited me to speak about the shifts in China's economy to a group of his graduate students at the University of Pennsylvania. I try to have dinner with him every year or two either in Philadelphia or Shanghai. I always enjoy hearing his views of changes in the legal and political science worlds dealing with China. Aside from being a professor, he is also Deputy Director, Center for the Study of Contemporary China; Director, Center for East Asian Studies; Co-Director, Center for Asian Law, University of Pennsylvania; and Director, Asia Program, Foreign Policy Research Institute. His research focuses on contemporary Chinese law and politics, including: legal reform and its relationship to economic reform and political change in China, the international status of Taiwan and cross-Strait relations, China's engagement with the international order, and U.S.-China relations.

His writing appears in *Journal of Contemporary China, Orbis*, and other foreign affairs and area studies journals, law reviews, edited volumes, and Internet and print media. He is co-editor of *China's Global Engagement* (with Avery Goldstein, 2017), *The Internet, Social Media, and a Changing China* (with Avery Goldstein and Guobin Yang, 2016), *Political Changes in Taiwan Under Ma Ying-jeou* (with Jean-Pierre Cabestan, 2014), *China's Challenges* (with Avery Goldstein, 2014), and *China Under Hu Jintao* (with T. J. Cheng and Deborah Brown, 2005). He frequently serves as an expert witness on Chinese law, consultant to U.S. government, Chinese, and international NGO projects relating to law and reform in China.[xiii]

Rein: Are American economic sanctions sufficient to dissuade Kim from his nuclear ambitions? Or does President Trump need to launch a strike on North Korea as he did with Syria? If he were to do so, how do you think China and South Korea would react? Would a wide-ranging war be inevitable?

deLisle: Many iterations of U.S. economic sanctions over many years have not effectively dissuaded North Korea from pursuing its nuclear weapons program, or its ballistic missile program. To the limited extent that U.S. sanctions could be made tougher (and it is a quite limited extent), it would be very optimistic to expect them finally to have the effect of getting Pyongyang to give up its arms programs.

Truly potent economic sanctions would require full cooperation from China. That has not been forthcoming, and is unlikely to occur. Moreover, although Kim's thinking is not exactly transparent to outsiders, there appears to be good reason to think that he considers his nuclear weapons program to be essential to regime survival. That is, having nuclear weapons is what deters the U.S. (and everyone else) from treating him like Gaddafi—from taking steps that could topple Kim and potentially end the DPRK regime, and, perhaps, an independent North Korea. If that is indeed Kim's assessment, then it is hard to see how any policy measures could induce him to give up nuclear arms.

Trump has talked of resorting to force, but the idea has generated near-unanimous opposition among experts and analysts in the U.S., and also among U.S. allies in the region, for obvious reasons. A strike akin to the one Trump launched over "beautiful chocolate cake" with Xi Jinping at Mar-a-Lago would not be nearly enough. The goal presumably would be, at minimum, to destroy Pyongyang's nuclear capabilities. The challenge would be somewhat akin to the Israeli attack on the Osiris reactor in Iraq in the early 1980s. But the task would be much more difficult to accomplish here, given the more advanced stage and greater scale of North Korea's nuclear program, and given that some of the targets are hidden or hardened to survive a U.S. strike. An attempt to take out all of Pyongyang's nuclear facilities, thus, would require large-scale action and very well might not be fully successful.

And, of course, there is the very high risk of devastating retaliation by North Korea and subsequent escalation of conflict. If any part of the North's nuclear arsenal survived an attack, a weapon could be used against Seoul, or perhaps Japan, or perhaps U.S. military assets in the region. Even without deploying a nuclear device, Kim could use his military's considerable capacity to lay waste to Seoul (and other places) with conventional weaponry. Attempting to cripple North Korea's capacity to retaliate with conventional arms would require very extensive U.S. strikes, with very limited prospects for success.

South Korea—more so under Moon but also under his predecessor Park (and for past, and likely future, South Korean leaders more generally)—would hardly welcome such a risky and likely catastrophic (for South Korea) course of action by the United States, under any but the most dire circumstances.

China would be vehemently opposed as well, for reasons that include opposition to U.S. military action on its doorstep, and concern that the result would be a disorderly collapse of the DPRK regime and all the cost and chaos that would entail for China.

Rein: Do you think China has been actively trying to contain North Korea's nuclear ambitions with economic sanctions? Or has China been playing President Trump by asserting its commitment to sanctions yet keeping trade routes open with North Korea? Does China view Kim Jong-un as an ally and useful buffer against America, or is he becoming a thorn in their side?

deLisle: The U.S. understandably has been frustrated for a long time with the weakness of the pressure that Beijing has been willing to impose on Pyongyang (whether through economic sanctions or other means). Trump has sought to push China to do more, after retreating from an initial, implausible view that he might outsource the North Korea problem to China. Trump's now more modest expectations of greatly increased cooperation from China are certain to be disappointing, as we have already begun to see. He already faced this during his first few months in office, and opted to give Beijing something of a pass (noting that "at least China tried"). There has been some talk of the Trump administration imposing secondary sanctions on Chinese firms that continue to do business with North Korea, but such action does not appear imminent. For U.S. policy, a key question is if—or when—Trump's apparently growing frustration with China on this issue will have major policy consequences.

China's approach well may be to promise a fair amount and deliver very little. U.S.-China relations with respect to North Korea face a fundamental problem in that Washington and Beijing have very different bad case scenarios. To be sure, a war on the peninsula is bad for both the U.S. and China, and neither favors a permanently nuclear armed North Korea. Beyond that, interests diverge. For China, a very bad outcome is a disorderly regime collapse in North Korea, refugee flows into China, and the prospect of a reunified Korean peninsula governed by a U.S.-allied government. For the U.S., a very bad outcome is North Korea becoming an even more potent rogue state, brandishing the threat of nuclear attack against U.S. allies in the region and, worse, the U.S. homeland, and possibly proliferating nuclear weapons or know-how to third parties with interests and agendas profoundly adverse to those of the United States.

This basic dynamic has been in place for some time. Recently, it has been shifting in two potentially significant ways. First, Pyongyang's pursuit of a larger nuclear arsenal and the development of missiles to strike U.S. territory changes the U.S. calculus and shifts the policy debate. The perceived imperative to act and the risks of action are both rising. Second, Beijing has grown increasingly unhappy with Pyongyang under the current North Korean leadership. As Kim's antics have become more outlandish, as other states have become more concerned about the threats he poses, and as he has begun to bite the Chinese hand that feeds him, Kim has become more of a liability and a risk for China. Supporting North Korea has become more awkward for a country that increasingly claims superpower or near-superpower status and that seeks to cast itself as largely supportive of the international status quo. And it is becoming more difficult for China not to accept that the Kim regime's behavior genuinely threatens the legitimate national security concerns of other states.

Kim Jong-un's North Korea remains a useful buffer against the U.S. (and, more specifically, the prospect of a unified, U.S.-allied Korea). But this benefit comes with increasing costs, and annoyance, for Beijing as the Kim regime's behavior increasingly threatens neighboring states' security and embarrasses Beijing. This surely accounts for China's willingness to take such steps as banning the export of some dual-use (military-civilian) goods, supporting UN Security Council-authorized sanctions and trade restrictions in response to Pyongyang's weapons programs, and suspending coal imports from North Korea. But the sanctions that Beijing has undertaken or supported have not always been fully implemented and have stopped well short of posing existential threats to the Kim regime (or even curbing China's overall trade with North Korea).

Rein: What do you make of North Korea's recent criticisms of China's economic sanctions. Is there are a real break between the two countries, or is Kim merely posturing? Does China have as much political control over North Korea as President Trump believes?

deLisle: Kim's criticisms of China's economic sanctions are one marker of the notable deterioration in recent years of a relationship that the Chinese used to like to describe as being as close as "lips and teeth." In reaction to the modest—but economically painful to the DPRK—measure of suspending Beijing's coal imports from North Korea in early 2017, North Korean state media's referring to China (albeit not by name) as "dancing to the U.S.'s tune" and, in effect, collaborating in an effort to bring down the DPRK regime, was a remarkable statement. But it is, at best, premature to discern a profound break. Absent a sustained, more radical turn in Kim's behavior or a determination in Washington that Kim is becoming an imminent fundamental or near-existential threat to the U.S. (or, perhaps, U.S. allies), China still sees its interests as largely consistent with the status quo. Unless conditions change significantly, Beijing's approach is likely to remain one of "hold your nose (increasingly tightly), and stick with Kim."

It is hard to know how much control Trump thinks Beijing has over Pyongyang, but he appears to think it has a lot. And it is difficult to define how much control China does have over North Korea, but it is limited, and complex. Beijing is in a difficult position. It does not have the capacity simply to issue orders to Kim—unless it backs them with threats that it does not want to have to carry out. The DPRK is, of course, utterly dependent on Chinese support. In that sense, China has awesome potential leverage, but it can exercise that leverage only at considerable risk and cost. The consequences of trying to use it—in terms of Pyongyang's reactions—are not entirely predictable, and the outcome might be at odds with China's interests and preferences.

Rein: Do you foresee a scenario where China could move to neuter Kim or push for a regime change? Do you think if America reduced its troop size in South Korea and Japan that China would agree to a grand bargain to push for reunification?

deLisle: So far, we have been talking mostly about marginal changes in a bad situation (on one hand) and the possibility of highly disruptive and possibly catastrophic change (on the other hand). An intriguing alternative is a "grand bargain," which comes in a couple of possible varieties: one in which China acquiesces in regime change in North Korea in return for significant (or total) withdrawal of the U.S. military presence in South Korea—a military presence largely premised, after all, on the threat posed by the North; and another, more sweeping one in which Korea is reunified but as a neutral or near-neutral state (and presumably a non-nuclear one).

These are bold visions that, if achieved, could resolve many of the problems and remove many of the risks that we have been discussing. But they entail major risks and do not seem at all feasible under current conditions. Xi and Trump seem extremely unlikely to reach any such agreement. Attempting to impose such an arrangement on the Kim regime, or effectuating regime change in North Korea, as a precondition would be an obviously risky proposition, fraught with many of the perils associated with the bad case scenarios that might follow U.S. military action.

Rein: China has punished South Korea economically for deploying THAAD. Now that the newly elected President Moon has halted deployment, undertaking a review of the system, do you think Sino-Korean relations will be close again as they were between 2013–2016? Or is there now too much mutual distrust? What can South Korea do to regain China's trust and thus access its markets and consumer base?

deLisle: It seems unlikely that THAAD deployment has deeply and permanently damaged what has been a pretty positive relationship between China and South Korea. Although Beijing of course did not welcome the deployment of THAAD and was concerned about the possible impact on China's security (particularly the spying that THAAD's radar could make possible), Beijing's public posturing against THAAD was out of proportion to the threat it actually posed and, likely, to Beijing's perception of that threat. Moreover, the replacement of Park by Moon as South Korea's president, and South Korea's ensuing pause in THAAD deployment, renewed (but wary) interest in engaging Pyongyang, and efforts to improve relations with Beijing (while also tending to ties with Washington) have given China reason to lower its level of concern and, thus, forego further measures that would gin up the Chinese public's antipathy toward South Korea and, in turn, Chinese consumers' and tourists' aversion to South Korean products, retailers, pop culture, and vacations. The THAAD controversy does not seem likely, in the long run, to loom much larger in China-South Korea ties than other ups and downs that characterize many dense and generally positive bilateral relationships.

As to Chinese consumer reaction to THAAD, it was dramatic, with tourism to South Korea and purchases of South Korean branded goods dropping steeply (by 40% on some reports), and with the role of South Korea's Lotte group in providing land for the THAAD deployment creating an unusually prominent link between a Korean commercial enterprise and offensive (to China) Korean government action. Chinese consumers' choices are affected—although, of course, not determined—by the tone the government sets, as well as by policy directives (for example, reportedly telling travel agencies to suspend sales of group tours to South Korea or denying requests for charter flights to South Korea). So, if the government-to-government relationship rebounds some from its recent troubles, as seems likely, that will remove one impetus to Chinese consumers' turn against South Korea. Popular Chinese attitudes toward South Korea are far less negative than attitudes toward Japan, which—despite occasional outbursts of strong anti-Japanese sentiments and boycotts—have not precluded robust Chinese demands for Japanese products, travel to Japan, and so on.

Case Study: Show That You Are a Friend to China

As we have seen, foreign companies face tremendous financial risk in cases of tensions between China and their home nations' governments. Typically resulting from political hostility, boycotts and consumer protests waged against foreign companies are quite common. American, Japanese, South Korean, Filipino, and French companies alike have all come under attack by Chinese consumers heeding their government's call. Usually in response to military threats or attacks on Chinese sovereignty, China's government rapidly mobilizes criticisms against adversarial foreign policies, bringing along its billion plus consumers and their wallets to the battlefield. While protests tend to target Japanese firms most fervently because of lingering tensions borne from Japanese atrocities during World War II in China, no nation's companies are exempt from the possibility of attack.

Take Starbucks, for example, when it was essentially forced to shut down a café inside the Forbidden City in 2007. Rousing furious protests from Chinese ultra-nationalists, Starbucks' presence within one of China's most historic sites was seen as a flagrant offense to Chinese culture and its respectful preservation. Incited by the placement of such an iconic American brand in the middle of Chinese heritage, online and in-person protests grew to such levels of ire that Starbucks finally decided to close up shop.

Likewise, whenever Sino-Japanese tensions blow up, Japanese companies like Toyota, Uniqlo, and Canon are immediately boycotted. Some protests grow so violent that consumers themselves fear buying Japanese brands lest they become targets of mob anger. When friction erupted between the U.S. and China in 2016 over the South China Sea, protests similarly went after iconic American brands like KFC. Although hostility toward KFC blew over after a month or two— and KFC continues to thrive in the Chinese market—it is still critical for all brands, no matter how popular, to both project their national origin and demonstrate a thorough respect of China and its culture.[xiv] KFC was smart in how it has built a long-term close relationship with Chinese consumers which allowed it to move on from the protests quickly and continue its market-leading position in the Quick Service Restaurant (QSR) sector. Chinese consumers know that KFC respects China not only by creating 430,000 jobs but also by creating free lunch and other programs on an ongoing basis for needy Chinese.

For example, it has often provided free food during times of natural disasters to rescuers and those injured and donated over 100 million RMB to poor children's lunch programs where it provides an egg and milk for poor school children. As Joey Wat, the President of Yum! China, parent company of KFC, told me, "Helping poorer kids or in disaster relief was the right thing to do—we have the food and they needed the help." It is important to note that you cannot perform outreach programs purely as a public relations tool. Companies must do it because it is, in Wat's words, "the right thing to do." As Wat told me, "I always tell our 430,000 staff to do the right thing. Do what is right for the country and have a higher goal. It is not just about making money."

At the same time, such benevolence also helps impart the brand as a friend to China. Reading and book programs geared towards children is also well received by parents—the program demonstrates that KFC respects the value of education that is placed in Chinese families. While protests about US-China tensions over the South China Sea flared up in the summer of 2016, it blew over quickly in large part because KFC has built such a closeness with the Chinese community and consumers appreciated the contributions KFC has made to Chinese society.

With an ever-present potential for politically driven hits to revenue, it is crucial that companies actively demonstrate friendship to China, respecting its people and government. Being a friend to China certainly does not consist of bowing down to all of the Chinese government's demands. Nonetheless, companies must make sure to be respectful when pushing back against Chinese political forces and indicate clear interest in China's long-term success.

How does a company achieve this? One must first note that it is insufficient to merely state one's status as a friend to China or donate perfunctorily to charities. In order to truly gain the loyalty of Chinese consumers and demonstrate friendship, companies must show a perceptive understanding of and respect for Chinese culture.

Revisiting our previous example, Starbucks has actually succeeded rather well in this endeavor—an important stronghold in the weathering of Chinese protests over issues such as their café's Forbidden City location. Making waves in early 2017, Starbucks announced that it would be granting medical insurance to more than 10,000 elderly parents of Chinese employees under its new Starbucks China Parent Care Program. Employees that have worked for Starbucks for over two years will receive coverage for parents under the age of 75 for 30 critical illnesses. Now Starbucks' second largest market worldwide after the U.S., China continues to be courted by the company. Conscientious about frequently reinforcing its popularity in China, Starbucks enjoys around 30 percent margins—some of its highest in the world.

Starbucks' Parent Care Program is much more than a desirable benefit used to lure in recruited candidates and retain talent, however. Capturing and keeping employees is certainly difficult for any company in China, given the nation's strong labor market, and especially for Starbucks as it seeks to double its current number of 2,300 outlets by 2021. But more than anything, Starbucks' coverage of employees' parents serves as a strong demonstration that it understands the pressure on so many young workers to take care of their families.[xv]

As we will see later in Chapter 6, China's medical system is woefully inadequate. Gathered through surveys conducted by my firm, lack of access to good medical care is one of the five biggest concerns shared by contemporary Chinese. Given the combination of the state system's weak medical insurance and a deeply ingrained Confucian tenet of filial piety, immense pressure is placed on China's only children to take care of aging parents. Starbucks' initiative was therefore a brilliant display of both empathy to its workers and Chinese cultural understanding, despite the company's American roots.

In a conversation with Belinda Wong, the President of Starbucks China, she claimed to me that Starbucks' provision of insurance was neither intended for public relations purposes nor to curry favor with the government, assuring me that it was simply the right thing to do for employees. Nevertheless, the Parent Care Program has served as a remarkably well-executed public relations move. Wong might naïvely assume that investors and everyday Chinese view Starbucks' initiative simply as a good deed, but the reality has been a significant increase in Chinese consumer respect for the company. As was exclaimed to me by one 24-year old woman from Jiangxi Province, "What an amazing benefit! Starbucks really understands Chinese culture, respects it and is doing a great thing."

Initiatives by companies akin to that of Starbucks will prove incalculably beneficial in mitigating political risk. While no demonstration of cultural sensitivity and friendship will fully immunize foreign brands to political crackdown and consumer protests, proving oneself a friend to China will radically reduce such risks and thereby improve one's standing in case of a political showdown.

Key Action Items

1. Treat Chinese employees well and understand the constraints they face in China, whether these consist of poor medical access, *hukou* or household registration issues. Offering employee benefits such as low-interest loans for them to buy housing, or helping to defray medical care costs for family members, is key to recruiting and retaining top talent.
2. Appoint Country Heads and public relations teams that are skilled at connecting with Chinese consumers on an ongoing basis by being active in social media and in programs on a daily basis. These representatives must also show consistent respect to both employees and customers, thereby regularly strengthening their company's brand. A great example of this is Apple which has consistently shown respect to the Chinese people and brand.

Chapter 3
America's Power Vacuum and the New Global Order: One Belt One Road and AIIB

Qatar, June 2017

"It is very bad," Nahib sighed. Cupping his hands around his chin, the Yemeni shopkeeper continued nervously, "the tension between Qatar and Saudi Arabia is getting worse and worse. There is too much religious tension in the world. How does the dispute get resolved? I have no idea. I am not sure it can be."

I was interviewing businessmen in Souq Waqif, Doha's main outdoor trading bazaar, when I met Nahib. Normally, traders overwhelm the bustling souk (marketplace), buying and selling spices, falcons, and various foodstuffs, Nahib told me. During Ramadan, Muslims living in Qatar often flock to Souq Waqif to enjoy a festive Iftar, the meal ending their daytime fast. Usually abuzz with celebration, restaurants and outdoor cafes lining the bazaar serve feasting families as friends smoke apple and other-flavored shisha from large hookahs.

But there was little to celebrate that night. The souk's winding pathways sat shrunken, relatively void of people. Just two weeks earlier, Saudi Arabia, Egypt, Bahrain, and the United Arab Emirates had cut diplomatic ties with Qatar—home to the world's highest per capita GDP given the Persian Gulf state's large natural gas reserves. In addition to launching a land and air blockade on Qatar, the Saudi Arabian-led coalition expelled Qatari citizens from their own countries, splitting apart families. Qatar's stock market and currency plunged as investors fled.

Nahib was one of many who were nervous. Earlier that week, there had been a run on supermarkets as fretful Qataris hoarded supplies. While Turkey and Iran increased food shipments several days later, anxieties were only momentarily calmed. One manager of an American luxury chain hotel told me they were "sharing eggs and other food products" with sister properties in case they ran out. But with so many vacant hotel rooms, this was unlikely to happen. Disquieted, the manager explained that they were running on less than 10 percent occupancy, and even those remaining guests were mostly long-term residents. Their business decimated, the hotel had shut down one of its two towers altogether.

Complicating political dynamics, U.S. President Donald Trump has appeared to confuse America's position on the matter. Causing alarm on Twitter, President Trump swiftly indicated his support of the Saudi Arabian-led coalition, despite the fact that Qatar houses America's largest military base in the region—stationed

DOI 10.1515/9781501507618-003

with 11,000 military personnel. Fearful of the President's unpredictability, many worried the U.S. might become a destabilizing force rather than a mediator in the conflict.[i]

Choosing Saudi Arabia as the destination of his first official visit overseas, Trump showed a bold divergence from predecessors who took less controversial routes to Mexico or Canada. Bewildered, governments in the region and throughout the world questioned whether President Trump would upend normal alliances or preserve long-term partnerships in the region. While Trump intends to keep enemies on their toes and forge better deals for the U.S., his tactics often confuse allies abroad. Alienated by the President's unsteady maneuvers, former American allies may feel forced to seek out and shore up new relationships, as happened in Asia as nations have gravitated toward China.

At times impetuously careless and at others tactical, President Trump's variable foreign policy moves have left traditional Middle Eastern allies unsure if they can rely on the U.S. As a result, many have looked to build stronger regional coalitions of power, as did those opposing Qatar. Having just established its first overseas military base in Djibouti, China has also caught the attention of Middle Eastern players. Several now seek expanded trade and military links with the eastern superpower.

About a week after Qatar was hit with the Saudis' blockade, I arrived in an empty airport. Maybe four people stood in the immigration line. Outside, taxi drivers dozed at exits, waiting for clients who would never arrive. On our way into the city, my taxi driver, originally from Nepal, bemoaned the country's losses. "Ever since the blockade, there has been no business. I wait for hours without a customer." When I left Qatar a week later, outbound queues stretched farther than I have ever witnessed in an airport. It felt as if Qatar's two million expatriates were all escaping to safer climes—an orderly yet nervous evacuation like that of Saigon at the end of the U.S. presence in Vietnam. No one knew what would happen next, and no one wanted to be in the country lest Kuwait fail in its diplomatic initiatives to mediate the situation.

"The Sunni and Shiite problem is getting worse. How does anyone solve this?" Nahib continued. Arriving in Qatar nearly seven years ago, Nahib had come to make his fortunes as a shopkeeper, while his wife continued to work in the UAE (United Arab Emirates). Though Nahib had previously lived in Saudi Arabia, it was only in Qatar that he earned enough money to send his children to study in the UK. But now he was apprehensive about the future. What if Qatar's moneymaking party was over? Few other countries in the Middle East offered him the same opportunities for wealth. "We have no idea what will happen. It is just like North and South Korea. Unsolvable. I don't know if I should stay here or go elsewhere."

While offering no proof of its accusation, the Saudi-led coalition had enacted its blockade citing Qatar's sponsorship of terrorism. In a tense departure from President Trump's position, U.S. Secretary of State Rex Tillerson demanded evidence of Saudi Arabia's indictment and a peaceful end to hostilities. The Saudi response was silence.

A few days after I met Nahib, Saudi Arabia and its allies presented Qatar with a 13-point ultimatum—Qatar's only way out of the stranglehold. In immediate objection, Qatar called the demands unreasonable, if not impossible, protesting that they interfered with its national sovereignty and internal affairs. Among its demands, the Saudi-led coalition required Qatar to sever its alleged ties with the Muslim Brotherhood; end diplomatic relations with Iran; block Turkey's use of Qatari soil for its military base; and shut down its Al-Jazeera television network, which had often criticized and embarrassed leaders of neighboring kingdoms.

But the true underlying cause of tension is Qatar's closeness to Iran. A mostly Shiite nation, Iran has long been at odds with Saudi Arabia, the predominantly Sunni state. Each vying for dominance in the region, the two similarly sized nations have drawn satellite states into the conflict, seeking support on their respective sides of the schism. A clash rooted in history, Saudi Arabia and Iran's divide—and more principally, the Sunni-Shiite divide—seems intractable to bridge.

Until recently, most American political analysts have lumped the Islamic World into one collective category (see Harvard Professor Samuel P. Huntington's *Clash of the Civilizations*, 2011). In reality, however, dynamics of the region are far more nuanced.

A whole series of books can and should be written to explain the Sunni-Shiite divide, and the further subdivisions between other brands of Islam—such as that which distinguishes Salafi Islam[12] (which prevails in Qatar and Saudi Arabia) from Shaykhist Islam (predominantly in Iraq). A pit of writhing anger and ever-shifting alliances result from the clash for religious and political dominance. Yet the issue is no longer a regional one. Given growing fears of radical Islamic terrorism and global reliance on Middle Eastern oil, clashes in the region have begun to affect the rest of the world.

---

[12] Salafi Islam is also known as the more derogatory term Wahhabism in the West—although some claim that Wahhabism is a separate brand of Islam altogether.

Thwarting any attempts at negotiation or peacekeeping in the region, the Sunni-Shia divide prevails above all other issues in the Middle East. And any reconciliation seems far from imminent. Nearly every person I interviewed in Qatar, from Yemenis to Jordanians to Egyptians, felt the blockade was just Saudi Arabia's first move in an attack against Iran, a Sunni-Shia power play far from letting up. Any real resolution was out of sight; the anger was simply too deep-rooted.

***

Outside the regional power struggle, another question with global repercussions concerns the U.S. and China: What roles will these two superpowers play in negotiating a resolution? And will their respective strategies undermine or bolster their global influence?

Under President Trump, America has seesawed in its position on the dispute, causing great upset in its allies who perceive a lack of support. Directly after the blockade's enactment on June 5th, President Trump tweeted his support of the Saudi coalition. But only a week later, America sold $12 billion USD in F-15 fighter jets to Qatar. On top of this, U.S. Secretary of State Tillerson firmly cautioned Saudi Arabia, demanding an end to hostilities. Were military conflict to erupt, it is uncertain whose side America would take.

Unlike America, which has made public its oscillating position, China has yet to declare a stance in the dispute. Keeping relatively silent on the issue, Beijing seems to be upholding its practice of non-interference—staying out of other countries' affairs and merely voicing its hope for a peaceful end to hostilities (much as it has done with regard to the Korean Peninsula). Developed under Deng Xiaoping and Marshal Ye Jianying in the late 1970s and early 1980s, China's strategy of non-interference reflects the country's own opposition to foreign meddling. Even today, China is wary of other nations seeking to intervene in issues of national sovereignty, particularly when dealing with Taiwan, Tibet, Xinjiang, and Hong Kong. So, in return for states' recognition of the PRC—acknowledging the one-China principle and isolating Taiwan—China will leave them well enough alone. Veering markedly from the standard Communist ideology of expansion as observed under the Soviet Union's Joseph Stalin (1922–1952), China consistently elects not to interfere in other nations' internal politics, regardless of their political systems.

However, non-interference gets complicated in the Middle East. Aiming to implement its One Belt One Road initiative throughout the region, China will face great difficulty if it insists on remaining neutral between two critically important coalitions. While China has expressed interest in helping mediate the conflict, the government may need to stake out a more radical position for regional players to take the nation seriously. Without a consistent stance and demonstrated support from the Chinese, Middle Eastern nations will find it difficult to trust China sufficiently to shift toward its camp of global hegemony.

In order to assess China's chances, we must first examine Chinese relations in the Middle East. Iran—Qatar's main ally, and arguably a crux of the dispute—has been a Hot Partner to China for several years, as both have sought to counterbalance American might. Somewhat similar to China's relationship with Russia, the two nations have found union more in fear of the U.S. than in any mutual linguistic, cultural, or ideological affinity.

Saudi Arabia and its coalition partners, on the other hand, have fluctuated between China's Warm and Cold categories, depending upon their closeness to the United States. During both Bush presidencies, Saudi Arabia shared close ties with America and had a cooler relationship with China. Brought together by the hunt for Al Qaeda, Saudi-U.S. relations were particularly close in the years following 9/11. But the relationship soon grew tense during Obama's years in office, when the administration sought closer ties to Iran and increased criticism of the Saudi kingdom. Accused of fomenting anti-American sentiment, Saudi Arabia was also associated with acts of terrorism against the U.S.—after all, fifteen of the nineteen 9/11 hijackers came from the oil kingdom, also home to Osama bin Laden. As a result of the widening gap between the two nations, Saudi Arabia sought to counterbalance American influence, thereby forging strong trade relations with China. By 2016, Saudi Arabia became China's largest trading partner in the Middle East. Sino-Saudi trade grew from $1.28 billion USD under President Bush, Sr. to over $60 billion USD by Obama's final year in office—a 47-fold increase.

More recently, President Xi has further accelerated trade with Saudi Arabia, moving it firmly into China's Warm Partner category. On March 16, 2017, Saudi Arabia's King Salman, on a visit to Beijing, signed an MoU (memorandum of understanding) for $65 billion USD of potential deals with President Xi. One of fourteen Sino-Saudi agreements, the deal included a significant partnership between giant state oil firm Saudi Aramco and China North Industries Group Corporation (Norinco), enabling projects to build chemical and refining plants in China.[ii]

While neither Qatar nor Saudi's coalition members have been Hot Partners to China, both camps are critical to President Xi's construction of a new silk road. Locked in obstructive divide, these nations have the potential to make or break China's One Belt One Road (OBOR) initiative—a master plan for continued Chinese growth that may even surpass America's Marshall Plan in scale and scope.[iii]

***

Aiming to attract one trillion USD in investment, OBOR primarily engages in mass infrastructure projects abroad. By establishing foreign dependence on China's wallet, OBOR seeks to spread Chinese influence from nearby Indonesia in Southeast Asia, to African nations like Ethiopia, and even deep into the heart of Europe. Already, OBOR projects in Pakistan have reached a $55 billion USD price tag. With a $2.5 billion USD power plant underway in Myanmar, China has announced further plans to build gas pipelines across all of Central Asia, not to mention a 3,000-kilometer train system linking China to Singapore. Thailand agreed to a $5.5 billion USD railroad project that will connect China to Thailand via Laos.

As China's economic growth rate decelerates, the nation faces a slowing domestic economy and overcapacity in key areas, such as construction equipment, cement, and steel making. By deploying its wallet to fund and construct infrastructure projects abroad, China will provide domestic businesses with vast new markets for trading. Focusing on 65 countries considered to benefit most from OBOR, this carrot approach will gain favor from nations most in need of Chinese investment. Furthermore, in a world increasingly troubled by President Trump's long-term foreign policy plans, more countries have been looking to OBOR for economic growth, thus the initiative by China is continuing to counter-balance American hegemony by creating long-term steady partnerships.

In terms of China's political benefit, OBOR is a route to power. By gaining influence abroad, China will have an upper hand in international affairs, shepherding more and more countries into its Hot and Warm Partner categories. Typically, both the builder and lead financier of its projects abroad, China plans to drive tremendous economic growth in the regions it targets. In a rapid rise to the top, China has already become the world's largest trading partner for many nations. For a handful of others, it comes in second only to the U.S. or the E.U. For President Xi, OBOR may solidify China's place at the top. Offering an unbeatable deal, the initiative shows promise in increasing countries' dependency on China's wallet for economic growth. And for countries susceptible to the West's moral critiques, China layers icing on the cake. Promising a policy of non-interference, China serves as an excellent alternative to the West for non-democratic nations, especially those run by strong-arm dictators or hereditary rulers. Deterred by America's almost missionary-like zeal to spread democracy, many Asian and African leaders welcome OBOR with open arms—a deal with ostensibly few strings attached.

The Middle East is a vital gatekeeper to OBOR's success. But the question remains: Can China implement OBOR successfully in the Middle East with all the internal divides and competing demands for its political patronage or support?

In practical terms, the threat of military confrontation and chaos in the region will pose tremendous hindrances to China's long-term, billion-dollar projects. Opportunities for investment may also face insurmountable challenges if conflict continues to spiral out of control. With nations focusing on re-armament and defensive maneuvers, private investors would inevitably seek safer economic environments, leaving the region a poor choice for China's businesses. Most importantly, however, China runs the risk of alienating both sides of the Middle Eastern schism if it continues to stand in the middle. Feeling insufficiently supported by China, each side may grow to reject the nation's presence, a dooming prospect for OBOR.

At the same time, taking a definitive stand flies in the face of China's very diplomacy. In a January 2016 speech to the Arab League in Cairo, President Xi expressed, "Instead of looking for a proxy in the Middle East, we promote peace talks; instead of seeking any sphere of influence, we call on all parties to join the circle of friends for the Belt and Road Initiative; instead of attempting to fill the 'vacuum,' we build a cooperative partnership network for win-win outcomes."[iv]

But China must consider its limitations when attempting to remain neutral. Most mediating nations—such as Kuwait in the current Qatar imbroglio and Belgium or Thailand during World War II—tend to be smaller states. Without a sizeable economy or military might, these nations are effective precisely because they *don't* threaten major players in a dispute. Using their unimposing nature to disarm countries, they are much more readily embraced as mediators in conflict.

In contrast, China simply cannot play the little guy. While it might like to stay out of the fight—enjoying warm relations with both sides—its sheer size and global ambitions prevent it from claiming a status like that of Belgium or Thailand. With its imposing economic might, China seems threatening by nature, especially as it attempts to implement an initiative with massive global ramifications. In a region where divides permeate everything from interpersonal dynamics to economic trade, China *might be forced* to take sides even if it does not want to because its might and size are big enough to threaten any of the powers in the region, and the divides in the Middle East are so great that any significantly cooperating nation must take a side.

***

China's insistence on neutrality in the Middle East is not without reason. In order for OBOR to succeed in the Gulf and beyond, warm ties throughout the region are essential. Even if countries are not in the Hot Partner category, China must keep them in the Warm Partner category because any countries in the Cold Partner category have the potential to become too disruptive.

In order to predict China's moves in the region—and the lengths to which China will go for support—we must first understand OBOR, both through the lens of history and that of China's future. Comprehending the reasons for which China has launched such a massive initiative is vital for companies to flourish when seeking profit from China's growth.

First, let's review some history. It is important to understand that, in many ways, China has become a superpower more by circumstance than by intention. A mere result of its size, China's explosive economic growth was largely inevitable in the aftermath of Deng Xiaoping's and Marshal Ye Jianying's sweeping political and economic reforms in the late 1970s and 1980s. In combination with its economic superpower status, China's growth as a political superpower was also largely driven by external factors. Under frequent American condemnation of its political system, China felt largely estranged from the U.S.-led system. Other countries like Vietnam and India have also felt isolated and never cozied up to America. Underpinned by vastly distinct ideological and cultural foundations, modern China felt compelled to develop institutions and initiatives that counterbalance America.

By the time President Hu Jintao assumed power in 2003, China was clearly becoming the world's second superpower. Yet even when China started to rival the United States for supremacy, many protested it was still a relatively poor country, tormented by centuries of disorder and abject poverty. Having experienced dramatic growth as a result of its large size and economic potential, China was not strategically pursuing a rivalry with the U.S., much less global dominance.

Quite the contrary, Hu's administration seemed to frequently dissuade other nations from the notion that China was a superpower. In reality, many political leaders, such as Zhou Yongkang,[13] seemed more intent on enriching themselves—often through corruption and graft—than in building a strong Chinese state. Having neglected their duty to the nation, numerous political officials under Hu were later arrested for corruption. Among them were several former Vice Chairmen of the powerful Central Military Commission, such as Xu Caihou and Guo Boxiong. Intent on personal gains, Xu and Guo had allowed the People's Liberation Army to fall into disarray.

---

[13] Zhou Yongkang served as a member of the Standing Committee of the Politburo, overseeing military and security affairs. He was later arrested for corruption after his son reportedly made $1.6 billion USD from a public works project in Chongqing.

In a 2010 issue of *Forbes*, I therefore argued that China was like a teenage boy. It had matured quickly and was therefore viewed by others as an adult. Yet its projection of superpower status to nations abroad saw little resemblance to its self-perception back home. Few within China's borders understood that others saw it as a superpower; internally, the Chinese considered themselves a developing nation. Even as late as 2012, Prime Minister Wen Jiabao used "developing" and "poor" to describe China's national condition. In adopting these claims, China therefore never had to foot the bill for global initiatives, such as safeguarding shipping routes from pirates or aiding in humanitarian missions. Instead, it let American-led coalitions take on the debt, shouldering both military and political risks. Lacking awareness of its perception abroad, the Chinese were largely oblivious that even small indicators of growth could be seen as a threat to neighbors.[v]

By 2013, however, there was no doubt of China's emergence as an economic superpower. China could no longer fly under the radar. While America sluggishly recovered from its Great Recession of 2008, an unfazed China continued to confound experts with 8 to 10 percent growth rates. Companies from Apple to Starbucks found that Chinese consumer wallets powered their largest or second largest markets globally.

In just a few years, China shifted from an economy dependent on exports, heavy investment, and low-end manufacturing to one powered by innovation, services, and consumption. This critical shift is further explored in my previous books, *The End of Cheap China: Economic and Cultural Trends That Will Disrupt the World* (2012) and *The End of Copycat China: The Rise of Creativity, Innovation, and Individualism in Asia (2014).*[vi]

By President Xi's ascension to power in 2013, China had become the European Union's second largest trading partner with $567.2 billion USD of trade, as reported by the Central Intelligence Agency Fact Book. For its neighbors in Asia, China became the giant in the room, accounting for 63 percent of Myanmar's trade and about 34.2 percent of Laos' trade. Even farther afield, China struck trade deals with Australia (33.7 percent), Yemen (28.3 percent), Zimbabwe (27.8 percent), the U.S. (19.9 percent), and even in Peru (21 percent). Quite simply, whether or not China had pursued the title of a superpower, by the early-to-mid 2010s, it had essentially become one.

But China's unintentional rise became purposeful in 2013. Superseding his predecessors in global ambition, President Xi is also more secure in his position at the helm than any Chinese political leader since Mao Zedong. Assuming office at the end of 2012, President Xi has set China on a path of greater economic, political, and military dominance. From a well-connected family, President Xi has set out to strengthen China's Communist Party and the country as a whole, crafting a place for himself and his family in China's pantheon of great families. In contrast to past Chinese political leaders who sought personal gain, such as Zhou Yongkang and Xu Caihou, President Xi is much more interested in building a legacy and fortifying China on the world stage.[vii]

While demanding more say in global institutions like the World Bank and the International Monetary Fund (IMF), President Xi has also created new institutions like the Asian Infrastructure Investment Bank (AIIB), installing a mainlander, Jin Liqun, as its first president. Opened in January of 2016, AIIB has grown to 52 member states—about a third as many as the U.S.-headquartered World Bank—each with $100 billion USD in capital.

While not necessarily attempting to upend the current world order, President Xi has clearly pursued a more equal position for China given the size of its national wallet. In an arena where institutions are still controlled by predominantly racially white leadership, Xi has also attempted to shed the dominance of colonial powers. In conjunction with this goal, China's government has made deliberate attempts to elevate Chinese heritage among its own people. In a statement by Chinese Prime Minister Li Keqiang, he underscored the importance of *zhonghua minzu* (that Chinese nationality transcends ethnic boundaries): "The Chinese race is a big family and feelings and love for the motherland, passion for the homeland, are infused in the blood of every single person with Chinese ancestry." In a response by Jamil Anderlini, the *Financial Times'* Editor in Chief for Asia highlighted China's emphasis on its race, claiming that the government "very deliberately and specifically incorporates anyone with Chinese blood anywhere in the world."

But President Xi's carefully laid plans to seize power slowly were soon upended on November 8, 2016, when Americans voted in Donald J. Trump as the country's next president. The businessman-entertainer turned politician holds extremely different views from his predecessors. Adopting a more isolationist approach, Trump prefers to make business deals with other nations than to criticize them ideologically for not adopting an American way of life.

Criticizing everything from America's free trade agreements to the member nations of various IGOs (intergovernmental organizations), President Trump has made waves in the carefully tread waters of international diplomacy. Aside from leaving a vacuum of power in Asia as a result of U.S. withdrawal from the TPP (Trans-Pacific Partnership), Trump has also unsettled European nations in his criticism of NATO (North Atlantic Treaty Organization), questioning its value and claiming that Germany and others should shoulder more financial responsibility.

For nations that have long relied on the U.S. for financial and ideological support, President Trump has generated both apprehension and distrust.

Seizing opportunity, President Xi has swiftly moved to occupy the global power vacuum left in Trump's wake, accelerating China's shift to superpower dominance. Moving swiftly, in 2017, President Xi hosted China's OBOR Summit in May, President Xi welcomed 29 heads of state and numerous senior officials from friendly nations, promising $1 trillion USD in investments. After President Trump signaled that he would withdraw America from the Paris Climate Accords, President Xi underscored his newfound global leadership position by stating China will adhere to the accords because climate change is real and hurts the world.

In an unexpected turn of events, business leaders throughout the world are now looking to President Xi as a standard bearer for globalization and environmental protection. However, this gradually rising trend still faces China's obstructive protectionism, a force impeding the introduction of western brands to the Chinese market. Although China indeed drives growth for Hollywood and other American industries, many Western companies and commodities—from consumer brands like Buick; to internet and technology platforms, such as Facebook and Twitter; and even financial service firms like Citigroup—are hampered by protectionist policies. Nonetheless, with China's wallet quickly securing a grip abroad, and a well-timed vacuum left behind by America's increasing protectionism, China may very well have a clear path to power.

With Trump's America First rhetoric, the world is looking for a new superpower to take the lead in world affairs. This is why countries became so much more welcoming to OBOR by mid 2017 than even at the end of 2016—they see China and OBOR as a driver for economic growth despite misgivings in some quarters for China's newly found central political power.

***

The Middle East plays a crucial role in China's successful implementation of OBOR. In recent history, most of the Islamic world has weathered delicate relations with the United States. In previous centuries, the Middle East has experienced drawn-out wars with Christian Europe, and is well acquainted with the continent's colonialism. Yet Middle Eastern nations have relatively new relations with China.

Presented with a fresh slate, China has the remarkable opportunity to forge strong relations with the Middle East and Central Asia, a task it must execute smoothly to ensure OBOR's success. As we have seen above, the conflict dividing Qatar and Saudi Arabia's coalition—and perhaps more importantly, the Sunni-

Shia divide—is an intransigent knot with far-reaching implications. In its pursuit of Warm Partners in the Middle East, China walks a thin tightrope. In order to secure OBOR's success, China will need to develop novel strategies—either remaining neutral or offering calculated support, somehow helping everyone and alienating no one.

*****

Dialogue:
Shane Tedjarati, President and CEO, High Growth Regions, Honeywell

Shane Tedjarati is responsible for driving Honeywell's business expansion in High Growth Regions of the world: Asia, Africa, Latin America, the Middle East, and Eastern Europe. Tedjarati is an avid aviator. He has lived in China for more than 20 years and speaks six languages. He has been instrumental in engineering Honeywell's success story, starting in China and India, and expanding globally to the High Growth Regions of the world where today Honeywell derives the majority of its growth.

Tedjarati is a Henry Crown Fellow of Aspen Institute and also the co-founder of its Middle East Leadership Initiative and China Fellowship Program; special advisor to Chongqing and Wuhan Mayors; member of the advisory board of Antai College of Economics and Management Shanghai Jiao Tong University; and industry Co-Chair of China Leaders for Global Operations (CLGO), a dual master's degree program by MIT and Shanghai Jiao Tong University.

As much as any American company, Honeywell is poised to benefit from OBOR, so I thought it would make sense to interview Shane to hear his thoughts on how Honeywell and other foreign companies can benefit from China's rise.

Rein: What are the greatest challenges facing China's One Belt One Road (OBOR)? Are they political? Financial? Logistical? How do you suggest the Chinese government go about resolving some of these obstacles? How should international businesses approach these challenges?

Tedjarati: Sporadic political instabilities along the Belt and Road countries or regions do impose high risk onto the OBOR implementation, however, this is not only pertinent to OBOR initiatives, rather, regional safety, political stability, and financial system stability, etc., have always been a major intelligent-risk-taking practice for international businesses.

Rein: Critics have argued that OBOR is a tool to protect Chinese industry and that only Chinese firms will benefit from OBOR. Do you agree, or do you see a way for foreign firms to profit from OBOR? If so, how and in what categories?

Tedjarati: The One Belt One Road initiative is a terrific opportunity for companies like Honeywell.

The initiative can help drive outcomes of both our "East for East" and "East to Rest" strategies and are creating growth for Honeywell throughout the region.

Honeywell continues to strive to be the better partner with other Chinese companies in order to fully embrace all of the OBOR opportunities in front of us. Honeywell has many partner companies and is aggressively working with them to better understand their needs and supply them with solutions that will help them best serve their customers.

Rein: What do you consider to be Honeywell's greatest opportunities in China's implementation of OBOR? In what sectors and what regions are these opportunities concentrated?

Tedjarati: The One Belt One Road initiative promises to raise the level of connectivity, cooperation, and trade between dozens of nations that have traded with China for thousands of years. Multi-national companies like Honeywell can bring a set of technology solutions to Chinese Engineering Procurement and Construction (EPC) companies, especially in the infrastructure and energy projects, which can help Honeywell create new opportunities in high growth regions such as Asia, Africa, and the Middle East.

Since 2008, Honeywell has been supporting leading Chinese enterprises to go out, especially in the industries of oil and gas, petroleum refining, chemical, power, and paper, which has prepared us well for the later Belt and Road initiative proposed by China in 2013. Till now, Honeywell Process Solutions and Honeywell UOP have participated in more than 20 overseas EPC projects located in Central and Southeast Asia, the Middle East, Africa. Compared with 2015, Honeywell Process Solutions achieved over 70% growth in term of EPC export business in 2016.

Rein: Are there any specific OBOR initiatives that Honeywell is currently benefitting from? Please explain.

Tedjarati: World Pensions Council experts stated that the Belt and Road initiative constitutes a natural international extension of the infrastructure-driven economic development framework that has sustained the rapid economic growth of China.

Honeywell's "Follow the Growth" (FTG) campaign was developed to help Chinese companies become more global. As part of this campaign, we began working with Asia Trans Gas to provide automation and safety technology designed to help them manage their operations and establish safer working conditions along the third pipeline of the Central Asia-China Gas Pipeline project. The pipeline became operational in 2015. The same Honeywell technology is in use in the first two pipelines of the project, which are already in operation. Asia Trans Gas is a joint venture of China National Petroleum Corp. (CNPC) and Uzbekistan national holding company UzbekNefteGaz.

Rein: A key component of China's statecraft is its non-interference approach to other countries' internal affairs. Do you think China will be able to continue its non-interference strategy when seeking to implement OBOR in divided regions like the Middle East, where tensions have split Qatar and Saudi Arabia—both key partners for OBOR?

Tedjarati: The initiative calls for the integration of the region into a cohesive economic area through building infrastructure, increasing cultural exchanges, and broadening trade. We believe in the Chinese government's consistent stance of non-interference of other sovereign countries' internal affairs, while promoting cultural, economic and trade cooperation and exchanges.

Rein: How important is it for multinationals to build up trust and warm relations with China's government in order to succeed? How has Honeywell established these ties so successfully? What should businesses keep in mind when seeking to build trust with the Chinese government?

Tedjarati: It is very important to build trust. Honeywell is committed to long-term growth in China and has invested more than $1 billion so far. There are now more than 13,000 employees located in more than 30 cities across the country. 99% of them are local Chinese and 1/5 of them scientists and engineers.

Honeywell identifies China-specific needs and meets them with locally-developed innovations. Becoming *The Chinese Competitor* is the key to transform how Honeywell does business in China. It combines our strong brand, international market access and global operational excellence with local competitor's winning attributes—leading us to becoming the better operating global company in China with better product, better quality, better value, and faster speed.

Case Study: Re-shoring and Attracting Chinese FDI

Escaping the Shanghai heat on a sweltering July Day, I dined with an old friend Mr. Xu in an ornate restaurant overlooking the Bund. While he cleverly keeps an extremely low profile, strictly avoiding media interviews of any kind, Mr. Xu is a billionaire many times over. Having made his money in real estate and manufacturing of cheap yet decent quality products, Mr. Xu is responsible for a great number of household items that populate American homes, from toys to tires to electronics.

Seeking his input and expertise, I discussed with him the central themes of my earlier book *The End of Cheap China*, particularly concerned with the climbing costs facing Chinese businesses. "You were right," Mr. Xu said. "Very prescient. We are getting hit by rising labor and real estate costs." In an effort to cut losses, Mr. Xu's business had pushed to automate production lines and improve worker efficiency, but only so much savings could be squeezed from such efforts. Automation in China grew 58 percent in 2016—certainly a helping hand to many Chinese manufacturers desperate to preserve profits. Yet companies that gained from China's growing automation levels were primarily limited to those at the top of the value chain, such as producers of construction, medical, and aerospace equipment.

Faced with rising costs, Mr. Xu had to determine what course to plot if he wanted to maintain his company's profits. He had looked into relocating or building new factories in Southeast Asia, deliberating over countries like Indonesia and Sri Lanka. Deterred by fears of rising protectionism in America, however, he justly worried about getting slapped with tariffs.

Mr. Xu ultimately made a drastic decision. "I am opening my first factory in South Carolina, to be followed by others across the United States." Mr. Xu chuckled, "I made my money relocating our manufacturing operations from the U.S. to China. Now I guess we are going back." Somewhat puzzled, I queried him concerning his rationale.

"Well, it certainly wouldn't have made sense a decade ago, but there are multiple encouraging factors now. First, I'm getting big tax breaks from the South Carolina government. When we calculated the costs, we found it is actually about the same price to manufacture in the U.S. as it is in China now—once you factor in all the travel costs and such. Second, I want to be closer to my customers in America. With consumer demands changing so quickly and unpredictably, we must be able to get our products into the supply chain and consumers' hands as fast as possible. By being located in South Carolina, we'll cut delivery time by a critical margin. And lastly, we're increasingly worried about rising anti-Chinese sentiment among Americans, not to mention protectionism in general. Having a factory in the U.S. will do a lot to help us garner favor with American politicians and their constituencies."

Many countries are currently focused on maximizing investment gained from China's government-led business efforts, and from OBOR specifically. But states and companies must be careful not to discount the broad array of profitable opportunities in attracting foreign investment from private factories. While China has little risk of losing its dominance as the world's factory, the costs of domestic manufacturing are becoming unsustainably high. As a result, many of China's private companies are looking to relocate or take operations abroad, building new manufacturing facilities in countries such as the U.S., attracted by tax breaks and proximity to the consumer.

The trend of Chinese companies moving manufacturing facilities to Africa, Southeast Asia, and even America will continue. China has gotten too expensive and companies are seeking out preferential tax treatment, and want to be closer to their end consumers and customers in Western markets. Moreover, many American companies will re-shore operations to America as costs get too high in China. American companies like K'Nex, a toy manufacturer; Trellis Earth Products, which makes plastic bags; and bra manufacturer Handful have all announced they will re-shore back to America from China because of soaring prices in China.

Key Action Items

1. Countries and their state and provincial governments should offer tax breaks and other monetary incentives to private Chinese companies relocating to or building new manufacturing facilities within local cities. Private Chinese companies will significantly invest in regions of the U.S. and elsewhere if they receive good tax breaks. They are also accustomed to working closely with local Chinese governments and seek a similar relationship with state and city governments overseas, cooperating for mutual benefit. Foxconn is a good case in point, announcing in July 2017 a $10 billion USD plant manufacturing liquid display crystals that will provide 3,000 jobs in Wisconsin.[viii]

2. Chinese firms want to build factories closer to their customers in order to gain an upper hand in the market. Countries and local governments should therefore spend time in China lobbying founders and CEOs of private Chinese

companies to extol the benefits of moving to America. Given that these business executives often have little overseas experience or lack English proficiency, a hard sale is largely preferable to waiting.

Chapter 4
Innovation and the State-Owned Sector

Beijing, China, June 2017

It was one of those rare and beautiful blue-sky days in Beijing—a reminder of just how magical the capital can be if its government would find a way to reduce the suffocating pollution that normally blankets the city. Under a brightly shining sun, the giggles of children running and jumping rope outdoors echoed through the streets.

Having sprained my knee the week before in a father-son basketball game against my son Tom's team, I lumbered on crutches through the expansive training compound of China National Petroleum Corporation (CNPC), the parent company of PetroChina. China's state-owned oil giant, CNPC was now the world's third largest oil and gas company by revenue and ranked third in Fortune Global 500. A training ground for CNPC's various divisions, the whole campus seemed to buzz with training sessions.

I had been invited to keynote a conference for two hundred of the most senior *cadres*[14] of China's state-owned enterprises (SOEs). With a focus on stimulating SOE growth, the conference was jointly organized by China's State-Owned Assets Supervision and Administration Commission of the State Council (SASAC), the umbrella organization that oversees 102 centrally owned companies, and a multibillion dollar European family-owned private equity firm. Plagued by excessive bureaucracy and myriad other issues, China's SOEs had become a drag on the efficiency of the national economy, falling behind on innovation and even standing in the way of China's private sector. Asked to advise SASAC's hosted cadres, I prepared to speak about the primary challenges hindering SOEs and how the system should be reformed in order to recruit and retain talent and promote a focus on innovation. Change was seriously needed if China wanted its state-owned companies to compete on innovation and grow globally through initiatives like OBOR.

***

---

[14] A cadre is an appointed CCP loyalist who oversees the SOE's activities and reports back to the Party.

DOI 10.1515/9781501507618-004

To understand why SOEs are struggling, particularly in retaining talent, we must first explore the system's purpose and organization.

All state-owned enterprises report back to SASAC. Even the CEOs of multi-division conglomerates with tens of thousands of workers have political supervisors at the top. As a result, they lack the autonomous command held by Chairmen or CEOs of American companies—who wield far more power. Unlike Exxon, where the CEO reports only to the Board of Directors, the CEO of PetroChina, for example, would need to report to the CEO of CNPC who would then have to report to SASAC.

Without much of a personal stake in their company's earnings or the possibilities of high salaries (which are capped by the government), many SOEs operate with political goals in mind at the expense of purely market-oriented ones. Executives of SOEs typically care more about getting promoted up the political ladder than on profits or increasing efficiency. Consequently, a senior bank executive from Bank of China or ICBC (Industrial and Commercial Bank of China) might loan money to another SOE even if he knows the loan will become non-performing; he'd rather garner the political support of other leaders in the system when seeking a promotion.

Yet this interplay with politics affects more than just the domestic realm. For instance, SOEs might become suspect when acquiring assets abroad that have security risks. Given that they report up the Communist Party chain of command rather than to profit-seeking shareholders, many foreign nations are wary of approving acquisitions by SOEs. In 2016, for example, the US-China Economic and Security Review Commission in its annual report to Congress recommended that Congress block all acquisitions in the U.S. by Chinese state-owned firms because the Chinese Communist Party (CCP) uses to the SOEs as an economic tool to advance national security objectives.

Tightly bound to complex incentive systems, China's SOEs are a conundrum for even the most astute economist—at once both the key to China's economic miracle and the greatest thorn in its side. On the one hand, SOEs are remarkably helpful. They continue business activities at the behest of politics even when it makes little economic sense to keep investing. Doing so shores up employment numbers and bolsters consumer confidence during economic hardship or increases investment in regions where returns are too low to attract private investment. A safeguard against unemployment, SOEs are also an effective tool for China's central government to pump up the economy when needed. This has been particularly helpful in the post Great Recession crisis of the past decade when SOEs kept hiring during the downturn even while multinationals in China implemented hiring freezes.

Yet the political aspects of SOEs generate numerous challenges. Slowing growth and impeding prudent decisions, heavy bureaucracy and political incentives pose threats to China's initiatives abroad. In the case of OBOR, for example, China's state-owned sector requires several important reforms in order to lead investment coalitions efficiently. Walking a fine line, SOEs must become more profit-oriented, and less a mere tool of China's political system or they will face opposition by the foreign lawmakers they need to grant approval for projects. In meetings with senior advisors to Vietnam's President, for example, I was told that there was distrust and suspicion in many circles within Vietnam with what the end goals of SOEs investing in the country were. Tasked with exploring these challenges and their solutions, I reflected on how I would approach my audience.

***

The conference was held using CNPC's largest auditorium. Decked out with cramped seats as a nod to President Xi's austerity campaign, the venue veered noticeably from a Shangri-La or Grand Hyatt where similar events had been hosted under Jiang Zemin and Hu Jintao. At the back of the auditorium lay instant coffee and DIY tea packets, further emphasizing Xi's anti-extravagance push. The only modern indulgence in the room—providing a minimal sense of comfort—were mobile phone charging stations installed at each seat. Even bureaucrats can't live without their WeChat.

Specifically, the conference had gathered these top SOE cadres to determine how SOEs should plan ahead in China's shift from an economy based on heavy investment and manufacturing to one based on services and consumption. Most critically, SASAC wanted SOEs to focus on innovation in order to lead the economy in initiatives like OBOR. I was therefore asked to discuss human resources and their importance in creating a culture of innovation.

Occupying a larger role in China's economy than most analysts realize, SOEs are critical to spurring domestic innovation. According to 2013 figures, while comprising only 30 percent of firms, the public sector accounted for 55 percent of assets and 45 percent of revenue.[i]

But SOEs were hurting. As anxiously reported to me by SASAC's officials, state-owned giants were now losing out to start-ups in Shenzhen and Hangzhou, struggling to compete with China's private giants like Huawei, Baidu, and Alibaba. Quickly surpassing China's long-standing SOEs, these latter companies had started to offer better employee benefits—housing, education allowances, even international travel jaunts. If SOEs failed to attract top talent, how could they possibly take a lead in operating OBOR abroad?

Absorbed in thought and daunted by these challenges, I approached the podium. While having spoken at the renowned *Three on the Bund* to launch my last book, *The End of Copycat China* (after being invited by owner and friend Cherie Liem)—an event chaired by the head of the Communist Party School in Shanghai—I had never faced such a large and senior group of SOE cadres. On top of the pressure, a key component of my speech required criticism of the very audience in attendance. Already unsettled by the fact that many cadres were still looking at their phones, I was painfully aware of my status as an American outsider, anxious that my critiques might be ill received and viewed through a nationalist lens. Many Chinese still feel Americans are trying to contain China's rise rather than help it along. Many Americans who formerly seemed to respect China and its government, like George Washington University Professor David Shambaugh, suddenly wrote that the Communist Party was on its last legs and ready to implode, creating ill will towards outsiders.

Taking a deep breath, I began by outlining why China's economy had to become more innovative—as both President Xi and Prime Minister Li Keqiang had exhorted. Innovation was critical both for sustainable economic development and for Chinese leadership through OBOR, I argued. In light of the state-owned sector's aversion to risk, this message was crucial to convey. Many of the cadres present had risen up the ranks precisely because they successfully placated political superiors, often keeping their heads down at the expense of generating revenue and taking risks. This had to change, I insisted. In the midst of rising real estate and labor costs, SOE executives had to take risks and prioritize innovation if they wanted to stay afloat. Looking out at my audience, I was heartened to see heads bobbing up and down in agreement. No one was looking at a phone anymore.

Much of their aversion to risk can be accounted for by the power structure in place. Given that SOE executives are politically selected—rather than having risen to the top by beating business odds—their long-term positions are fairly stable regardless of company profits. Because of this, SOEs grow intellectually ossified, especially at the top, unable to generate and unwilling to welcome fresh ideas. Yet even bringing in more profit-oriented business directors has often had its problems as they are not always accepted. Bureaucracy's permeation of SOE culture has hindered Chinese who developed careers in the private sector. As one senior Chinese executive of a European tool company who had been educated at IMD (International Institute for Management Development) in Switzerland told me, "I tried taking a senior role in an SOE but left after less than a year. The culture made it impossible for outsiders like me, trained in European and American businesses, to get anything done. It was far too political."

An additional frustration, SOEs often become too spread out and unfocused in one business line. SOEs in silk, grain, and dairy, for example, often seem more like real estate investors or mini hedge funds than firms targeting a single industry. Normally holding a remarkable amount of real estate, SOEs also decisively scoop up shares in the stock market whenever they see potential for returns.

Recognizing these inherent problems and the need to build a more market-oriented economy, Prime Minister Zhu Rongji took on China's first great SOE reforms in the late 1990s. Highly successful, Zhu's reforms eliminated several of the problems discussed above and ensured the nation's last two decades of strong economic growth.

To the initial shock of the country, Prime Minister Zhu forced SOEs to lay off workers. Over 30 million workers lost their jobs, hundreds of SOEs privatized, and thousands shut. Until then, employment by an SOE was nicknamed the iron rice bowl. One simply never got fired. But as SOEs grew bloated and slow-moving, Prime Minister Zhu was compelled to make sweeping cuts. After taking a number of SOEs public, Zhu saw many become more profit oriented and productive.

However, while Zhu's extensive reforms worked for nearly twenty years, by the mid-2010s, the same rot had started to seep in again. Too many SOEs had leveraged their political connections to fend off competition from the private Chinese and multi-national sectors. With this advantage over private companies, SOEs could more easily get away with lower quality goods and services. China's telecom sector, for example, is largely closed off to private investment and has some of the most expensive yet slowest data plans in the world. Multi-hour-long waits are not unusual before seeing a teller at one of China's state-owned banks. Good luck trying to open a credit card account or do Internet banking. State-owned hospitals are no better—seeing a doctor can take hours, even days, of queuing to spend just a few minutes with a doctor.

Treading on sensitive ground, I explained to SASAC's cadres that rot begins at the top of an organization. If SOEs were to be truly competitive, the very leaders sitting in front of me needed to foster a culture of risk-taking, not squelch it. Equally imperative, SOE executives had to place far greater importance on consumers; ensuring customer satisfaction was key.

Having remained sluggishly static, too many SOEs failed to cater to consumers' dynamic demands. Seemingly indifferent to the needs of non-SOE clients and consumers, SOEs particularly in the financial services and retail sectors were being swiftly overtaken by the Alibabas and JD.coms of the world. Even with their dominant political position, SOEs in the communications industry were losing out to private Chinese companies like Tencent—developer of WeChat. Offering consumers a far cheaper platform for communication, Tencent seemed almost a no-brainer for frustrated consumers who relied on state-owned companies for ex-pensive voice calls and text messages. In a similar vein, Alibaba far outpaced state-owned department stories with its Taobao and Small platforms. Alibaba also outcompeted financial service SOEs in development of its Alipay division. Swiftly attracting hundreds of millions of Chinese users, Alipay offers consumers a way to buy goods online, transfer money, and buy wealth management products with-out even a credit card or securities brokerage account. Private hospital chains like Shanghai United or Parkway Health also saw wealthy Chinese flocking to their top-notch equipment, stellar doctors, and trusted medical care.

SOEs could no longer relegate consumers to a list of secondary priorities. In-novative products and services would be critical for customer retention. Unfortu-nately, however, consumers were not the only ones needing to be retained. One of the greatest challenges to China's SOEs was their increasing inability to recruit and keep top talent.

Once a prime destination for top university recruits, SOEs have long enjoyed their pick of the best by providing generous benefits and relatively secure posi-tions. In the Great Recession of 2008, when even huge multinationals experi-enced hiring freezes, SOEs refused to lay off workers. In recent years, however, China's private companies have progressively offered greater job security and lu-crative benefits. In conjunction with a declining reputation, SOEs have conse-quently lost their pull.

Perhaps the only benefit SOEs could offer that private companies were una-ble to guarantee are China's coveted *hukous,* or residence permits. *Hukous* are the tickets for those seeking a life in China's big cities, allowing them to buy homes and gain cheaper access to both education and medical care. But even the dream of securing an urban, tier 1 city[15] *hukou* no longer sufficed to attract top talent to SOEs. Soaring salaries in the private sector quickly overcame concerns about ac-cess to education and medical care. Only housing remained a major stress point for young Chinese hoping to make a life in China's crowded urban centers. Many cities imposed limits on the number of non-residents purchasing homes— regula-tions impervious to bribery or wealth. In Shanghai, for example, non-residents not only have to work in the city and pay income tax for a full five years, but also need to be married before they can even consider purchasing a house.

---

[15] China's 613 cities are divided into four tiers based on their GDP. Tier 1 cities have a GDP of over $300 billion USD; tier 2 cities' GDP is between $68 and $200 billion USD; tier 3 between $18 and $67 billion USD; and tier 4 GDP is below $17 billion USD. Political administration and popu-lation are also considered.

Salaries and benefits aside, cultural changes have also accounted for much of the state-owned sector's falling retention rates. As China's cultural psychology shifts away from political movements and collectivism, younger Chinese have increasingly prized individualism. In light of this trend, today's top new talent often view SOEs as a doddering force, unable to compete in an environment of innovation and creative solutions. For those born after 1990, most popular brands—Tencent, Alibaba, OPPO, Mengniu, Yili—are all private Chinese firms. By contrast, companies most frustrating to China's high-standard millennials—doomed by exorbitant prices and poor customer service—primarily consist of SOEs like China Telecom or Bank of China. Were private companies to have such issues, they would simply go out of business.

Seeking trendy avenues for creative expression, young people are wary of the SOEs' corporate cultures, known for prizing political expedience over business acumen. Loath to adopt the lifelong careers of the past, young Chinese prefer to switch between jobs and companies every few years, seeking fortune over long-term stability. SOEs might offer a decadent package, but everyone knows the state-owned sector is no route to billions. And as President Xi's corruption crackdown gains an ever-stronger grip, glamor-less SOEs continue to lose their talent.

Seeking to advise the cadres on how they might retain young talent, I shifted from talking about innovation in the finance and retail sectors to more groundbreaking sectors like biotech, Internet, and technology. To succeed in these industries, Chinese firms had to consider buying technology from abroad, either incorporating foreign parts into their own products, or buying out entire manufacturers. SOEs simply lacked the technical expertise to survive on their own in this way.

Providing better tech products through the incorporation of Western-manufactured parts would be critical not only for the retention of young Chinese workers but also for generating greater profits. And nothing was more central to making OBOR a success than being perceived as profitable.

Seeking to drive home this latter point, I emphasized that no one would be interested to be a mere political pawn in China's play for global influence. Countries would take part in OBOR if, and only if, they could see themselves making profits. Consequently, to thrive both domestically and internationally, SOEs had to prioritize innovation, revenue, and the needs of their beneficiaries.

Upon finishing my speech, there was a smattering of applause. It appeared that the cadres had agreed with what I'd said, but most were waiting to deduce the views of others before publicly displaying their own. But once their clapping began to indicate my speech's general acceptance, the cadres' applause turned to a chorus.

Most revealing, however, were the questions and feedback that followed. Expressing wholehearted agreement, even the most senior SOE executives communicated that they wanted to reform. They understood they needed to change in the context of China's global expansion. Doing so, however, would not be easy. Still anxious about other executives in China's state-owned sector, many cadres remained concerned by the political ramifications of their decisions—both for their companies and their own personal careers. Without the assurance of system-wide changes, a prisoner's dilemma would remain.

Having accepted my premise, many cadres now asked me for specifics. One executive raised his hand. Head of one of China's large conglomerates, the executive had directed his SOE through the buyouts of American and European auto and aircraft parts makers. Now seeking to make his company more innovative, he asked, "How do we organize internally to promote innovation? And how do we get buy-in from senior executives and government officials who might not care about profits?" Within seconds, hands shot up throughout the audience as cadres piped up around him, asking similar questions. I quickly realized their barrier was not lack of will; if anything, they faced greatest resistance from the system's internal workings.

What surprised me most, however, was my audience's openness to criticism. Implicitly targeting many of the cadres I had spoken to, I argued that China's legal order needs to be more fair and transparent. By using political maneuvers rather than competitive initiatives to compete with China's private sector, SOEs were not only gaining an unfair advantage but were also holding back progress on a *national* scale. Expecting my audience to recoil, I was taken aback by the cadres' affirmative nods. Equally surprising, they showed little objection when I presented uncomplimentary consumer data: 86 percent of the consumers interviewed by my firm, the China Market Research Group (CMR), had reported moderate or strong dislike of the service provided by the Bank of China. Many complained that SOE executives were far too focused on doling out loans to other SOEs, leaving little regard for retail business. The cadres seemed to agree with my conclusion of SOE customer dissatisfaction—an unintended opportunity for Alibaba's Alipay or Tencent's WeChat Wallet as alternatives to Bank of China. This would continue to be a failure of SOEs, and a failure of the entire system, if priorities did not change.

Yet even with the will of cadres present, the question of *political capital* still remains. The executives may want it, but will the government, in its continued efforts to control the economy, allow for more unfettered competition? With current incentive systems in place, how can decision-making be oriented around economic efficiency rather than political gain?

***

In China's campaign to build international power through OBOR, SOEs may serve as the nation's greatest help or prove to be its greatest hurdle. To achieve the former scenario, China's state-owned sector must adopt the necessary skills and structure to lead investment and growth. Targeting areas rife with conflict, a great number of OBOR's projects will operate on decades-long time horizons, taking years to reach break-even points. It is therefore highly unlikely that companies in China's private sector—which are constrained by the requirement to report to shareholders seeking short-term profits—will take any substantive lead in these long-term investments.

Because they have the ability to shoulder these burdens, SOEs must gain a handle in recruiting the talent to be sufficiently competitive for expansion in these regions. Fortunately, even SASAC understands the need to continually improve its cadres' management talent. I learned this after finishing my keynote and Q&A period, when I met with Zhang Hong, the Deputy Secretary General of SASAC in charge of training. Having served as a university administrator prior to his position at SASAC, Zhang Hong has kept the pleasant demeanor of one. Curious about his role within SASAC, I asked him what type of training he focused on most. Holding a kind but firm gaze, he said, "Any and all kinds of training that can help prepare cadres for the future. In an environment where innovation remains critical for creating sustainable businesses, the executives must change and improve for the better."

I have been quite critical of SOEs for the past decade. Aside from their staggering inefficiency, they have hurt competitiveness within China. Nonetheless, I was heartened by Zhang Hong's resolute and thorough approach. He and SASAC clearly recognized the need for continual training and SOE reform. Yet a combined effort between China's SOEs and its central government has yet to be determined.

By the time President Xi took over the government in late 2012, he knew the state-owned sector was in dire need of modernization. But it remains to be seen whether Xi intends for SOEs to be truly competitive and take risks in the pursuit of profit. Some speculate he might instead want them to serve as a tool in advancing his political aims and to ensure a stable, moderately prosperous economy—not maximally efficient, but a fair provider of employment. So far, it looks like President Xi is following a mix of the two routes; he aims to make SOEs more competitive, but does not intend to follow a Wall Street, profit-at-all-costs mentality.

In approaching the sector, President Xi's first step was to cut down on corruption, force mergers of SOEs and rotate executives among the competition. Former Chairman of China Unicom Chang Xiaobing, for example, was named Chairman of its main competitor, China Telecom in 2015. He was detained a few months later for corruption. One concern I have is whether these super-sized SOEs will become more innovative or even more bureaucratic and stifling.

As we saw in Chapter 1, President Xi has also tightened his control on more facets of China's bureaucracy, primarily by installing loyal military men in positions of power. The state-owned sector has not been immune to such actions. Establishing such large SOEs with loyal cadres, Xi has ensured they will have the girth to benefit from OBOR. Perhaps even more importantly, these SOEs are poised to follow President Xi's directives to invest in regions that are politically strategic to China but which pose little profit-making ability. As a result, while some SOEs may adapt to China's increasingly innovation-driven economy, and thus focus on profits, a large portion of the sector will be channeled towards Beijing's political motives—sacrificing revenue in favor of Chinese influence abroad. It will be critical for foreign firms to also profit substantially from OBOR or else the whole initiative will be seen as a tool for China to achieve power and profits, and thus face pushback from other nations' citizens.

***

In light of these new developments under President Xi, foreign brands have a momentous opportunity to sell to SOEs as they vie to become global players. To capitalize on the trend, brands must first understand Xi's concept of the *Chinese Dream*—a notion heavily promoted by the President, and now a critical component of China's national discourse.[16] Upon assuming office, Xi challenged the nation's citizens both to reflect on what it means to be Chinese and to consider how they wanted to build a strong Chinese society.

Results spanned the gamut. Many Chinese began turning to religion, such as Christianity and Buddhism. Seeking greater meaning and purpose in life, these citizens had come to reject the craven push for money, now looking for spiritual wealth. Greed for profits had resulted in a seemingly endless stream of counterfeit

---

[16] President Xi's China Dream was introduced by him in a speech in November 2012 when he said "dare to dream, work assiduously to fulfill the dreams and contribute to the revitalization of the nation." The term became popular in 2013 starting in China's state-owned media to follow Xi's words, and meant to recreate pride in their nation among the Chinese.

medicines and poor quality foods flooding the market—harming vast numbers of the population. China's buildings suffered too. Hoping to increase profit margins, many Chinese contractors and real estate developers began cutting corners in construction projects producing shoddy results, a trend later termed "tofu construction" by former Premier Zhu Rongji. Hurt by the effects of greed, many Chinese embraced the Chinese Dream as a calling to higher, more civilized ideals.

But in business and political terms, President Xi wanted the nation to promote indigenous innovation and Chinese brands. Hoping to discourage consumers from slavishly purchasing Western European and American brands, Xi instead wanted to instill pride in the "Made in China" label. And Chinese consumers were open to the shift—they loved that Chinese companies like Alibaba and Tencent were among the most innovative in the world. As first-rate domestic brands began to flood the market, many consumers were proud to discuss Chinese brands in a context other than complaints about shoddy quality, even if those fears indeed still existed.

Chinese attitudes towards brands—both domestic and international—are critical for foreign businesses to understand. Perhaps more than consumers from any other nation, the Chinese have a tremendous wealth of knowledge when it comes to the heritage of different brands. A typical 26-year-old young woman from Chengdu will be able to rattle off that Chanel is from France, Moncler from Italy, and Shiseido from Japan. Furthermore, she will have a keen understanding of the stereotypes by which brands from those countries are judged in China.

In fact, it is exceedingly difficult for brands to overcome country-level stereotypes or even distance themselves from the identity of their national origin. For example, Korean products are always seen as cheap and a good value. Similarly, food products from Eastern Europe or Southeast Asia are considered safe but cheap. These inalienable stereotypes provide excellent opportunities for food companies from Eastern European and Southeast Asia; nations like Poland, Bulgaria, or Thailand. They can easily position themselves as cheap but safe, finding their way to the third slot of Chinese grocery shelves, between cheaper domestic Chinese brands and expensive Western European, Australian, Scandinavian, Chinese, or American ones. Companies from negatively stereotyped nations, on the other hand, like Mexico, may struggle to find a spot on the shelf at all.

While consumer-held stereotypes are no doubt grounded in reason, many also take their root in the historical influence of Chinese government propaganda on the Chinese mentality to buy or shun certain brands. Given that China was cut off from much of the rest of the world during the Cultural Revolution—not to mention China's isolation during and prior to the Qing Dynasty beforehand—contact with foreigners was largely restricted to port cities like Shanghai and Tianjin. As a result, much of the population experienced little to no interaction with foreigners until the 1980s. Opinions have thus largely been formed in the past four decades. Even when I first arrived in the mid 1990s to study Chinese at Nankai University in Tianjin, China, many Chinese peasants told me I was the first American they had ever spoken to.

While not politically correct, Chinese tend to look at the world through skin color. White is good and dark is bad. Part of this mentality stems from associations founded in China's feudal times. Darker skin historically meant that its bearer was relegated to working the fields and getting sunburnt, while the wealthy protected their light skin under parasols and by staying indoors. Deeply ingrained, these cultural relics have led Chinese consumers to assign a higher value to brands from predominantly white nations, accompanied by a desire to get closer with their governments.

This is one reason why Chinese flock to members of Britain's Commonwealth to buy real estate or send their children to school, as we shall see in Chapter 7 on Immigration and Real Estate. Three major recipients of Chinese investment in housing and education, Australia, New Zealand, and Canada, have also received an enthusiastic welcome by Chinese markets. Selling everything from Manuka honey, to kiwis, to dairy products, to beef, many of these countries have been able to export into China at a higher price and with the guaranteed trust of consumers.

But aside from the profits one can derive from selling directly to China's consumers, foreign brands must learn to capitalize on President Xi's more recent fight for indigenous brands. Currently, the drive for indigenous innovation and Chinese products is not well understood by many western observers—even those who have resided in China for many years. For example, China-based American businessman James McGregor, Chairman of communications agency APCO China, has erroneously criticized China's moves as protectionist with the goal of stopping foreign brands from growing and making money. While his arguments may hold some truth, the reality is much more nuanced. President Xi's vision of making great Chinese brands does not exclude collaboration with or opportunity for foreign businesses.

Quite the contrary, there are plenty of opportunities for western brands to profit and thrive in Xi's promotion of indigenous products. Let's take aircraft maker Comac (Commercial Aircraft Corporation of China, Ltd.) as an example of a SOE building a brand while sourcing their products from western brands.

Comac's new C919 airplane17 is intended to compete with the dominance of Boeing 737 and Airbus 320. Positioned as a Chinese brand, the Comac actually sources most of its foundational technology and mechanical parts from Western brands. In its development of the narrow-body twin-engine airliner, Comac offered tenders for the engine to Pratt & Whitney and CFM International—a joint venture between GE Aviation and Safran Aircraft Engines (a division of France's Safran). Nexcelle was chosen to provide the engine's nacelle,18 thrust reversers, and exhaust system. Belgium's Solvay, an international chemical group, was critical in developing the coating technology for the Comac C919's maiden flight.

In other words, although the Comac C919 is considered a Chinese brand, it has actively used foreign components. Although protectionism exists, it certainly does not mean that foreign brands cannot have success. Foreign brands that will do best in catering to China's prolific construction of indigenous brands will be ones like CFM, which has stakeholders in both France and the United States. As SOEs use their wallets to gain political support in different regions, it is more likely that a U.S.-French joint venture will get a deal over a purely American one. It also means that smaller countries like Belgium or Sweden will benefit. In the pursuit of numbers, China seems to use its Wallet to gain political favor and currency across as many nations as it can reasonably move into its Warm or Hot Partner categories.

Ignorance of these motives has left many Western companies in the dark when attempting to sell to China's state-owned conglomerates. Few understand that the considerations of SOEs do not merely concern the quality and price of a service or good. Operating well outside the boundaries of business, SOEs must also evaluate a whole host of political factors given their accountability to SASAC and President Xi's political motives. A Chinese airline like Air China or China Eastern will most likely always buy a certain number of Boeing planes as well as a similar share of Airbus ones, seeking to placate businessmen in both America and Europe if they also start to buy Comac planes. Whichever region is most in favor will get more planes, but a sufficient profit will always be handed to the competitor. It is only politically expedient to do so. See GE, for example, a vocal supporter of Beijing's OBOR. Given GE's role as a political heavyweight in the U.S., China's SOEs and central government will always dole out enough deals to the corporation. So, if Washington starts to criticize China for some reason, a well-treated GE can be relied on as China's proxy.

---

[17] The Comac C919 had its maiden flight on May 5, 2017, in Shanghai.
[18] Nacelle is the outer casing of an aircraft engine.

In many ways, China and its SOEs will single out and identify companies as Hot, Warm, and Cold Partners, just as they do with countries. GE and Honeywell, for instance, will always benefit from their seat at the Hot Partner table, while Google and Twitter, because they and their founders have publicly criticized the government, will remain banished to China's Cold Partner category under their current leadership. And when considering the Cold Partner category, companies that dwell in this position will be blocked altogether from even a penny of China's Wallet. While Cold Partner countries might have a foot in the door, China's government excludes Cold Partner companies from even the chance to thrive in China.

To succeed, foreign brands need to show that they will not only provide the right services and products to Chinese companies, but also that they will adhere to Chinese laws and regulations and for which the Chinese government is willing to allow foreign investment. For example, LinkedIn has succeeded in China as a social media company—while Facebook and Twitter remain blocked—precisely because it has shown a willingness to follow China's laws. Other companies, such as GE and Honeywell, have so publicly supported OBOR that the government will use its Wallet to support them.

There is, however, too much protectionism in the country that does need to change. For example, there are far too many restrictions still in the auto and financial services sectors that force American companies to establish joint ventures with Chinese counterparts. There is a concern that the Chinese government uses these partnerships to force technology transfer so that the American companies essentially are partnering with companies that will become their competitors in five years. Yet, despite the protectionism, China can still be a major driver of growth for even the largest companies.

******

Dialogue:
Victor Shih, political economist at University of California at San Diego and the founder of China Query, LLC

I first reached out to Victor Shih online several years ago after reading some of his analysis on China's debt and political system. Shih has researched China's banking system for nearly 20 years and was one of the first if not the first person to make public China's local debt problem. Perhaps he brings such strong analysis on China because he has experience in both the academic and business worlds. Aside from being a professor at UCSD, he is also the founder of a consulting company that focuses on China's debt dynamic and elite political economy. Shih also worked a stint in the Global Market Strategy Group of the Carlyle Group and assisted on macro trading in the group. Shih holds a Ph.D. in Government from Harvard University and a B.A. summa cum laude from The George Washington University.

Rein: Do countries have cause to worry about SOEs acquiring assets abroad, as they are tools of the CCP, or are fears generally overblown?

Shih: For non-high-tech, nonstrategic industries, I don't think governments have to worry too much because Chinese companies have to obey the law of their host countries just as much as any other companies. For high-technology industries, especially those that have dual-use potential, countries do have to worry because China has an explicit plan to take over a number of high-technology industries and become the leading power in Asia. Recently, it has taken a very aggressive military posture in the Asia-Pacific region.

Rein: What role will SOEs play in initiatives like OBOR? What do SOEs need to do in order to be successful? Hire enough local employees? Ensure profits are spread to other companies? Actively seek to avoid and counteract environmental degradation?

Shih: SOEs will likely take a major role because they are willing to be "patient investors" who take losses on their investment. Of course, they also will receive preferential loan packages from China's policy banks. If, by success, you mean that these companies will become acceptable to the host countries, then I think they indeed have to hire more local employees and to subcontract out more to local companies. That will build strong local constituencies in favor of Chinese investment which is the only viable long term strategy. If contracts all go to Chinese companies which bring their own workers, serious backlashes will be inevitable. If, by success, you mean generating returns that are higher than putting one's money in a wealth management product in China, it will be much more challenging because Central Asia is plagued by a number of factors that deter growth such as geography, low human capital, and weak contract enforcement. Generating healthy returns without strong partnerships with local insiders will be very challenging.

Rein: Do you think there is a level enough of a playing field in China for private Chinese companies and multinationals to compete against SOEs? To what extent does protectionism get in the way of this competition? How should private Chinese companies go about leveling this playing field and competing successfully?

Shih: At the retail and light industrial level, the Chinese market is highly competitive as your work has shown. The more capital intensive a sector is, however, the more partnership with or at least acquiescence of the Chinese government is crucial for success. If the Chinese government favors an SOE or a privately owned national champion, foreign competitors would have to contend with billions in financial subsidies, protectionist policies, and preferential government procurement policies. This definitely creates an unfair playing field for foreign competitors, but some companies have overcome obstacles with partnerships with large Chinese companies and a ton of lobbying. Some domestic private companies resort to "partnerships" with relatives of high-level officials, but that has its own risks.

Rein: How would you recommend China reform its SOE sector? Should it continue to privatize companies? Or reduce the number of companies that report to SASAC directly?

Shih: We have seen many SOEs that are losing money in their traditional production take advantage of the cheap financing they have access to and branch out into other sectors, thus crowding out the private sector. This is rational behavior on the part of the banks because they view central SOEs especially as risk-free. The government has to begin to allow even larger State-owned companies to go bankrupt and for banks to take haircuts in the process so that the banks no longer privilege state-owned companies in making credit decisions. Of course, given the recent instructions to banks to stop all signs of financial instability, allowing a wave of SOE bankruptcy is unlikely.

Rein: The Chinese government is pushing for a greater focus on innovation within SOEs. To what extent do you think this goal is achievable? What are the challenges to innovation in the state sector? What should SOEs do to better compete in innovation?

Shih: As you know better than anyone else, there are some success cases. However, there is also incredible waste. The reason is that policies encouraging innovation also come with generous fiscal and financial subsidies, which every state-owned company would like. Thus, even SOEs without the technical skill to develop certain technology will try to do it in order to obtain central subsidies or financing. On the one hand, production in "new" sectors such as solar panels and industrial robotics can take off in a short time. On the other hand, cheap and substandard knockoffs often crowd out the genuine innovators. The government's tendency to massively subsidize "strategic" sectors then becomes a problem for the world as cheap Chinese-made products in these sectors soon flood the global market.

Rein: Now and in recent years, SOEs are losing good talent to private Chinese companies like Alibaba and Tencent. What do you think are the reasons for this? To what extent does this trend have to do with political factors over profit-oriented incentives among SOE executives?

Shih: There was a time in the recent past that, including grey income from corrupt activities, an executive in a state-owned company could do very well for herself. Those days are over for most people and thus it is natural that talented individuals may think that their lifetime income would be much higher in a successful private company. However, for people who think that they probably will not succeed in the private sector, a steady paycheck from an SOE is still the preferred option.

Rein: Do you think the government's crackdown on corruption is changing how SOEs do business? How so?

Shih: For rank and file SOE employees, the perks they receive have diminished substantially—such as gift cards and fruit baskets around New Year time. For high-level executives, they clearly have to be much more careful, but some corruption probably still exists. The moment that anti-corruption organs in China relax their grips, SOE executives, who still have enormous power within their firms, will become tempted to engage in corruption again.

Rein: To cut down on corruption and inefficiency, the government has been merging SOEs, such as in the upcoming merger of ChemChina and Sinochem. Do you think these mega mergers are economically expedient, or should the government focus on streamlining giants instead of making them bigger?

Shih: We have seen this play out before. Mergers do not make state-owned companies more efficient. Mergers just make it much more difficult to cut off financing to them and much easier for them to lobby for government subsidies and bailouts. As long as political objectives are more important, SOEs, no matter their scale, still will have no incentives to improve bottom lines in the medium term.

Case Study:
Don't Underestimate the Ability of SOEs to Innovate and Move Up the Value Chain

One of the most common perceptions of China's state-owned sector is that its SOEs are a lumbering bureaucracy, kept from market-oriented goals by senior executives whose exclusive focus consists of moving up the Party ranks. While these perceptions are true in several respects, it would be a mistake for foreign multinationals to underestimate the innovative ability of many SOEs. It would also be a mistake to pin SOEs as static forces, unable to evolve. As demonstrated by the response to my SASAC keynote, many executives earnestly want to increase their focus on quality control and build significantly more profitable, market-oriented businesses. SASAC, for their part, have also offered the requisite support and encouragement.

Take Comac, for example, the aerospace manufacturer poised to compete with Boeing and Airbus. Given that nearly all of China's small cities have their own airports and rail links, Comac has evolved to meet this China-specific demand, catering to smaller cities with its scaled-down airplane models.

An even better example can be found in Bright Food, China's second largest food and beverage manufacturing company. While it may appear surprising given China's widespread food safety concerns, Chinese food companies are likely today's most innovative firms precisely because of present fears. In a race to counteract consumer anxiety, Chinese companies have been compelled to go upmarket, developing higher quality and more numerous premium brands. Equipped with insight into Chinese consumer fears regarding the food sector— and particularly the dairy sector, Bright Food has led the wave, becoming one of China's greatest success stories in the food business.

Take its yogurt line, for instance. Positioned as a high-end product, Bright Food yogurt is full of probiotics, marketing its healthful attributes. At the height of China's melamine scandal in 2008, executives from Bright Food decided to visit Momchilovtsi, a small Bulgarian village of fewer than 1,500 inhabitants, famed for the longevity of its citizens. Taken with the village's clean air and natural environs, Bright Food soon thereafter launched an entire brand of premium yogurt named after the village. Bringing back large quantities of the village's Lactobacillus bulgaricus bacteria to put into its yogurt,[ii] Bright Food capitalized on the pure origins of its ingredients, attracting otherwise panicked buyers.

In order to further underscore the product's use of imported, high quality ingredients, Bright Food used high-end packaging embossed with Cyrillic writing. The SOE even created folklore, using Momchilovtsi's imagery on their yogurt packaging and in advertising campaigns. By 2015, sales had hit $250 million USD, driven by safety- and health-conscious Chinese consumers.

Key Action Items

1. Foreign brands have an opportunity to learn about evolving Chinese consumers through the various adaptive efforts of China's SOEs. One important lesson to learn is that Chinese equate good packaging with high quality, a reason for which Tetra Pak has experienced great success in China. Brands must focus on expensive, sturdy packaging as China's Bright Food has done. Conversely, they must avoid seemingly cheap packaging—an error committed by Nestlé when it adopted more environmentally friendly packaging in its water lines. While the move was one of ecological conscience, many Chinese consumers considered Nestlé's new packaging to be flimsy and unsafe.

2. Companies should be careful not to discount the rise of Chinese brands. In general, Chinese consumers prefer trusted domestic brands to foreign ones, with the exception of products in the luxury and auto sectors. Having understood fears of the "Made in China" label, Chinese companies have been aggressive in their efforts to move up the value chain. By acquiring ingredients from overseas to emphasize the safety of their products, numerous Chinese firms have created novel brands that sound as if they are imported. Other Chinese companies simply purchase foreign brands entirely. As a result of these trends—not to mention Chinese pride in domestic industry—Western brands cannot assume that their foreign heritage will automatically attract Chinese consumer trust or a premium reputation.

Chapter 5
China's Outbound Investment: Clash of Cultures

Vancouver, Canada, August 2016

"Please call me now!" Squinting at the phone in my hand, I drowsily pieced together the email that had just arrived in my inbox. Just a few minutes before 5 a.m. Vancouver time, my university classmate Claire had emailed me with an urgent plea. "There's a big Chinese corporation that just contacted me to do a huge deal with my company. Can we talk?"

Nearing the end of my family vacation, I responded that I was on holiday in Canada and promised to call her in two days when I arrived back home in Shanghai. She emailed back immediately: "Man... it is moving a bit fast. Is there any way I could talk to you earlier? ASAP?" Fighting the urge to fall back asleep, I rolled out of bed and called Claire.

My former classmate, now CEO of a UK-based lifestyle brand and a media darling, briefed me quickly. Just hours before, Claire had received a call from a young Chinese woman representing one of China's biggest and better-known conglomerates. Regularly written about in the Western press, such as the *Financial Times*, the conglomerate is a household name for all Chinese yet also owns brands widely known in both Britain and America.

Claire explained the situation: "The young woman said she is close to the chairman. Apparently, he wants to buy up my whole company or co-invest in a new lifestyle company focused on China with a British branding. They're willing to fund the whole venture and give us a 50 percent stake so that we develop a brand and manage its growth. What a potentially game-changing opportunity."

But then came the kicker: "They've given me just three days to prepare a term sheet and five-year business plan with the goal of hitting $100 million USD in revenue in three years. According to the woman, their chairman needs the plan immediately so that he can choose which option to take. They want to turn this into a billion dollar company if we go public with it." Taken completely off guard, my friend had never faced such a fast-moving potential partner or acquirer and now sought the most strategic approach given her circumstances.

She continued somewhat perplexed, "This could be a really big payoff. What do I do? They want everything in three days. They said that after they get my proposals, they will choose which path to take within a week and it's basically a done deal because the chairman loves my company's brands! They're even talking about term sheets. Is this normal for Chinese companies?" I could hear the

DOI 10.1515/9781501507618-005

excitement in Claire's voice, tinged with slight apprehension as she remarked on the speed at which negotiations were taking place.

The potential business opportunity and payoff were huge—a once in a lifetime opportunity afforded by one of the few Chinese companies making it onto western business radars. Nearly every month in recent years, business media headlines from the *Wall Street Journal* to *Bloomberg* featured Chinese companies' scooping up of Western lifestyle brands. Turning heads in 2015, for example, Dalian Wanda Group bought Ironman Triathlon for $650 million USD and Anbang Insurance followed suit in its acquisition of the Waldorf Astoria from Hilton Worldwide for $1.95 billion USD.

What if Claire's company could also make it to the big league? While excited by the prospect, Claire feared moving too fast, and getting cheated or losing control of the company she had so laboriously nursed to strength over the years. Having never before faced a deal of such scope and speed, she was determined to be as methodical as possible in analyzing the present situation.[i]

Contextualizing Chinese business speed, I explained to Claire that the rapidity and magnitude of the conglomerate's demands were a standard tactic of Chinese businesses—both within China and when dealing with mergers and acquisitions overseas. Yet there are several reasons why Chinese companies far outpace American and Western European management standards. Sometimes China's conglomerates genuinely do operate at breakneck speeds in order to seize fleeting opportunities. At other times, however, haste may be used as a negotiating ploy to throw others off-balance and thereby extract a better deal. More nefarious companies might even be seeking a free business plan. Lacking the brainpower or adequate resources, these companies essentially appropriate Western companies' proposals to construct new operations, all under the guise of partnership.

"But speed is not always sinister," I told Claire. Often, profit-making opportunities in China exist for a mere matter of weeks, whether in public equities, commodities, real estate, or some other asset class. Reliably vigilant, the government is known to intervene at a moment's notice, shutting everything down to avert a bubble. Windows of opportunity may only be open for a couple of days before China's government enforces new restrictions on anything from real estate purchases to license plates, inevitably sending prices soaring. Prompted by ever-present volatility, two CEOs may have dinner together one night and decide to raise billions of USD the next, one from the other. Take Alibaba's Jack Ma, for instance. Just days after having drinks with Evergrande Group Chairman Xu Jiayin, Ma self-reportedly bought half of the soccer club Guangzhou Evergrande for $192 million USD with minimal knowledge of the sport. Final discussions, according to Ma, took only 15 minutes.[ii]

Negotiating at such speeds is something I have had to deal with often throughout my career. A few years ago, for example, I was interested in starting a small $150 million USD private equity firm under CMR's umbrella. After engaging a close friend in China—one I trust almost as much as I would family—we had resolved to collaborate on the project with one of his closest friends whom I had yet to meet. Assembling for the first time at the Kunlun Hotel in Beijing, we had a one-hour long meeting, at which we discussed how the fund would invest in IPOs just weeks before they were to go public. Companies would take our money to signal the markets that, through us, they were well-connected in China. One of my responsibilities involved endeavoring to raise money from wealthy individuals and institutional American investors, and perhaps a Middle Eastern royal family or two. After concluding our initial discussion, the three of us planned to meet again a week later.

A week went by and my friend called me. "Have you raised the money yet?" Stunned, I questioned him: How could we possibly raise money before even agreeing to do a fund, let alone have a formal fund structure, legal framework, bank account, or even registered company? Shocked, he was under the impression I could just call up three to four friends and get everything committed. He explained that it was impossible to wait months to set up everything legally because the IPO market was about to be shut off. We had only a week, two maximum, to deploy the funds before China's government stepped in to close off any opportunities. He therefore reasoned it was essential to get the commitments, make the investments, and exit them within a tight interval, essentially on the basis of our word—forget written contracts.

We quickly realized that the barriers were insurmountable. It was simply too rapid a process for American financiers to invest even relatively small sums. Institutional investors in the U.S. typically need months of due diligence and meetings with investment committees before they can even consider investing in a PE fund. Left with little choice, we put the fund on hold. Ultimately, however, my friend was right on the need for speed. Within less than a month, the Chinese government indeed stopped all IPOs for an extended period of time, leaving slower movers out of luck. In stark contrast, funds that had seized the opportunity to go public skyrocketed as investors tumbled into them with mounting momentum—speculative play more than anything.

With firsthand experience of Chinese negotiation speed, I counseled Claire to gather a few brief ideas and craft a mini-proposal. Yet I warned her against including too much detail lest the Chinese company attempt to steal her ideas or simply waste her time. She had to tread a cautious middle ground. On the one hand, Claire in no way wanted to turn off a potential suitor that might prove a big break for both her and her company. Her proposal needed to be sufficiently meaty to pique interest. On the other hand, however, she had to avoid preparing an entire business plan or thorough case study for what might become a competitor under the initial guise of friendship.

Heeding my advice, Claire put all other work on hold for three days to compose two succinct yet informative plans—fairly in-depth but not to the extent she had originally aimed for. Meeting the conglomerate's deadline, she then sent off her proposal to the young woman who had contacted her, purportedly with a direct line to an excitedly expectant chairman keen to read Claire's materials.

About a week later, I emailed Claire to see what the response was. "Nothing," she wrote back. "Girl didn't even let me know that they had received my two potential paths forward." After I followed up a month later, Claire sent the same response with an additional, "What is the matter with these people?" After three months of waiting, she gave up. Claire never heard from the Chinese company again.

Perplexed and irritated, she expressed to me months later that she still failed to understand how such a famous and purportedly reputable conglomerate could conduct itself in such a way. "How can they contact the CEO of another company, show such extreme interest, even talk about term sheets, and then never respond again? It just does not make any sense."

***

Unfortunately, stories like Claire's are not uncommon. In fact, I am contacted several times a year by CEOs of large corporations expressing bewilderment at the manner in which Chinese firms operate culturally. They come on so strong, negotiate so hard and seek commitment so quickly it almost feels as if they lack any interest in building long-term relations. As a result, they seem merely intent to maximize short-term profits at the expense of longer-term yield. Almost flying in the face of the common stereotype that Chinese think in centuries rather than quarters, this supreme focus on the short-term has caused many a conflict between Chinese and Western businesses.

As Chinese companies follow the State's agenda and increasingly do business offshore, these corporate culture clashes are sure to grow more frequent in coming years. Largely directed by efforts in Beijing, the next phase of growth for both state-owned enterprises and private Chinese firms is to become global players, often through full acquisitions and stake investments. Consequently, just as American consumers grow accustomed to Chinese brands and Chinese conglomerate-owned foreign makes, Western corporate chieftains must learn to deal with Chinese firms doing business abroad. The days of China's relegation to a manufacturing label are long gone.

Quite the contrary, many factors are stacked in favor of Chinese business success. Armed with ambition, Chinese companies have access to low interest credit lines from state-owned banks and are frequently supported by regulators. As long as outbound investments conform to their company's core business lines, follow the government's list of supported sectors, and are not deemed a conduit to getting capital out of China, corporations will amply profit from regulatory backing. In addition to growing profits, business abroad effectively dovetails with President Xi's ambitions for the country. Aiming to move China up the value chain and gain influence on the global stage, China's government recognizes SOEs as a critical component of President Xi's OBOR initiative. And in order to kick-start such a massive international enterprise, SOEs and private corporations have no choice but to adopt outbound strategies in facilitation of Chinese political and economic influence abroad. As explored in Chapter 4, OBOR's success hinges upon a successful mix of public and private Chinese money, and political support of the latter is necessary to drive the two. One must also remember that while China's private companies operate on a mostly sovereign basis, their organization usually contains a Party committee that regularly reports to government officials.[iii]

Bolstered by the above combination of factors, many private Chinese firms are steadily and organically growing abroad. Take Chint, for example. A low-voltage electrical power transmission company that made $6 billion USD in revenue in 2013, Chint now sells its products in over 13 countries. When I travel to any of a multitude of Southeast Asian nations, I cannot even walk a few blocks without glimpsing Chint's red, white, and blue signs lining city shops. Green signs touting Chinese handset maker OPPO's mobile phone line intersections throughout Ho Chi Minh City.

Historically, Chinese firms that trend toward organic growth have focused first on Southeast Asia, Africa, and Eastern Europe in order to minimize risks and strive against relatively weaker competition. In recent years, however, private Chinese companies have gradually begun moving into America and Western Europe. Think Haier home appliances or electronics maker TCL Corporation, which, in 2013, bought the naming rights to Grauman's Chinese Theater in Hollywood.

Other private Chinese corporations have demonstrated faster growth targets and acquired entire companies in a bid to become immediate global players. Dalian Wanda Group stands as a perfect example, sweeping through cinemas in its acquisitions of Ironman, AMC, and the Odeon & UCI movie chains, as well as Hollywood's Legendary Entertainment film studio. Acquirers like Dalian Wanda and

Fosun Group often originate in the real estate or insurance sectors, from which they derive ready capital bases to spread into new sectors. They have essentially attempted to master Warren Buffet's strategy of attaining capital from one main line of trade to then deploy it in higher return businesses. At the same time, their fast expansion has drawn the attention of Chinese regulators determined not to allow overseas investments gained by risky capital raising initiatives.

For Western firms, it can therefore be highly lucrative to sell entire companies or stakes to Chinese conglomerates, often with higher valuations than those found in public markets. Exceedingly eager to join global ranks, many Chinese firms are even willing to overpay in their ambitions to scoop up prized brands and coveted technology. Typically run by founders who are already rich, such Chinese corporations acquire Western businesses and sports teams more as trophies than for profit-making purposes. This trend marks a clear divergence from many Western multinationals, often run by professional managers obligated to focus on profits when making acquisitions.

Accordingly, CEOs like my friend Claire have the opportunity to make enormous profits if they have significant shareholding stakes in their companies and can manage to successfully close a deal with a large enough Chinese firm. However, they can also run into serious problems if they lack an appreciation for how to deal with potential private Chinese acquirers and investors. To sell well, Western firms have a stake in understanding two key components: (1) Why Chinese firms are looking to go abroad; and (2) what challenges they face when doing so.

The next section will be dedicated to exploring these critical issues.

***

There are four general reasons why Chinese firms are attempting to go abroad:
1. *Brand Building*: Chinese companies typically buy Western brands for one of two reasons: (1) To bring them back to China and introduce them on the domestic market, or (2) to inject investment and facilitate their global growth. Chinese meat and food processing company Shuanghui did this for the first reason, for example, when it acquired American pork producer Smithfield Foods for $4.7 billion USD in 2013 to bring the brand into the China market. One of Smithfield's biggest shareholders told me over dinner that he was "very satisfied" with the purchase price and that it was a better valuation than he could have gotten in the public markets. These types of outbound investment for the purpose of bringing foreign brands back to China most commonly occur in food, medical, and other sectors fraught by consumer fears over domestically sold counterfeits and shoddy quality products—a phenomenon we will explore further in Chapter 6.

2. *Technology Acquisition*: Facing more limited resources on the mainland, Chinese companies are intent on purchasing foreign technology to integrate into home operations. By investing in tech start-ups overseas, Chinese firms can also project themselves as innovative global tech leaders, and thereby strengthen their customer base. Illustrating part of this trend, Tencent, Alibaba, JD.com, and Baidu have joined the ranks of Silicon Valley's biggest foreign investors. In the past two years alone, they have, in aggregate, invested $5.6 billion USD in Silicon Valley—focusing on companies such as Snapchat and Lyft. Having gained a stronghold in the innovation hub, these tech giants expect to either integrate some of their newly acquired technology into current operations within China or to secure their titles as funders of the future.[iv]

Chinese companies in the industrial sector, for their part, are more interested in incorporating foreign technology into their current product lines or for the purpose of automation; often buying from America, Germany, and other Western European states. A classic example can be found in Xuzhou Construction Machinery Group (XCMG)'s acquisition of a majority stake in German machinery manufacturer Schwing GmbH. Keen to get hold of German industrial proficiency, XCMG invested prime capital in the premium concrete pump maker as early as 2012.[v]

3. *Diversification*: As a result of anxieties over slowing growth and squeezed profit margins, many Chinese companies seek to diversify revenue streams away from China. Such efforts are particularly common among real estate firms—painfully aware of the fact that China's halcyon days of real estate profits have long since set sail. At the front of the wave, Dalian Wanda Group offers an archetypal example, having shifted away from real estate and into lifestyle, entertainment, and other consumer-oriented brands through its various acquisitions.

4. *Management Know-How*: Looking to obtain management know-how, many Chinese acquirers keep foreign companies' management teams in place specifically for the purpose of learning from them. In Geely's acquisition of Volvo, for example, Geely quite purposefully preserved the senior management team and simply offered Volvo administrators more latitude and capital than their former owners, Ford Motor Company; and, in addition, helped them penetrate China's market. It is important to note that Chinese companies usually differ greatly from Japanese firms of the 1980s, which often fired Western senior managers after making an acquisition, installed Japanese executives in their stead, and established a hard "bamboo ceiling" for non-Japanese employees. As one Ivy League educated former employee of a

Japanese-owned firm in the 1990s told me, "It is hell being a non-Japanese in a Japanese company. They will never promote us above a certain level and we always have to report through Japanese managers." Yet even in the biggest of Chinese-owned firms, placing a bamboo ceiling on Westerners is not commonly seen. Alibaba even installed former Goldman Sachs Vice Chairman Michael Evans as its president in 2015 precisely because of his sought-after foreign expertise and extensive network.

Tracy Wut, Principal of the M&A Global Practice Group for multinational law firm Baker McKenzie, underscored to me the major reasons behind China's outbound M&A: "A growing appetite for *cutting-edge technology, manufacturing capabilities, consumer brands, and safe haven assets* in advanced economies have been driving China's outbound investment as Chinese companies seek to diversify their businesses and make inroads into international markets. According to our firm's report, Chinese direct investment in North America and Europe more than doubled in 2016, reaching a total of USD 94.2 billion."

For those eager to sell to Chinese firms, it is imperative to appeal to these four categories. Those that position themselves accordingly—appealing to both private Chinese companies and, in some cases, SOEs—have the opportunity to cash out completely and otherwise gain smart money partners. These partners can critically facilitate both business growth and the long-term wealth of their network.

Yet even with these guidelines, Western brands may be frustrated by Chinese business challenges—a factor outside foreign firms' control. As Chinese companies strive to become global players, it is plainly evident that many are not yet ready for prime time and will most likely fail—even those that have repeatedly made forays abroad. For every successful M&A accomplished, there are hundreds of failures. As deals fall through and Chinese companies flop on their promises, such miscarriages often leave a bad taste in the mouths of CEOs worldwide. Having experienced this frustration firsthand, my friend Claire conveyed to me, "I doubt I will entertain selling my whole company again to a Chinese conglomerate. If another one contacts me, they will have to move slowly and on my terms." Yet many of these issues are simply due to cultural and communication clashes. In some cases, Chinese firms are brash and oblivious to the rules of international business. In others, they quite frankly mean to break the system's model, hoping to bend others toward China's less rigid and rapid fire manner of doing business.

Overall, there are three fundamental challenges hindering Chinese firms from succeeding in outbound M&A. Companies aiming to sell to Chinese businesses must therefore comprehend and account for such challenges in order to minimize risk in negotiating deals and in general collaboration.

1. First, there exist various internal challenges that consistently prevent Chinese companies from growing abroad. Many Chinese firms simply lack a comprehensive understanding of and savvy approach to the global trade system, and are therefore debilitated when attempting to close deals at the senior level. As seen in my classmate's case, her Chinese business counterpart sent a junior employee to talk to a UK-based CEO and then never responded to three days of hard work. As a result, the company burned bridges not only with Claire but likely with many other British companies who were apprised of the incident. It is quite possible, however, that many of these Chinese firms are attempting to disrupt the system and deliver their own methods of conducting international business. It is therefore essential that Western companies hire trusted employees or professional service firms—such as strategy consulting firms or investment banks—to serve as a bridge between Western and Chinese C-level executives.

2. Second, many private Chinese companies lack the internal manpower to grow abroad or have not yet developed the necessary structure to empower mid-level managers. Far too many firms are still run by the founder or a small select group of executives at the top. Without having professionalized a sufficient percentage of their management ranks, these companies are downright unable to fill leadership positions at the national level and, consequently, pay a high price. While this framework enables rapid decision-making, it causes disarray as too much is controlled either by one exceedingly busy individual or a small group who cannot possibly maintain adequate oversight of global operations.

    Moreover, a great number of Chinese firms lack the experienced and business-battle-hardened forty- to fifty-year-old group so typical of mid-level management positions in Fortune 500 companies, such as Procter & Gamble or Unilever. Given historical factors, many Chinese of this age group had neither the educational nor business opportunities to develop the necessary management skills. As a result, many vice presidents in U.S. companies find themselves working with Chinese counterparts in their late 20s with relatively little experience who might have had five jobs in five years in order to job hop to get higher and higher titles. By contrast, China's most talented 40- and 50-year-olds are usually either entrepreneurs or struck it rich during China's real estate boom. Relatively few are likely to work in large corporate operations as do the majority of their American and European contemporaries.

    As opportunities to get rich quickly dwindle in China, today's 30-year-old will most likely become a solid mid-level manager in ten to twenty years.

While the number of qualified individuals is undoubtedly growing, it will therefore take a decade or two before China's junior managers are capable of powering meaningful business growth abroad. And even this scenario depends on the willingness of company chairmen to delegate decision-making power and managerial authority to underlings.

3. Third, China's government weighs in heavily on the ability of domestic companies to become global players. Chinese firms are influenced by Beijing's shifting political desires, as the government decides to support specific businesses and sectors in the context of its global ambitions and the macro economy. When confronted by too much capital outflow, China's government simply shuts everything down.

In December 2016, I received a panicked call from an American-based hotelier. At the time, he was in the middle of conducting a joint deal with a large Chinese conglomerate that had extensive overseas investments in the hotel, real estate, and leisure sectors. Having committed to the purchase of the hotelier's U.S. hotel chain, the Chinese company was compelled to back out at the last minute. Caught in a regulatory fiasco, the Chinese firm had to pay a $50 million USD break-up fee simply as a result of their inability to get money out of their home country.

What caused the sudden debacle? In the first half of 2016, outbound mergers and acquisitions grew 60 percent year over year. Billions of dollars of investments were being made. But suddenly, as capital flows hit $100 billion USD a month in early 2016, fears of the Chinese *renminbi*'s (RMB) depreciation took hold of the nation, and Chinese government regulators immediately intervened. As a result, outbound M&A in the second half of 2016 plummeted dramatically and was practically left at a standstill by early 2017. However, outbound M&A by SOEs remained constant through the first half of 2017 showing the political importance of outbound investment that was consistent with Beijing's political goals.

Already confronted with a dizzying collection of market opportunities to invest in abroad, Chinese companies are frequently called to navigate the ramifications of political regulation. Often abrupt and offering little warning, China's government may restrict overseas investment at a moment's notice, offering no one an exemption from the law—as it did in July 2017 when it put limits on high-flying companies Wanda and Anbang from expanding overseas. Yet, Baker McKenzie's Wut welcomes the new guidelines because "it provides more clarity on how China will regulate its outbound investments" and shows "investment in industries that would generally help China to move up the value chain or improve people's livelihood are likely to be encouraged ... such as investments across different sectors in life sciences and healthcare, in particular in technologies, products, services that can be imported into China."

***

For acquisitions, companies are typically acquiring assets of companies from wealthier Warm Partner and Cold Partner categories. Germany, Australia, New Zealand, America, and the United Kingdom are the regions with the most vaunted brands. Aside from New Zealand, all the other assets come from countries that are not political allies. Part of this makes them more exotic and wanted by Chinese brands.

Although outbound Chinese M&A dropped 46 percent in the first part of 2017 year over year (again, especially from the private sector), there exist many opportunities for Western companies to sell stakes or entire companies to Chinese firms looking to buy innovative technology, management expertise, and desirable brands. When my firm interviews Chinese companies, outbound M&A is a tool many want to employ to diversify assets. The main barrier is government regulation. In 2017, the government put a halt on much outbound investment because they are worried about capital flight, a depreciating RMB, and too much debt used for investment that could cause a systemic risk.

However, the underlying demand by Chinese companies to grow through acquisition remains strong. Once the government lessens the restrictions, when fears of debt and capital outflow diminish, the outbound trend by both private Chinese companies and SOEs will continue.

******

Dialogue:
Winston Cheng, President of International, JD.com

Winston Cheng has had a storied career. Before joining JD.com as President of International, he was Managing Director, Head of Asia Media, Telecom and Technology for Bank of America Merrill Lynch. Before that he was Managing Director, Head of Asia Ex-Japan Technology, and IBD for Goldman Sachs.

Rein: What are JD's plans for overseas investment? Are there specific regions that you are looking to invest in, and why is JD targeting these?

Cheng: We have been enjoying significant growth inside China, but we've been predominantly within China. Yet as we examine and maintain our growth rate, we are also interested to replicate our experiences from China elsewhere, in terms of helping bring in international brands, improving retail environment efficiency, and offering a better consumer experience to domestic customers.

Regarding the regions targeted, we seek markets in a development stage or environment similar to what we saw in China more than fifteen years ago. We considered Indonesia to fit this category, for example, so began the planning stage and entered Indonesia almost two years ago. And as we continue our growth in the international market, it is important to identify the most opportune regions. The U.S. is an extremely large market, for example, but quite mature. China and India are also huge markets, drawing numerous investments, but India has reached a development stage ahead of what Chinese investors are seeking, so the criteria by which we assess regions for expansion in the international market are quite stringent. We look for markets that currently lack a clear leader and in which we haven't considered the regulatory environment, and then we examine whether we can add value to the local market, providing a differentiated and superior service to local consumers.

When examining investment opportunities, it is also vital to consider the financial and developmental risks involved in targeted regions and countries. When looking at India, for example, we saw the country get extremely 'hot' about five years ago, looking at India in a stage that was still rational. So three years ago I would deem it highly overvalued, but then we have seen some divesting in the last year by which valuations have come down somewhat in India. Indonesia, on the other end, is enjoying that up cycle right now, rising exceedingly quickly. However, local markets all have their challenges. Chiefly, it is important that people be careful not to look at Southeast Asia as a bloc. The size and internal variation of different Southeast Asian countries are both important distinguishers. While Indonesia has an enormous population, for example, it consists of many islands and domestic disparities pose difficulties. As a result, China and India are still much more attractive given their respective concentrations and uniformity of law enforcement and infrastructure. So while different nations present distinct disadvantages, Southeast Asia is certainly attracting many; valuations are high. Yet there will be opportunities. And within this context, JD is fixated on the long-term view and takes entry points into strong consideration.

Rein: What are your underlying reasons for investing abroad? To bring products and services back to the Chinese market? To invest in start-ups to get access to innovative technology? To service the local market, such as in Indonesia?

Cheng: As the President of International, I think it is critical not to look only in one direction. We cannot narrow-mindedly bring Chinese expertise elsewhere or focus solely on JD's launch outward into international markets. In fact, I dedicate a significant amount of time to bringing foreign companies into China via JD's platform, helping them access Chinese consumers, and effectively grow their revenues inside China. This actually occupies over 50% of my job today. Much of JD.com's tremendous growth—in excess of 40% a year, even at our over 100 billion dollar GMV run rate—derives from our significant GMV [gross merchandise value] increase within China alone. For that reason, we're always looking for markets that are growing in excess of that for our next stage of development, making sure to service local markets abroad and contribute to their domestic consumers.

In the meantime, however, we cannot forget about our opportunities inside China, which is why we dedicate significant resources to helping international companies with their entry to the Chinese market and, once inside, ensuring the entry of superior products, services, and technology to China. In the last couple months, for instance, we've announced a focus on luxury brands. We now have a partnership with the Kering Group, one of the high profile global brands keen to work with us. Working directly with Yves Saint Laurent, Swarovski, and premium watch brands, among others, we've been sought out by a great number of brands that work with us on an international basis and have opened their flagship stores with us.

We have also developed an effective system for working with smaller brands, differentiating us from competitors. By buying products into our inventory from these brands, we can actually provide them a much more efficient service. Almost two-thirds of our revenue today actually comes from first parties, meaning we buy and hold inventory. For an SME [small and medium enterprises] business owner in the U.S., Africa, or Europe, it is therefore better to work with JD because we take on inventory and a significant portion of risk. As a result, these SMEs have a guaranteed sale that we then push actively in marketing, more so than our competitors, many of which essentially serve as a mere platform.

Without this type of assistance, many smaller brands are unable to gain a hold. Lacking brand recognition, they spend a debilitating amount of advertising dollars for ranking and exposure on pure marketplace models. Yet these don't necessarily translate to sales. Using our model, we already buy inventory and therefore don't require small brands to spend additional dollars in vain. Because our buyers include large retailers like Walmart and other department stores, our buyers are powerful and know which products will sell. Moreover, given our use of big data, we manage our inventories very efficiently and know what will sell on the market. And as our inventory turnover rate continues to decline—one of the lowest in the industry—we're trying to continue to improve on that.

Rein: Are there certain sectors in which you are working to get more inventory?

Cheng: Given that we are China's largest inventory for consumer electronics already—not to mention one of the more important partners for major brands such as Apple in China—we can be extremely helpful to most players. Given that we are one of the largest general retailers both on an offline and primarily online basis, we are not specifically focused on any category. Consequently, we are looking to develop the categories for which we haven't reached the top or second highest position, primarily those categories which are broad and fragmented, such as the apparel industry. Certainly in 3Cs (Computing, Communication, and Consumer) and other realms, however, dynamics are easier to track and we are definitely a leader in those areas. Therefore, while all products are important, the fashion apparel industry (which provides significant business for us already) is one area that we plan to focus on more. We have also noticed that the number of female users on our platform is growing significantly so we are seeking out more products to sell to female customers.

Rein: What is your thinking process when considering an acquisition or investment abroad?

Cheng: Somewhat diverging from our competitors, we always look at the market first to determine whether we have the capability to grow organically in that market. When growing organically in the market, we both contribute Chinese talent and predominantly hire a significant amount of local talent. Hiring sufficient local talent is essential for us to grow our business. In places such as Indonesia, we are actually working to foster the growth of IT professionals, to build our executives, to train people in working closely with a diverse team and improve our approach. It's therefore critical that there be a sustainable, long-term local work force because we enter foreign countries for the long haul. So, this capacity to grow organically is an integral component of my thinking process when considering investment overseas.

With regard to acquisitions, we work more on a case-by-case basis. Of course, sometimes we need to watch out for competitive moves. In the Internet space today, many seem to be playing a capital game, seeking to store more and more capital in the sector until everyone else is ultimately forced out and the entire space is occupied. As one can see, it's a dangerous game but unfortunately there is plenty of capital out there to engage in it, so we certainly need to be aware.

Rein: The Chinese government has announced its move to crackdown on certain types of outbound investments, deterring companies from buying into sports teams, casinos, and real estate, for example. Do you predict that some of these outbound investment controls will stop JD from investing abroad? Or since you are part of the tech sector and have better compliance and risk controls, do you think the government still supports you?

Cheng: Overall, I don't think JD necessarily gets overt government support. We are certainly subject to government policy like any other company based in or operating out of China, so I don't think we enjoy special treatment by any means. Given that we are a U.S.-listed company, a sizeable portion of the capital we've raised in the past is already sitting offshore and our cash flow is fairly strong on an onshore basis. We have also run our investment like a regular committee and have not made outrageous bets akin to some of those that have caught political attention in recent years. JD has not historically been excessively acquisitive externally, investing in a manner similar to most regular enterprises. And in addition to having a certified board, we undergo highly formal processes with our best committee and have had feasible valuations throughout the past. Needless to say, all our operations have been carried out according to the regular Western book from the government's perspective.

Rein: President Trump has criticized China for stealing American jobs. Yet it seems JD might be able to create jobs in the United States because U.S. brands that were not able to sell to the Chinese consumer ten years ago are now able to do so using your store. Do you see JD as assisting in job creation and balance of payment issues abroad?

Cheng: As a retailer that doesn't necessarily manufacture, we actually do not dictate where things are made necessarily, yet we are not agnostic. Based on our experience and knowledge of consumer behavior in China, in some instances we in fact recommend that brands manufacture products in their home country to offer more authenticity. Ultimately, however, manufacturers and brands determine where products are made, accounting for cost structure and competitors in their industry. Therefore, while we don't dictate where products are manufactured, we do often encourage brands in the design stage to make products domestically if we think local manufacturing will result in higher quality, better brand positioning or other advantages. So in that regard, while we can't pinpoint how many jobs we are creating exactly, we are certainly helping to some extent by driving the entry and growth of foreign companies—not just U.S. firms—in China, allowing them access to China's growing mobile internet consumer base and encouraging them to manufacture and hire talent in their home countries.

Rein: Are there any investments that you think could significantly help JD's bottom line in the future, such as your acquisition of Farfetch perhaps?

Cheng: Our partnership with Tencent in 2014—in which Tencent contributed their e-commerce business to JD—has been remarkably powerful. At the time, Tencent was entering the Chinese trade market but realized that backing JD would be more profitable than attempting to make it on their own, largely given the challenges of e-commerce and of differentiating oneself in the arena. Our exclusive partnership with their WeChat app—now home to 940 million mobile users—has given us an exclusive window into the Chinese version of the app as we are now placed right next to the gaming and shopping sections. We have also enjoyed strong ties with Walmart as it contributed its Chinese Yihaodian e-commerce marketplace to JD in exchange for close partnerships. As a result of these two alliances, we now have online mobile traffic connected to e-commerce procedures, our own logistics, and over four hundred plus Walmart stores, forming a competitive setup. To put it in concrete terms, what you have in China today is as if Facebook, Amazon, FedEx, and Walmart in the U.S. were all tied together to provide a streamlined service. A powerful combination, this union offers a wealth of excellent experience to our respective teams.

Rein: When we interview wealthier consumers in tier 1 cities especially, they tend to report that they trust buying from JD over buying from your major competitor platforms, often saying they think you offer stronger service as well as more genuine and higher quality products. Is it part of JD's strategy to be more upmarket than the competition and bring more trust to the transaction?

Cheng: It is certainly our strategy to provide an authentic product and the best service possible to our customers. We don't necessarily target upmarket, but it is clear to us that the upmarket consumer is particularly attracted to our services. Given that the upmarket consumer's time is limited, these customers are looking for a platform that is hassle-free, on which they know they are guaranteed the best product, the most competitive prices, and the highest levels of authenticity at the fastest rate possible. So, JD definitely seeks to ensure these qualities consistently.

Furthermore, as China's per capita GDP continues to grow in conjunction with increasing consumption power and a rising white collar workforce, upmarket consumers want to use their time more purposefully, whether at work, enjoying leisure with their families or going on weekend excursions. They thus have less time to browse through a tediously constructed setup and then negotiate with the purchasing platform. They want a hassle-free, top quality, competitively priced, and expedited customer experience. While going to a physical shopping arena certainly has its benefits, consumers will rarely return home having efficiently found everything they want for the best possible prices. We therefore believe that over time people will want to increasingly buy from trusted online platforms like ours.

Case Study: Selling a Company or Stake to a Chinese Acquirer

An enthusiastic go-getter with a slight frame, Little Zhang was a middle-aged woman who helped lead acquisitions of foreign companies for her own Chinese conglomerate. Holding a large glass of Coke when I met her, Little Zhang had a pleasant face that would have fit well in a kindergarten setting. She worked for ASIC, a large state-owned enterprise in the aerospace sector and once the parent company of Comac—China's airplane initiative set up to rival Boeing and Airbus.

When I first met her, Little Zhang had just heard me give a speech on how foreign companies can best sell to Chinese companies while minimizing risks. Approaching me after the talk, she told me, "You are right, Xiao Shan [my Chinese name]. The Chinese companies that have fared best in overseas acquisitions are just like Geely in its acquirement of Volvo." During my speech, I had argued that China's most successful overseas acquirers tend to bring in capital and resources but leave management teams largely intact. China's Dalian Wanda Group, for instance, injected tremendous capital into AMC when it acquired the movie chain, but made sure to keep AMC's executives in place.

Even more striking has been the success of automaker Zhejiang Geely Holding Group Corporation, which acquired Volvo in 2010 and more recently bought a huge stake in Malaysian automaker Proton. After buying out Volvo, Geely similarly left the company's Swedish managers in place for the most part. Investing both capital and expertise regarding China's distribution network, Geely subsequently saw a remarkable rise in profits as well as the release of its critically acclaimed SC CXC 600 line.

Elaborating on Chinese firms' M&A strategies, Little Zhang continued to speak of her own company, ASIC, "We have made a slew of acquisitions across America and Europe in auto and aircraft parts, and results have been excellent so far. Our strategy has been to buy either an entire company outright or a stake, but we are more passive in day-to-day decisions. We don't try to bring our compensation, travel, and other similar elements into the mix." Outside of full acquisitions, most investments have been fairly small, ranging from $5 to $100 million USD. As a result, most foreign investments fly below the radar of Western financial journalists. Most importantly, however, these investments are small enough not to produce anxiety in the companies and countries targeted.

Chinese conglomerates will either (1) buy out an entire company, inject capital, and generally leave successful management teams in place, or (2) make a fairly small investment, flying under the radar and not causing anxiety. Chinese firms understand that current employees can be disquieted about a stake sale to an unfamiliar Chinese firm, and that regulators are concerned about ties to the Chinese government, even for private companies. Regulators and politicians often claim private Chinese companies, like telecom maker Huawei or real estate developer Wanda, are simply fronts for the Chinese government or military and thus place a lot of scrutiny on deals.

Speed, as we saw in the case of my classmate Claire, often marks typical dealings with Chinese firms.

Key Action Items

1. When selling to Chinese firms, foreign companies should either sell small stakes or their entire company—it is unwise to sell a major stake until it is a full 100% stake, as cultural issues will be difficult to surmount. Integration of Motorola Mobility into Lenovo, for example, has been challenging as a result of Motorola's already deeply embedded culture. At the time of Lenovo's acquisition, the Motorola branch was neither large enough to stand on its own, nor small enough to be fully absorbed by Lenovo.
2. Selling to Chinese companies does not entail the same risks as does selling to Japanese firms. Most often, Chinese firms are looking to buy brands, technology, and management know-how when they make acquisitions. Few are interested in replacing executive ranks and expelling foreign expertise. As evidenced above, Geely kept Volvo's management teams, as did Wanda after acquiring the AMC cinema chain.
3. It is important to understand that Chinese companies operate under fundamentally different moral and business codes when making acquisitions.

Often focused on extremely short-term gains during the courting process—usually by necessity—Chinese firms look to maximize profits and throw potential partners off balance by moving rapidly and delivering unreasonable demands. Once a deal is consummated, however, Chinese companies quickly reposition themselves to home in on long-term strategies. Foreign companies need to hire internal employees or outside advisors who understand Chinese business processes to determine whether the need for speed is a legitimate pocket of opportunity or if it is a strategy to put the foreign company off kilter.

Chapter 6
Fear, Wellness, and Understanding the Chinese Consumer

Shanghai, China, 2016

"Two months to live," Carrie sighed. She went on, "Doctors at a famous public hospital in Hangzhou gave my mother two months before she would die from cancer." Carrie then smiled, "But then I took her to see doctors in Hong Kong. They gave her cancer treatments not available on the mainland, and she is still living two years later."

I was interviewing Carrie, a forty-five-year-old woman, about why so many Chinese were seeking medical treatment abroad rather than at home. We were dining in a bustling restaurant nestled next to the Bund's Peace Hotel, an Art Deco masterpiece built between 1926 and 1929 by Sir Victor Sassoon, a British Sephardic Jew. Like Sassoon, many Jews came to Shanghai in the 1920s and 1930s because of its visa free policies and built many of the landmark buildings in the city like Grosvenor House and Cathay Mansions. In the 1930s, the city drew 30,000 Jewish refugees fleeing Nazi Germany. Rumor has it that the Bund was named after the bunds and levees along the Tigris river by immigrating Baghdadi Jews.

Carrie told me how her mother had been diagnosed with cancer by doctors at a top public hospital in Hangzhou. They said her mother was going to die soon and nothing could be done. In preparation for death, Carrie began to put all of her mother's affairs in order.

As a last-ditch effort, she flew with her mother to Hong Kong to get a second opinion. The oncologists in Hong Kong offered drugs not available in the mainland—and they worked. Two years later, Carrie's mother, was alive and well.

Carrie thus began a routine of monthly flights to Hong Kong for her mother's medicine. While many of the prescriptions were not yet available in China, equally important was Carrie's distrust of drugs bought on the mainland. The only choice, therefore, was to visit Hong Kong directly or pay a premium for third-party *daigou*[19] who purchase the products in Hong Kong and bring them back into the mainland.

---

[19] The word *daigou* means "buying on behalf of."

DOI 10.1515/9781501507618-006

Having to navigate and wade through China's medical system is remarkably tedious and time consuming so Carrie quit her job as a lawyer to take care of her mother full-time.

Introduction of new medicines to the mainland takes years if not decades, as approval processes linger in the bottlenecks of China's bureaucracy. An example can be found in the HPV vaccine Gardasil, produced by the U.S. pharmaceutical company Merck. Approved in 2006 by the U.S. Food and Drug Administration (FDA), Gardasil has yet to be permitted in China, more than a full decade later. Instead, rumor has it that an early version of a drug—covering only a fraction of the HPV strains protected against in America—is to reach China's market in late 2017 or 2018. Following the lead of many other frustrated mainlanders, one of my employees at CMR actually took time off several times to get the full vaccine course done in Hong Kong. In the meantime, millions of Chinese children who could benefit will miss out on the vital immunization because of the sluggish regulatory process.[i]

Yet even for treatments approved by the China Food and Drug Administration (CFDA), purchasing domestically available medicines is a frightful process. Many Chinese simply don't trust the quality or even authenticity of most mainland drugs. And such distrust is not merely limited to the medical sphere. Suspicious of a wide range of products—from baby formula to diapers—countless Chinese tourists buy products while traveling abroad, and many others purchase directly from foreign e-commerce sites that ship into China, such as vitamin maker GNC. Consumers are scared of buying shoddy products and pirated versions sold online in China, even on famous sites like Alibaba's Taobao or Tmall sites, or in brick and mortar stores.[ii]

Carrie echoed this anxiety, complaining, "I go to Hong Kong even for medicines *accessible* in China because I'm worried they may be expired or counterfeit in local stores. Have you seen all the media stories of people getting arrested for selling fake drugs?"

She was right. Every several months, a new story comes out in the Chinese press featuring the police as they raid warehouses full of counterfeit or expired medical products. In March 2016, state media outlet *Xinhua* announced the arrest of 130 suspects in Shandong Province. Triggering a massive outcry, those arrested had sold over 20,000 batches of suspect medicine and vaccines for a total of $88 million USD. Many were reminded of the public health crisis of 2008, in which 300,000 children were sickened by melamine-tainted milk, produced by money-grubbing farmers and then distributed by those looking to gain an extra buck in the dairy supply chain.[iii]

To ensure her mother got genuine medicine, Carrie essentially had to smuggle Hong Kong-bought drugs into the mainland. Medicines—and similar products, like baby formula—brought into China by suitcase exist in a legal grey area. They have not been approved for sale and resellers do not pay mainland taxes. Customs authorities usually turn a blind eye to medicines intended for self-use rather than for resale. But it is common to hear of Chinese being fined or even arrested for entering the country with such products in their luggage.

But even in light of the risks, the practice is common, particularly among younger Chinese attempting to care for family members too old or ill to travel on their own. As Zoey, a twenty-six-year-old from Beijing told me, "Every time I travel to America or Hong Kong, I take a shopping list of medical products to buy for family and friends. My elderly parents want glucosamine for their arthritic joints; my sister wants waterproof Band-Aids for her daughter. I buy vitamins for myself." For many, the benefit of attaining genuine medicine and health products for loved ones outweighs any risks encountered in Customs.

"I just don't trust the Chinese medical system," Carrie continued. "Our doctors might be good. But because of President Xi's crackdown on corruption in the medical sector, eliminating bribery, how can I ensure the doctors will give my mother good care if I don't bribe them? Even non-corrupt, well-intentioned doctors lack access to the resources available in Canada or Hong Kong. And besides, they're too overworked."

Paradoxically, the anti-corruption crackdown intended to ease patients' minds has—at least in its initial stages—caused even greater worry. Seeing no sure incentives, patients and their families fear doctors will not give them good care unless they are bribed. As one family of a patient from Nanjing having back surgery told me, "If we cannot bribe the doctor, what motive does he have to take care of our elderly mother? Doctors are far too busy, and we have no personal connection with them."

Fear of poor quality products and the mediocre services of doctors too busy to care for non-bribing patients is exceedingly widespread—occupying the minds of patients diagnosed with everything from cancer to cardiovascular problems to brain disease. In 2016, my firm explored these issues further, interviewing 100 wealthy Chinese (with liquid assets over $2 million USD) from four cities. Each interviewee either had family members who had traveled outside of China or had personally left the country for medical treatment, visiting the United States, Japan, Hong Kong, Germany, Thailand, or South Korea.

In our interviews, over 70 percent of respondents told us they either distrusted Chinese care for critical illnesses like cancer or cardiology—often because doctors lacked access to the newest medicines and equipment, or because hospitals themselves were so over packed. Particularly in China's best public hospitals, doctors often see between one and two hundred patients a day, leaving literally no time to care for individuals for more than a minute or two—forget bedside manner.

Facing rising apprehension about subpar care and suspect medical products, China's smarter hospitals have begun to counteract public fears. At Parkway Health in Shanghai, for example, nurses now break the seal of inoculation packages in front of patients, demonstrating that vaccines are to be trusted. Drug expiration dates have also been shown to patients in an effort to establish public trust.

***

When approaching these contemporary health care issues, we must take stock of three fundamental problems plaguing Chinese society today: (1) lack of trust; (2) inability to access products and services as a result of overwhelming state control; and (3) overt individualism in the often-unscrupulous pursuit of money. Wielding a huge impact on the Chinese consumer psyche, these three issues are essentially intertwined and can even be summed up by the first and most fundamental problem—lack of trust.

Permeating a variety of spending categories, lack of trust impacts consumer behavior in everything from immigration and tourism (as we shall see in Chapters 7 and 8) to routine local shopping. With far-reaching implications, it is a concept essential to anyone dealing with China—be it brands or policy makers. Diverging markedly from the American ethos of 'trust unless burnt,' Chinese nowadays do not trust anyone until they prove themselves trustworthy.

Given China's contemporary lack of trust in the domestic market, foreign companies have the opportunity to tap into the Chinese consumer wallet by offering products and services not readily bought or trusted in China—such as the cancer treatments required by Carrie's mother, for example. Growing nationalism and technical expertise have indeed seen many now flock to top quality domestic brands—trusted companies like Mengniu, Bright Food and Yili Dairy. However, Chinese consumers still demonstrate an overwhelming desire to buy imported brands in key categories, particularly those pertaining to health or the well-being of children.

One of the most popular purchases among Chinese tourists, for example, is condoms. Fearing the quality of China's domestically produced condoms, many Chinese consumers get the contraceptive from Japan. Manufactured with faulty materials, too many condoms sold in the mainland are counterfeit, rendering them inadequate in prevention of sexually transmitted infections or pregnancy.

In 2015, for example, Shanghai police announced the seizure of three million knock-off condoms containing toxic metals. In an attempt to offset distrust in domestic brands, savvier Chinese firms have begun buying foreign brands. Humanwell Healthcare Group and CITIC Capital China Partners, for instance, teamed up to buy Ansell Ltd.—the Australian producer of gloves and surgical masks that owns the popular Jissbon condom brand. In a similar pursuit, China's Biostime baby formula company recently acquired Australian supplement and vitamin maker Swisse Wellness.[iv]

To take advantage of this trend, foreign brands must position themselves as offering higher quality and trustworthiness—it does not make sense for them to compete with domestic brands on price. Local brands can always undercut pricing, often via unsavory means, and have consistently demonstrated willingness to take squeezed margins. As such, the only way foreign players should shift into cheaper categories is through purchase of local brands. If they otherwise attempt to compete on price, Chinese consumers readily assume that foreign brands are cutting corners in quality control.

And it is not surprising that they would do so. Given all the dangers of shopping in China, most consumers are extremely wary of even marginal indications that a product might be faulty or unreliable, from less glue to seal labels on a water bottle to thinner bottle caps. Even in the purchase of everyday consumer goods, Chinese buyers go to extremes in ensuring safety. I have interviewed dozens of shoppers, for instance, who not only rotate the milk and eggs brands they purchase in case one brand is bad, but also rotate the outlet from which they buy the foods. Diversifying risk however possible, they might buy eggs from one online one week like JD.com, at Carrefour the next, and then buy from a different online vendor like Yihaodian the week after. As one forty-something-year-old woman told me, "I run all water through two purifiers and then boil it afterward. I must take precautions in case the purifiers are counterfeit or bad quality. I tend to do this for about a week and then buy imported water from brands like Evian or San Benedetto the next."

***

While many analysts are well aware of Chinese consumer distrust, both of brands and their distributors, few understand the underpinnings that have given rise to this culture. If Chinese society is for the most part free of crime and relatively safe, it seems quite paradoxical that lawbreakers in the business community, and fear of their illicit behavior, are so widespread. I have absolutely no hesitation walking anywhere in Shanghai at 2 a.m.—something I would never do in many U.S. cities, particularly big urban centers like Chicago or St. Louis, yet a trip to the supermarket presents myriad risks to the contemporary Chinese consumer. How do I know if my baby formula provider has cheated his way to profits by selling me poor ingredients? How do I know if the oil used by the restaurant is not recycled gutter oil?

To understand why China has become a no-trust society, it is important to home in on the underlying reasons for which many offenders have tainted the market and still continue to do so.

At the core of these factors is a paradoxical phenomenon that permeates modern Chinese psychology: extreme individualism brought about by the lack of civil society and an utter reliance on the Communist Party to fix all societal issues. Everything from China's Non-Governmental Organizations (NGOs), to the majority of charities, to schools from elementary education through university, is essentially run by the government. In examining modern China, various analysts like Tom Doctoroff, the author of the book, *What Chinese Want: Culture, Communism, and China's Modern Consumer* tout Confucianism as the lens through which to understand China—a country whose citizens sacrifice and sublimate individual desires for the betterment of the whole. Yet a closer look at the Communist political structure reveals that such a view may be somewhat shortsighted, particularly when probing consumer behavior. Much more attention needs to be channeled toward grasping the effect of collectivism on China's modern day dynamics of trust.[v]

Tom Doctoroff is certainly accurate in claiming that Confucianism still retains a strong influence on contemporary Chinese culture—much as the Judeo-Christian tradition shapes the ideologies and social dynamics of modern America. Yet while his work holds validity, it largely glosses over the extent to which Communism plays a role in shaping 21st century Chinese culture—a phenomenon often left unrecognized. Many of China's political critics have argued that Communism generates a culture of fear within the country, citing the state's one-party system, lack of free speech, and heavy media censorship.

But these analyses largely miss the mark in explaining how China's Communist Party exerts power internally today. Particularly in the past several decades, the Party has no longer gained its legitimacy through fear and violence. Prior to the 21st century, this was certainly not the case. The Communist Party often used violent means to consolidate legitimacy during the Cultural Revolution (1966–1976) and beforehand—notably when the Communists first came to power in 1949—and it still puts an immediate halt to violence by today's criminals. Even when I first arrived in Tianjin, China in the 1990s to study at Nankai University, people I interviewed regarding political issues would bow their heads down and refuse to say anything. But these dynamics have shifted dramatically in the past few decades. Now Chinese feel relatively free to criticize problems in the system as long as they are not calling to rally for a protest or overthrow of the system.

Having matured and stabilized since its early days, China's government now maintains its power by adjusting to the needs and demands of its citizens, a skill it has mastered quite well. Confirming this development, Harvard's Daewoo Professor of International Affairs Anthony Saich and the bipartisan Pew Research Center have respectively found that 85 percent of Chinese tend to support the direction in which their central government guides the country. Such support is largely derived from government response to the needs of China's population, rather than the Party's cudgel of violence to maintain power through fear. Even the Big Brother-like camera system set up throughout the country by China's public security bureau is typically applauded by the population. Providing a sense of security, it offers hard evidence in the case of an accident or crime.

In a different context—such as the police state of Stalinist Russia or Mao's Cultural Revolution—fear of cameras and government violence would likely permeate the everyday behavior of common citizens. Yet there is little if any fear present among contemporary Chinese civilians on a day-to-day basis. As long as they are not rallying in protest, Chinese feel relatively free to express their opinions and criticisms. As Harvard professor Gary King[20] has shown in a number of studies on China's online world, Chinese netizens are free to express their thoughts, while the Communist Party merely seeks to guide public discussion rather than arrest those who offer criticism.[vi]

But while the Communist Party no longer consolidates power through fear, it does exercise an often-unintended effect on national culture given that the State takes credit for everything—from China's economic boom of the past forty years to construction of a sports powerhouse in its 2008 Olympic games. As a result, the Party leaves little room for praise of individual achievements: Basketball player Yao Ming achieved world fame because he began his training under state tutelage; Wanda Real Estate's Wang Jianlin succeeded as a result of his beginnings in an SOE where he built the needed connections; actors, actresses, and directors like Zhang Yimou or Chen Kaige made it to the big screen given their tenure at state-owned Beijing Film Academy, not on the basis of their own merits.

However, while such ascription of credit may seem harmless at face value, the Communist Party's monopoly on recognition has unwittingly caused an over

---

[20] King is the Albert J. Weatherhead III University Professor and Director for the Institute for Quantitative Social Science at Harvard University.

reliance on the government to solve most problems. As a result, a large majority of Chinese focus solely on bettering themselves or their *guanxi* group,[21] and care little for the well-being and prosperity of others. Why help total strangers when that responsibility belongs to the Party? Why invest effort in halting the distribution of counterfeits if that is the job of China's police force? Besides, a corrupt official might be involved so why risk crossing him?

Such entrenched absorption in the self stands at the core of people's disregard for their external environment. Even walking down the street can be risky at times as a shopkeeper might throw refuse on the ground and hit pedestrians—someone hired by the Party will come and clean up anyway. The insides of Chinese homes and stores might be sparkling clean, but most homeowners and merchants don't bother to think twice when littering or negatively intruding on the lives of surrounding passersby. Drivers weave in and out of traffic to go faster for themselves, even if it slows drivers behind them. Or they park shared bicycles from Mobile and OFO on sidewalks blocking others from walking by. In a reinforcement of the vicious cycle, Chinese will thus do whatever they can to protect their own *guanxi* group, quality of life, and fortune, yet expend little to no investment on others.

I have seen several serious car accidents, for example, that precisely underscore Chinese over-reliance on the Communist Party in resolving communal problems. When I run up to help, I see numerous Chinese crowding about—perhaps with a desire to give assistance, but often just standing around aimlessly. Part of their reason for remaining bystanders involves fear of getting into trouble (China only implemented Good Samaritan laws in October 2017). There are many cases of people assisting others only to be sued by the people they were helping in the first place.

However, the greatest cause of their hesitation stems from a general conviction that the Communist Party will fix everything for them. I often hear onlookers screaming above the crowds, ordering others to call 110 or 120 for the police or ambulance because they will be able to solve the problem best. And if either is slow to arrive, people feel justified in anger, decrying the government for not hurrying to help, yet all the while leaving their injured countrymen largely unassisted. A deeply ingrained conviction, issues and accidents in the public sphere lie within the jurisdiction of the central government—individuals simply lack the wherewithal to contribute. People therefore rarely take first aid courses to learn

---

[21] I define *guanxi* as a circle of trust, as opposed to a circle of good connections as it is commonly defined.

how they should help others in the case of injury. Acting on an embedded primary response, most Chinese simply call the government for assistance.

Yet the Party's disproportionate absorption of credit has implications far beyond the realms of everyday accidents and neighborhood littering. Because the Party is credited for just about everything, any positive *individual* impact on society tends to be washed out by state praise. Either China's media organizations applaud the Communist Party or praise the individual as a laudable Party member or product of the system.

Presented with virtually no avenues to accrue renown in the enactment of good deeds, many Chinese are thereby driven to selfish pursuits and individual gains—why contribute to society when I can profit more on my own? With a mentality of personal profit at all costs, large swathes of opportunistic Chinese individuals have found their own prosperity at the expense of others. As a result, while China's homicide and theft rates may be lower than those of other nations, Chinese criminal behavior in the production and distribution of counterfeits or in general selfish behavior (like parking bikes anywhere convenient for them) has been much more widespread.

Few Chinese feel charged with the responsibility of improving their communities or working toward the greater good—even at a local level. For those more interested in local politics than in a lifelong Party career, it is impossible to run for city council or involve yourself on a school board without sacrificing involvement in the private sector. Limited by the rigidity of the system, you must choose at the start whether to become a government official, an SOE executive, or a member of the private sector. Barely any crossover exists between government stationing and jobs in the private sector.

However, while people may refrain from civic duties as a result of over reliance on the government, this is not to say that Chinese do not care for their communities. Many simply focus within the absolute micro-level—we might say *mini civil* societies—such as their families, their children's sports teams, or school homerooms. Markedly distinct from governmental territory, these spheres are so minute and insignificant that government organizations do not even deign to get involved.

But Chinese want to do more. As witnessed during the Sichuan Wenchuan Earthquake in 2008—in which 69,000 people died and between 4.8 million and 11 million lost their homes—Chinese nationals from across the country donated incredible amounts in charity. Yet even when millions responded to calls of help for the motherland, the government led and controlled all aid work. Individual efforts have consistently been relegated to the margins, as people even now donate money directly through WeChat Pay or Alipay to those advertising their plights on social media. The Party thereby effectively replaces a true civil society while scattered individuals engage in one-off donations and *mini civil societies.*

In examining this phenomenon, I often contrast China's *mini civil societies* with the stake placed by most Americans in building local communities. Habitually distrustful of the federal government, Americans tend to invest greater faith in local communities and thus demonstrate major interest in local political involvement—running for city council, joining school boards or volunteering for firefighter groups. A significant percentage of civil societies have also been established endogenously, such as the Elks Club or religiously affiliated organizations like synagogues and churches. In light of this contrast between American local civic engagement and Chinese reliance on the central government, we see an inverse relationship between Chinese and American perceptions of government branches. While Americans gravitate toward local politics, disparaging an unreliable federal government, Chinese do the opposite. Distrustful of corrupt local officials, Chinese citizens have largely invested their faith in the Communist Party and Beijing. Perhaps this is why you might notice Chinese parents getting more involved in their children's classrooms, while American parents seek a voice in the school board or alumni organizations—realms often controlled by state organizations in China.

In business terms, however, this Chinese sacrifice of macro responsibility in favor of personal or familial gains has detrimental consequences. Without the institutionalized reward of contribution to the public good, companies in China's private sector have consequently trended towards greed. Lacking the innate desire to build a stronger Chinese society, many businesses have therefore sold counterfeit or poor quality products, scheming their way to profits. And as we already explored above, Chinese consumers have grown painfully aware of the business sector's highly prevalent trickery. With the exception of one's own *guanxi* circles, it is woefully uncommon for Chinese to trust one another in the realm of trade.

A driver of Chinese immigration, outbound capital flow, and brain drain, this psychosocially embedded issue is not one easily overcome. On the endogenous level, a solution will require generations of morally oriented labor force members seeking avenues for civic engagement. And even then, such movements will likely require the coupling of government efforts to empower sovereign citizens— granting more accountability to common civilians in cooperation and local problem-solving.

Under President Xi's administration, however, it appears unlikely that NGOs and similar organizations will be granted much sovereignty. In fact, the opposite seems to be occurring given the Communist Party's tightening of control over

NGO day-to-day business activities. Having effected new oversight laws on January 1, 2017, Beijing is now implementing closer supervision of Chinese NGOs as well as more stringent NGO application procedures. In some ways, it is important that the government begin codifying what NGOs must do to become legal entities, especially given that many operated illegally without paying taxes and failing to offer employees the requisite social security and healthcare benefits. However, many NGOs now face debilitating obstacles when seeking the government sponsors they need to register legally. And as all are now subject to stricter state control, many NGOs that stray from Party objectives have been labeled illegal and forced to shut down while other, more conforming, NGOs receive immense political support.

Even if the government is not pulling its weight in the pursuit of a civil society, it is clear that individual efforts have trended toward civic engagement. Evidenced by interviews with contemporary Chinese, especially younger citizens under the age of thirty, a large proportion of the population yearns to do more for its fellow citizens. Simply witness the rise of online giving, as people have begun to send money directly to those in need via WeChat and other online financial channels. Nonetheless, it is critical that more civic and charitable outlets be granted to Chinese seeking a qualitative say in their nation's societal development. Otherwise, severe lack of trust will continue to permeate both China's domestic market and the interrelations of Chinese citizens themselves.

***

As China's domestic market continues to be plagued by consumer distrust, and as Chinese brands attempt to counteract it, foreign brands have an enormous stake in understanding the low-trust environment and in launching the right strategies to capitalize on it. Brands that remain oblivious to Chinese consumer red flags—product components most focused on by buyers—may often miscalculate, thereby losing an entire market. Take Swiss food giant Nestlé, for instance. Ever since its launch in China, Nestlé's baby formula unit has continually underperformed expectations. Given the brands general approval, one might be perplexed by this data. According to my firm's research, Nestlé even stands out to the Chinese as a trusted foreign brand, and most of its products have not done poorly. But Nestlé's baby formula has struggled in China precisely because the company sources its formula dairy from Northeastern China. Widely considered China's rust belt, the region's soil was heavily polluted in the 1970s and 1980s, deterring even modern-day Chinese from consuming its produce.

When we interviewed Chinese mothers and mothers-to-be, they overwhelmingly stated that even if they trust Nestlé, they refuse to feed their babies any dairy products sourced from China. Curious as to Nestlé's choice of China's Northeastern producers, I asked one of Nestlé's executives about the decision. In defense of the political tactic, he explained how Nestlé wanted to show China's government that the brand was creating jobs in Northeastern China while also respecting local farmers. Its intentions were indeed good, but Nestlé had completely overlooked the extent to which Chinese mothers avoid feeding their infants Chinese-sourced dairy products, particularly as a baby's main form of sustenance. Additionally, by competing so successfully on price, Nestlé unwittingly raised suspicion and lost clout among its key consumers. Unable to understand how a foreign brand—particularly from the expensive, developed nation of Switzerland—could be as cheap or cheaper than domestic Chinese brands, many Chinese simply assumed that Nestlé was cutting corners.

After all, even the most trusted of Western brands do not always boast a perfect track record. Leaving a foul taste in the mouths of Chinese patrons, several renowned Western brands have sold inferior products in China, while marketing them with the same label. Johnson & Johnson participated in the trend with a carcinogen-containing baby shampoo that had earlier been removed from American stores. Procter & Gamble (P&G) behaved similarly with its Pampers diaper brand. Many mothers told us they found domestic Chinese-made Pampers absorbed far less than Hong Kong versions, causing unhygienic leakage. Recognizing the problem, P&G started selling imported diapers as well as domestically produced Chinese versions. This unfortunately had the effect of causing parents not to trust domestically produced diapers even more.

By tainting the image of American manufacturers, these foul plays have opened the door for other foreign brands, particularly those from the Netherlands and New Zealand (and other countries that never set up domestically manufacturing facilities), with products with different ingredients than those produced in Western facilities. Projecting a coveted Western lifestyle, these areas are considered pure and trustworthy among China's buyers, often enabling their brands to sell directly into China via online portals and *daigou* middlemen. For this reason, major supermarkets from the UK to Holland to Australia have had to impose limits on the number of baby formula cans allowed to individual buyers. As Chinese mothers depleted in-store supplies to bring formula back to China, local mothers were soon left without formula to feed their own children. This is especially true for smaller brands that have never created a China-only product version (unlike both P&G and Johnson & Johnson). Such smaller firms import the same products they sell in Western markets, garnering enthusiastic trust from Chinese. If embraced by Western home markets, these products are believed to be sufficiently trustworthy for China's shelves.[vii]

On the basis of such convictions, brands positioning themselves in foreign, high-quality categories will do well in China's domestically suspect markets—offering goods such as baby formula and health products. Apart from their own sales, however, foreign brands must also be aware of savvier local Chinese brands. Angling to inhabit the niche of trusted Western products, several domestic companies have recently created foreign-sounding brands, sourcing either raw materials or whole products themselves directly from overseas. In a concerted attempt to reassure consumers, these brands have jumped through all the hoops necessary to define themselves effectively—charging high prices; investing in top-of-the-line packaging; and simply expressing empathy to consumers via communication and guarantees of safety. Some companies, such as the previously referenced Humanwell Healthcare Group, CITIC Capital China Partners, and Biostime, even go as far as to make acquisitions abroad.

In order to capture market share and dissolve concerns over trust, foreign and Chinese brands alike need to position themselves as the most trustworthy brand. To do this, they need to focus on two key areas: (1) packaging, and (2) pricing. Unlike Nestlé's water division which has focused on creating flimsier yet environmentally friendly packaging, brands should learn from Chinese water brands, Kunlun Shan or Tibet 5100, that both have rigid, luxurious feeling bottles. Chinese won't sacrifice personal health to be environmentally friendly. Moreover, both of the domestic water brands have understood the importance of having a high price to signal safety to consumers. Kunlun sells for two to three times the price of Nestlé's main line of water, Tibet 5100 four to five times as much (on par with imported Evian). Chinese equate higher price with better safety.

The fear of safety when buying products extends to products far removed from anything ingested or used on babies. For instance, one 28-year-old woman told me that she buys IKEA furniture products because she thinks the glue and varnish that IKEA uses must be of higher quality than those of regular Chinese brands.

As incomes rise, Chinese will continue to spend more money on healthy products. They will buy more natural products that are good for the health—from Manuka honey to blueberries to eggs fortified with DHA Omega-3s —but will spend more on more expensive products in categories. For example, the vast majority of 5,000 mothers my firm interviewed told us they would never buy domestic Chinese brand diapers in case the product quality was bad—yet at the same time would buy a conceptual foreign brand of diapers that was owned by a Chinese company because the processes were already in place to ensure safety. So while foreign brands need to focus on pricing and packaging to increase market share, the smart move for domestic Chinese brands is to go abroad and bring trusted

Western consumer brands back into the country. Despite rising capital outflow constraints, regulators have been fairly flexible in approving consumer product acquisitions when the product is brought back into China.

Going forward, the lack of trust is an element that all companies need to deal with, whether they are selling into China or to Chinese consumers as they travel abroad. Focusing on building trust as either a large, trusted brand or a small but focused brand in a specific niche is the best way to gain that trust.

★★★★★

Dialogue:
Frank Lavin, Chairman and CEO Export Now, Former U.S. Undersecretary of Commerce, Former U.S. Ambassador to Singapore

Rein: During the beginning of his term, Donald Trump has criticized China for unfair trade practices. Alibaba's Jack Ma, however, told President Trump he thinks he can create jobs in the U.S. by having American small and medium enterprises (SMEs) sell to Chinese consumers online via Taobao and Tmall. Do you think a lot of jobs will legitimately be created in the U.S.? Will enough jobs be created to placate President Trump in his demands that China open up more to American businesses? Basically, are there good opportunities?

Lavin: Yes, although I think one has to look at Jack's comments both symbolically and substantively. Symbolically, I think Jack Ma is doing exactly the right thing by signaling American businesses and government decision-makers that, when it comes to consumer retail products, China is generally open and American brands are well-respected. Chinese consumers have a real preference for U.S. premium products, lifestyle products, and so forth. So, his overt communication of this message has been well-executed, and it is one that should be heeded.

The substantive dimension of Jack's comments, however, is more of an open question. In this realm, it raises questions such as, how many new companies are going to sign up? And how many jobs will be created? Such tangible considerations are more difficult to determine and predict. In fact, I spoke in June 2017 about this in Detroit while participating in Alibaba's launch activity, Gateway '17. Proceeding from the meeting between Jack Ma and Donald Trump, the conference hosted over 3,000 people, and we had numerous meetings. While there, Jack Ma expressed that he was going to reach out to U.S. SMEs to get them exporting into

China. And I see that he's been getting a lot of response and interest. How that translates into new stores, new sales, and new exports is a bit of an open question; it's really a long-term project. But I'd say this stimulus of dialogue is where Jack really deserves applause. Regardless of the ultimate outcome—the ultimate statistical value of this exercise—both countries are better off if the Chinese e-commerce market is as open as possible to U.S. consumer goods. This also requires purposeful dismantling of the bureaucratic, regulatory, and functional impediments that now stop or hinder U.S. SMEs getting into that market. So I think Jack's heart is in the right place, and I think he's got a good message. He's certainly doing everything he can to strip out those barriers to make it as easy as possible for many of these SMEs. So while we're definitely going to see an upside to this, Shaun, the entry of a whole host of U.S. businesses to China's market is rather difficult to measure in the first year or two.

Rein: Regarding the barriers you've mentioned, what types of barriers are there? How difficult is it for American SMEs to get through Customs or deal with tariffs? Are these true barriers, or are these relatively easy processes right now? Also, is it easier for companies to sell directly on Taobao or JD rather than setting up physical stores?

Lavin: I think there's a cluster of barriers, all of which are navigable. But as a cumulative difficulty, the real barrier is lack of familiarity with the market, or just intimidation by the market. When selling into Canada or Mexico, U.S. firms tend to have a much higher level of familiarity, information is more accessible, and travel is easier. But given that many U.S. businesses have little acquaintance with the Chinese market, and China in general, these relatively standard barriers are viewed as insurmountable. However, when you simply peel apart these issues and ask, "What are the labeling requirements? What are the tariff barriers? How do you open up a store online?" they're all very navigable. I would say it's no more difficult to open up an online store in China than to open one in, say, Britain. But most Americans don't approach the Chinese market from this premise. So, a lot of what Jack is doing involves consciousness-raising, cheerleading, and pointing people toward firms such as Export Now, because overcoming such entry barriers is precisely what we do. We work with any number of companies, resolving issues such as getting regulatory approval, determining the right labeling for the product, coming up with an optimal strategy, the right SKUs, the right price points, and so forth. In the realm of e-commerce, we talk about whether companies should establish a store on Tmall, Taobao, JD, or a standalone '.cn' website platform, additionally identifying other aspects of the right e-commerce strategy. So oftentimes, while many of these strategies are not impossible to establish, companies need an advisor and friend to help them execute in China's market.

Rein: So, are these services what Export Now provides? Can you give me an example of how Export Now works with American companies? What specifically do you do and what parts of the market entry process do you take on? If I am a producer of ginseng or chia seeds, for example, does my first call come to you?

Lavin: What we do is offer a cluster of services that allows any U.S. company selling online in the U.S. to now replicate their store in China. We'll take care of inbound logistics, regulatory approval, testing, labeling, and all of the strategy work regarding products, price points, and all store operations—we'll actually run the store. We have our own warehouses, our own fulfillment team, and our own customer contact team. Along with this, we conduct all social media efforts, take care of all the execution and contact work, and even cover financial settlement. So, you can run a China e-commerce store and never have to go to China. You don't have to hire anybody in China or even legally set up in China. Providing a turnkey solution, we'll deliver all these activities on an outsourced basis so you can replicate your domestic market activity in China for a nominal expense. In essence, Export Now is a one-stop shop and the end state covers all the functional barriers I discussed above.

Within our company, we refer to our services as providing a mirror image—meaning that both Chinese consumers and the Western businesses catering to them operate within their respective comfort zones. Chinese consumers can now access U.S. or international products through their favorite websites in their own language—customer support is in their language; support and delivery are both operated within their time zone; delivery cost matches that of domestic products; they use local payment instruments; etc. So, every functional aspect of the transaction is in their comfort zone.

Similarly for the U.S. exporter, every functional aspect of the transaction with which they have contact also remains within *their* comfort zone. They access information in their language; they work with a U.S. contract and a U.S. service provider; they pay and receive in U.S. dollars; they receive all reports in English; all of their account support operates in U.S. time zones. And in terms of account support, American servicers help them think through how to take advantage of the next Tmall sale or promotion, or assist them in determining how to enhance social media outreach in China. Companies therefore have a consultant, if you will, a U.S.-based brand manager who can help them execute in China. Just as articulated by our mirror image services, everybody stays in their comfort zone and products move ahead with expedience.

Rein: You've spoken fairly extensively about e-commerce and online platforms such as Taobao and Tmall. However, do you think that American companies need to also set up physical stores in addition to selling online? Or can they solely operate on the web? Tell me a little about your strategy in this realm.

Lavin: What we're really recommending is an inversion of the traditional sequence. It's important to first remember that there is a much higher density of e-commerce activity in China than there is in the U.S. In the U.S., about 10 to 12 percent of retail constitutes e-commerce activity. In China, this figure more than doubles, as about 20 to 25 percent of retail comprises e-commerce. And these figures are even higher for premium brands, reaching about 30 to 40 percent. This is because, when you're online in China, you're talking only with the more affluent half of the market, so premium brands tend to consistently outperform other brands in this group. To sum it up, we typically say that in China, every brand is a Dollar Shave Club; every brand can be a pure play, conducting most or all activity via e-commerce. But to your question, this doesn't mean businesses need to operate exclusively online, even if it does mean that companies will likely perform better by starting off online in China. First, beginning through e-commerce is just simpler and less expensive than starting off by stocking physical stores in Shanghai, or even nationally. Operating online is also a very inexpensive way to refine your product slate, hone your pricing, adapt your messaging tactics, and develop your social media presence. Within a few months, you've already learned and grown significantly from all the online, real-time data that your business has accrued. Once you've established these fundamentals, it's a lot easier to begin transitioning to offline distribution as well. Something we've seen time and again, in fact, is that offline distribution looks at online success as a validation point. As a result, brands that have already established online operations are much better off when talking to a firm that might own a dozen department stores in Shanghai. Naturally, you're a lot better off having this discussion on the back of saying: "We've been online for six months. We're selling at a run rate of about 20 million RMB a year. Can we talk about working together?" That's a much more powerful discussion opener than, "I'm new in town, will you be my friend?" In this latter case, you would be negotiating from a position of much greater weakness given that you haven't built out your online basis yet.

Rein: Right. So once businesses decide to build out online, what type of categories do you think American companies will see most success in? For example, are they better off selling food, selling apparel, or capitalizing on other categories? And regarding those categories that do best, what are some of the underlying reasons for their success in China? Are China's versions simply too expensive? Do consumers not trust the "Made in China" label? So, to summarize, what categories do you think will do well specifically for Americans and why?

Lavin: There are a few answers to that question, and no single one can fully encapsulate an answer. But think about this general point: Almost anything imported into China from America is going to be a little bit more premium-priced. This is because American purchasing power is greater than that of China, and American consumer tastes, even in the mass to premium space—think Levi's and Nike—tend to revolve around brands that are more expensive in China. As a result, it is critical for brands starting out to have enough brand strength that Chinese consumers are willing to pay that difference. You cannot compete on price, and certainly not in the commodity space. You therefore need to be able to say something compelling about your product that engages consumers in a way that makes them feel good about buying the product—in other words, they must feel compelled enough by the product that they don't mind paying a price differential. American consumers are similar in many ways, but skill in courting the consumer is an attribute mastered by some brands and far more weakly developed by others. Typically, the apparel and cosmetics brands have done well in this realm, establishing a lifelong conversation with the consumer, but several other brands have largely missed the mark. These latter brands simply don't engage consumers as a matter of course, failing to explain themselves well. Another issue is that some brands are so well-established in their home market that when they enter a new market, they find that their ability to court the consumer has atrophied or lacks versatility. Therefore, with regard to what you just asked, Shaun, one of the questions we ask ourselves is: "If you bought this product for yourself, or someone gave this to you as a gift, would you tell your friends about it? Is there a conversation going on about this brand and about this product?" And, of course, if the answer is yes, we realize that there must be a buzz here, and we can make this work.

Businesses need to realize that Chinese consumers are going to be every bit as sophisticated, curious, and conversational about products as American consumers. And the point is that if nobody's talking about your product at all, it's more of a commodity product. It serves as something purely functional. Think of a stapler, for example. You might need a stapler, and you might have to go to the store to buy one. But you're certainly never going to give someone a stapler as a gift, and if you got any stapler, you're certainly not going to e-mail your friends and say, "you won't believe what I picked up today, I want to share this with you, here's a photo of my new stapler." It's a purely functional product. So, if you were the largest American stapler manufacturer, and you said, "I've got a great line of staplers, I want to take them into China," I'd have real qualms about that. Because with all respect, there's nothing about this brand or this product that the Chinese consumer's going to get excited about.

Rein: Your second largest stapler maker is our client. (*laughs*) And it hasn't been easy!

Lavin: (*laughs*) Maybe we want to change the metaphor for this book so we don't burn bridges there. (*laughs*)

Rein: We've primarily recommended a B-to-B strategy.

Lavin: B-to-B is not a bad idea. We've had clients like that too, and we typically tell them something along the lines of, "Look, the only people who are really going to buy this product are the other multinational corporations in China. The retail consumer is not going to seek out your product."

Rein: So, for those brands just entering the Chinese market, how do you go about creating a buzz? If you are an SME and you're using Export Now, what are the avenues used to reach consumers? Do you use WeChat? Do you use Facebook? Do you use Twitter? What other tools are there?

Lavin: Yes, we chiefly use social media. And to your point, China's social media environment has its own distinctive participants, most of whom differ qualitatively from American social media users. Nonetheless, you can typically start by taking the content created for American users and localize it for different channels, such as WeChat or Weibo. Of course, specific channels will differ depending on what a company seeks to do and whom it wants to reach, but all brands need to have indigenous platforms so that they are inside the firewall, and then must localize their content accordingly.

To assist in this, Export Now undertakes a great deal of content analysis. And one methodology we follow when launching a new brand consists of first asking companies who their large to international competitors are. We then follow this up by probing their competitors' activity on social media—specifically looking at their last 90 days of activity. Last year, for example, we did a major project for Victoria's Secret, in which we took care of all of their launch activity. Comprehensively surveying Victoria's Secret competition in China, we mapped out the main international lingerie brands selling on Chinese online sites, asking: Who are the main local brands selling to Chinese? What are they saying? How are they positioning themselves with the consumer? What's their message to that consumer? And finally, in what ways, if any, must Victoria's Secret modify its core message to reach the Chinese consumer more effectively?

Of course our clients at Victoria's Secret were a highly sophisticated group, so our project for them included an extensive set of activities. The point, however, is that these launch and planning processes must be done through a well-established methodology in which firms play to their strengths and demonstrate integrity in their message. Now what does that mean? Integrity of message means that the same value proposition in a firm's home market is equivalent to its value proposition in China. While the competitive map will be different, as will consumer culture, a firm's value proposition can only be modified superficially to meet nuanced disparities in taste. As we say internally, there is one cup of Starbucks in the world. The cup of Starbucks you get in Shanghai is the exact same quality and the exact same phenomenon as that of the one you'll get in Seattle, Paris, or Mexico City. And Starbucks quite appropriately claims that the Chinese consumer values its product in large part *because* there is only one cup of Starbucks in the world. So we would say the same thing to Victoria's Secret or any other brand—there must be one level of quality; one reason or cluster of reasons for which a consumer segment is in love with this brand. And this will hold true for the Chinese consumer just as it does for the American consumer. One thing Chinese consumers *really* don't want to hear is, "Well, this is the Chinese version of our product," or "this is the third-world or emerging market version of this brand's products." Companies need to protect a universal phenomenon, ensuring that if a consumer were to visit one store location in the U.S. and pick something out, that the product would be exactly the same as one found in the firm's Chinese stores. Of course, colors might be different, there might be other somewhat superficial elements of a product that will be adapted to the tastes of different consumers—the same reason for which Nike shoes might be colored differently in different nations—but quality must always remain consistent.

Rein: So it's vital to maintain the same quality standards, or even heighten them in China, rather than reduce them to a third-world product line—something many multinationals might consider doing?

Lavin: Precisely. I would not go downmarket; companies would thus be destroying brand value, right? And such firms may have spent decades, if not a century, building up a message and a brand. It is critical that they keep both of these intact. The formulation and experience of a brand's product itself must remain the same in every single market.

Case Study:
Bring Chinese Consumers Overseas Products and Services They Cannot Get in China Due to Lack of Trust, Lack of Availability, or High Prices

As we have seen at length in this chapter, Chinese often look to offshore destinations for products and services they are otherwise inclined to distrust in the mainland. Seeking better quality goods and services—particularly in the categories of critical purchases and prestige-granting goods—Chinese will either enjoy services abroad or bring their foreign buys back home with them.

In addition to individuals stuffing their luggage with self-care products, many official distributors have long since begun capitalizing on Chinese demand for offshore goods and services, particularly in the healthcare sector. Populating China's market with foreign medicine, vitamin, supplement, and health food brands, many are selling to Chinese consumers through gray-area online markets and sales channels called *daigou*, where people buy products offshore and then re-sell them in China at high markups. Riding the wave, Hong Kong pharmaceutical retailers from Watson's to ParknShop have profited handsomely, selling healthcare products either directly to Chinese tourists for the purpose of individual consumption or for domestic online resale.

Moreover, as Chinese buyers shift from spending on products to services, foreign brands now have the opportunity to bring such services directly to the consumer—but with a twist. Instead of merely establishing operations in China and serving Chinese at their doorstep, companies are beginning to bring Chinese consumers to their own overseas operations. Take medical tourism start-up MedBridge Health Management Consulting Co., Ltd., for example, a group funded by Kamet, the private equity arm of French insurance giant AXA.

Mindful of the reality that wealthy Chinese regularly opt for overseas treatment of critical conditions for both themselves and their family members, MedBridge is setting up a program to transport Chinese patients overseas for cancer care. And luckily for both MedBridge and its clients, many Chinese—even wealthy nationals—lack medical insurance, leaving the company unburdened by rigid insurance terms, which often restrict a patient's pick of hospitals and doctors. Or they have expensive international insurance that gives them the flexibility to choose whichever doctor in the world they want to see.

Regardless of where Chinese patients want to travel for optimal medical care, Medbridge wants to meet consumers on their terms. Facilitating everything from finding doctors to booking hospital rooms, MedBridge essentially plans to arrange the whole trip. As Pierre Janin, the CEO and Co-Founder of MedBridge, explained to me, "Cancer in China is a growing health concern creating a huge pressure on the healthcare system. In cooperation with Chinese doctors, we connect patients to the best medial teams and hospitals in the world not on in the U.S. but also in Europe to be treated. Patients seek a high quality of care and doctors connect with the best international oncology experts. We are a bridge. It is a full journey from second medical opinion up to rehabilitation."

Other popular destinations are South Korea for cosmetic surgery. Chinese trust the quality of care, as well as the expertise, in South Korea. Drawn by how Korean television drama stars look, over 60,000 Chinese travel to Seoul annually for medical treatment, with much of the trips to have plastic surgery in hospitals like BK Hospital or JK Plastic Surgery Center.

The results of the surgery can be so dramatic that some women are having problems getting back through Customs because they look so different.

Overall, until more private clinics and hospitals at the high end open up in China, the outbound trend of medical tourism will continue. This is especially true in critical care and in beauty treatments that patients consider critical, like a nose job.

While more and more hospitals are indeed opening up, they are limited in speed of growth by lack of suitable real estate locations and regulatory challenges. The anti-corruption campaign too is slowing the constructions of medical facilities as well because officials are worried about green lighting large, new heath care projects and getting accused of being corrupt.

Key Action Items

1. Do not build your entire business on grey-area sales channels like *daigou*. Regulations can change quickly, and the government is capable of closing off all *daigou* business operations practically overnight. That said, *daigou* is an important sales channel and should not be disregarded as an avenue to build revenue and reputation. If your products do well in the *daigou* world, then they will likely gain traction in brick-and-mortar chains on more favorably stable terms.

2. Cater closely to Chinese outbound tourists as they travel overseas to buy products both for themselves and for resale in their home market. Strong examples: Chinese-owned stores in Melbourne have gotten it right, packaging Manuka honey, chia seeds, Blackmores vitamins and other health supplements in a luggage-friendly manner. Attracted by convenience, Chinese tourists are able to tick off all shopping list items quickly and pack their goods without much hassle.

3. Increasingly, companies can sell services to traveling Chinese tourists, from education to medical treatment to summer camps. Companies can follow the trend of Medbridge—not just bringing products to China but bringing Chinese people to products and services outside of the country. We will also see in the Chapter 7 case study on the Boston Celtics summer camps how many Chinese parents are bringing their children to summer camps in the United States to learn English and sports.

Chapter 7
The New Global Chinatowns: From Ramshackle to Luxurious Enclaves

California, February 2015

"Welcome to Arcadia," Jimmy Zhang beamed as he opened up the door to his Mercedes S600. Behind him, the San Gabriel Mountains towered regally. We had just arrived in Los Angeles the night before. Traveling through the United States during the Chinese New Year holidays, visiting with family and friends, had become an annual tradition. We had come to America for the past several years to scout out potential real estate investments. A few years prior, we had visited Maui, another year Boston.

While none of us had yet bought anything, we were coming close in part, with the hope that our kids would eventually attend boarding schools like St. Paul's or Exeter and then Ivy League universities, many of us were looking to buy a spot that would enable easy visits to our offspring. Some of us were considering retirement abroad and wanted to prepare for that eventuality. Others of us simply sought to diversify assets outside of China using money already parked abroad—capital established while having worked overseas after graduate studies in the U.S. and before returning to China, or gained from investments that went public outside of China—in Hong Kong or the United States. With looming concerns that the RMB would soon be devalued, most of us were in search of legal means to diversify.

At the recommendation of another Beijing-based billionaire friend, we were all to visit Arcadia—commonly nicknamed "The Chinese Beverly Hills." Upon his glowing reviews, we determined to scout out Arcadia's homes before embarking on a several-week hiking trip through Zion National Park and the Grand Canyon to soak up their clean, fresh air. Telling us to skip a hotel, our friend insisted on hosting us at his sparkling multi-million-dollar mansion, free of charge. While he himself would not be there, he had arranged for his personal real estate agent to let us into the house and show us around the area. Having accepted his offer—or really, his order—I now looked into the face of a grinning Jimmy Zhang who came by early to show us around Arcadia's opulent neighborhoods.

Originally from Sichuan province, Jimmy had arrived in America two and a half decades before. At a time when China's jobs paid meager salaries and offered little security, twenty-somethings like Jimmy hoped for better work prospects in the U.S. But Jimmy's first decades in the States were tough. Speaking insufficient

DOI 10.1515/9781501507618-007

English, he was relegated to jobs cleaning dishes and waiting tables at cheap, grimy Chinese restaurants selling General Tso's Chicken and Moo Goo Gai Pan.

He had missed out on benefitting from the first wave of immigration from Hong Kong to the U.S. in the 1990s, just before China's takeover of the island in 1997. Lacking the linguistic ability and wherewithal to build trust with their Cantonese-speaking counterparts, he and other mainlanders were often deemed poor, country bumpkins by the Hong Kongese.

But Jimmy's bitter, itinerant life all began to change around 2008 when new money Chinese mainlanders began investing the riches they'd gained during China's real estate gold rush from 2003 to 2008. Bringing their money to the West, mainlanders who had cashed in on Chinese real estate began scooping up homes in California, almost like children grabbing handfuls of M&Ms—the bigger the home, the better. A prime target, Arcadia became the centerpiece for mainlanders looking to buy 8,000-square-foot or larger homes. Prices soared to the point at which $5 to $10 million USD mansions were fast becoming commonplace; heads only turned when one hit the $15 to $20 million USD range. In 2013 alone, over 90 homes in Arcadia sold for more than $2.5 million USD.[i]

In the meantime, Arcadia's racial make-up was quickly transforming, soon to become a mini China. As we drove along the streets of Arcadia, strip malls displayed more Chinese language signs than English ones, touting Chinese food, acupuncture, and other health care products largely foreign to American consumers.

A predominantly white city in the 1930s—much like other upper middle class cities throughout the country—Arcadia, Compton and other municipalities in the Los Angeles area were examples of the many cities where depression New Deal policies including one dubbed "redlining", which effectively mapped out areas where non-whites might gain mortgage insurance, served as effective tools to segregate communities. In addition, existing homeowners signed pledges agreeing to cooperate in enforcing the segregated sale of their home. Together, these and other factors caused bitter and sometimes violent disputes. This left the growing number of, African-Americans in particular, Chinese and Latinos to reside in poor conditions, often far from the city center. Many forget how widespread U.S. regulations and homeowner covenants were until the 1960s, strictly limiting non-whites and Jews from moving into certain areas. African diplomats, for instance, confronted immense frustration when searching for suitable homes within reasonable commuting distances of their nations' embassies—even in Washington D.C. restrictions were widespread. Only under the Civil Rights Act of 1964 and Fair Housing Act of 1968, enacted under President Lyndon B. Johnson, were many of America's race-based regulations fully outlawed.

As Americans began internalizing the values promoted by the Civil Rights Act, shifts in racial make-up of residential areas were a common phenomenon in the mid-to-late 20th century, particularly in cities like Arcadia. Soon after 1965, Arcadia received a wave of Chinese immigrants from Hong Kong, but numbers remained small for the next two decades, amplified slightly by Taiwanese newcomers. By 1980, only 85,000 Hong Kong-born immigrants lived on U.S. soil. Not until the 1990s did Hong Kongese immigrate en masse, buying out large quantities of land in California and Vancouver. Fearing Hong Kong's handover to mainland control in 1997, numerous Hong Kong residents had rushed to secure safeguards abroad. By the dawn of the millennium, Arcadia residents began to embrace Asian money, especially that of affluent Chinese—it had become an economic savior.[ii]

Taking advantage of the influx, Jimmy had opened up his own small real estate firm, serving only Mandarin-speaking clients. This was a move of great prescience. By 2017, the number jumped 38.63 percent from 2000. Hitting $80,147 USD in 2017, Arcadia's median household income was accompanied by an outstanding three percent unemployment rate.[22]

Quite literally, mainland Chinese money had saved Arcadia's local economy from the dire straits faced by so much of California and the country at large, debilitated by the Great Recession of 2008. Unlike the rest of America, whose empty strip malls and deserted downtowns gaped with shuttered restaurants and abandoned storefronts, Arcadia boomed.

Flooding the city, manicure shops, luxury auto dealerships from Mercedes to BMW, massage parlors, Chinese grocery stores, and restaurants eagerly catered to the new money flowing from the East. Along with Chinese language signs sprouting up throughout the city came an initial wave of service firms, like Jimmy's real estate company, as well as designers and architectural firms specializing in Chinese home-buying tastes.

Formerly alien concepts like *feng shui*[23,] south-facing homes, or in-law apartments within mansions joined the regular lexicon of real estate agents, as Chinese homebuyers' preferences differed markedly from those of typical Americans. Architectural design firms—such as Sanyao International, started by Robert Tong, and PDS Studio—thrived from new home designs that fit mainland Chinese tastes. Houses with high ceilings, circular driveways, and kitchens set up

---

[22] http://www.areavibes.com/arcadia-ca/employment/
[23] *Feng Shui is a philosophical system with Taoist roots where people and designs need to be harmonized with the surrounding environment, especially looking at wind and water flows*

properly for woks—a keystone of Chinese cooking, used in lieu of western pots and pans—enjoyed wide acclaim among mainland buyers. Few of these new homes were decked out with fireplaces or big, manicured lawns, the Chinese had no desire for such accoutrements. Additionally, prime property spots for Chinese stood in the center of neighborhood blocks as opposed to the corners typically preferred by more traditional American buyers.[iii]

Arcadia rapidly and uniquely developed an understanding of how these new mainland consumers diverged both from earlier waves of Chinese immigrants—mainlanders, Hong Kongese, Taiwanese—and from most Anglo Americans. Armed with a native's perspective and having taken advantage of the trend, Jimmy did quite well for himself during Arcadia's rise, now driving his S Class Mercedes and hobnobbing with China's wealthiest elite as they ventured through California.

As we spent the next several days in Los Angeles, touring Arcadia and neighboring cities, it became obvious the speed and scale at which mainland Chinese immigrants and their money are changing entire city landscapes. Disrupting supply chains, inbound Chinese continue to create tremendous opportunities for local businesses and industries. Tall, luxury apartment buildings have rapidly replaced downtrodden single-story homes, gentrifying vast expanses. Drawn by institutions of higher education, many Chinese homes have proliferated within commuting distance of UCLA and other universities now populated by record numbers of Chinese students. Armed with 24-hour security, these compounds are similar to those back in China, walling off residents from strip clubs and lower-end establishments nearby.

In mimicry of mainland style, entire strip malls opened to specifically accommodate Chinese consumers, offering products and services similar to those in Beijing and Shanghai—herbal medicine, acupuncture treatments, skin-whitening products, umbrellas to block sun rather than rain, after-school tutoring, and Chinese clinical care. Local auto dealers like BMW swiftly learned that Chinese drivers favored models less popular among other Americans. Formerly overlooked by American customers, models like the X6 saw a remarkable uptick in sales, hugely popular in China.

Consumerism and Cold Partners

Just as China's government wallet benefits the economic prospects of countries that fall into its Hot and Warm Partner categories, and conversely hurts economies of errant Warm and Cold Partners (as we have seen in Chapters 1 through 3), the wallets of Chinese consumers are starting to show a similar impact on international businesses. But the orientation of Chinese consumer wallets may differ from that of their regime. Deviating somewhat from a commitment to China's Warm and Hot Partner countries, Chinese consumers often power sales of brands and real estate in Cold Partner countries. Even if politically distrusted by the Chinese government and consumers themselves, Cold Partner countries still stand superior in attracting Chinese wallets with the promoted lifestyle and quality control of their brands.

In light of this divergence between China's state wallet and those of its consumers, however, understanding the categorization of Hot, Warm, and Cold partners remains vital for companies in the context of consumer spending. Chinese consumers may be free to invest where they like, but China's political hand still holds its grip. Brands and local governments seeking to attract Chinese foreign investment therefore need to keep abreast of their country's partner categorization. Doing so will not only enable them to burnish brands accordingly, but will also guide them in counteracting potential tension at the nation-to-nation level. For example, while the U.S. may be politically categorized as a Cold Partner country, Chinese consumers trust American brands for their quality control and, more importantly, covet the various lifestyles afforded when living in the United States. Brands needs to be aware of their country's categorization from a political standpoint so they can counteract negative positioning with strong brand positioning and advertising campaigns.

In fact, one of the best ways Cold Partner countries can benefit from Chinese wealth creation is via immigration, facilitating acclimation and opportunities for Chinese newcomers. America's EB-5 program, for instance, has successfully attracted well-educated and wealthy immigrants since its establishment in 1990, thereby stimulating economies in poorer regions by granting immigration papers to those who invest enough in these areas to create job growth. Through the EB-5 program, when investors invest $500,000 USD into a rural area or area with high unemployment, investors are granted conditional American permanent resident status, or as green card holders, that allows them to immigrate to America for two years. If the investments create 10 new jobs with a reasonable time frame, they can extend then the permanent residence status to become permanent.

While some have indeed abused the program—many argue, such as Brooklyn journalist Norman Oder, that the current $500,000 USD threshold is too low or that real estate developers find loopholes to use the money for skyscrapers rather than entrepreneurial ventures—the program overall has brought in wealthy Chinese immigrants whose contributions are invaluable to American society.[iv] Similar programs in Australia and other nations have seen comparable returns.

In terms of Chinese immigrants' regional preferences, however, the past decade has primarily witnessed an influx of Chinese to English-speaking nations formerly part of the British Empire, like the United States, Canada, Australia, and New Zealand. As explained in previous chapters, Chinese gravitate towards historically racially white nations, meaning very few will immigrate to Pakistan, South Africa, or Myanmar, where most citizens are darker skinned. While some of this stems from racial intolerance of dark-skinned ethnicities—a phenomenon still prevalent in Chinese society—much of Chinese immigrants' preference for English-speaking countries are rooted in their belief that English-based educational institutions are the best in the world. Keen on securing a brighter future for their progeny, Chinese parents naturally elect to immigrate to areas where they believe their offspring will be afforded a better education.

The Four Waves of Chinese Immigration into the U.S.

In light of the trends delineated above, this chapter and the next will focus predominantly on the evolving Chinese consumer as they spend and live outside China. As China's nationals increasingly spend time abroad, whether as tourists or immigrants, their domestic and international spending habits will also continue to shift. Comprehending the ramifications of these shifts will allow companies and states to capitalize accordingly. To start, this chapter will look at the arena of Chinese immigration, delving into the ways in which companies can adapt to the demands of Chinese consumers abroad—both in terms of their underlying life aspirations and their more tangible desires.

In order to profit from the fundamental life ambitions of the newest wave of Chinese immigrants, companies must first distinguish between China's most recent newcomers and previous immigrant waves of the Chinese diaspora. There are immense divides between those who moved to the U.S. to work during the California Gold Rush (1848–1855) and those fleeing Communist control of the mainland from 1949 to 1965, for example. Spending habits, lifestyle preferences, and long-term aspirations also differ accordingly. To inform a prudent business approach, let's therefore gain some historical context on these divides.

***

The first wave of Chinese immigrants in the mid-1800s tended to be dirt-poor Chinese from Guangdong and Fujian provinces, driven to Southeast Asia or the United States by prospects of starvation in their hometowns. A part of this wave, my ancestors left behind their life in Guangdong province and moved to

California. Like many Chinese immigrants of the time, they worked in low-end tin or gold mines, or performed other types of menial labor for minimal pay. It is this segment of the Chinese diaspora that gave rise to the term 'coolie,' which some argue derives from the Chinese word *kuli*, or bitter hard. Often never learning more than a smattering of English, these immigrants were responsible for seeding the cramped, smelly Chinatowns that grew through large metropolitan areas.

Restricted from living elsewhere by municipal authorities, most immigrants of this wave of the diaspora never had the opportunity to integrate into American society, discriminated against by both social and political forces. Prompted by fears that Chinese urban pockets were responsible for declining wages and economic ills despite their tiny population, the Chinese Exclusion Act of 1882 effectively blocked Chinese immigration to the U.S.. Even Chinese men who had already immigrated could no longer bring their wives to the country, leaving many of America's Chinatowns heavily male-oriented. As a result, many men returned to China to marry and have children, but often came back to the U.S. to work and repatriate their limited earnings. In the meantime, a large proportion of Chinese women who made it to the U.S. became prostitutes as their services were in such high demand. Having relegated Chinese immigrant pockets to more seedy areas in the hopes that they would share less contact with white middle class workers, U.S. metropolitan authorities in large part spurred the development of Chinatown's red light districts, even if unwittingly. Political fears of Chinatown's opium dens, and the spread of leprosy caused authorities to move these neighborhoods out of the city center. The authorities thus unintentionally assisted the growth of seedy, underground behavior.

Facing both institutional and day-to-day racial discrimination, these Chinese immigrants rarely learned English at a native, fluent level. Even though many spent most of their lives in the U.S., Chinese like my ancestors were simply kept too isolated to assimilate into American society. Lacking English skills, most remained relatively poor and uneducated for generations. After mining and railroad work dried up, early wave Chinese immigrants often operated laundromats or Chinese restaurants. Descending from humble beginnings and surviving by the hardest labor, this group therefore gave rise to the stereotype of Chinese as cheap and frugal—coating furniture in plastic vinyl sheets to keep them in better condition or carefully peeling off onion and garlic skin at supermarkets that sold them by weight.[v]

About half a century later, a second wave of the Chinese diaspora arrived in the U.S. following the repeal of America's Chinese Exclusion Act by the Magnuson Act of December 17, 1943. These new immigrants principally consisted of those fleeing China after Mao Zedong's Communists seized control of the mainland in 1949, rising victorious over Chiang Kai Shek's Nationalists. In a mass exodus, many had first moved to Taiwan after Mao's rise to power before immigrating to the United States. Yet unlike the first wave that fled starvation, this new wave of Chinese immigrants in the 1960s primarily consisted of China's landed gentry. Having supported Chiang Kai Shek's Nationalist Party, many feared retribution after the Communist takeover. Affluent and well educated, Chinese in this group brought with them both savings and prestige. Many even had preexisting ties in the United States—remnants of their military and academic cooperation with American counterparts in the run-up to World War II. While still confronted by institutional racism, this later wave of immigrants enjoyed far greater opportunities for economic and educational advancement.

As a result, descendants of the 1949–1965 immigrant group have tended to outperform the early wave of cohorts in the U.S., both academically and economically. Concentrated in wealthier suburbs, mid-20th century Chinese immigrants have largely avoided the more derelict Chinatowns, thereby integrating more smoothly into American society. Sometimes considered Taiwanese, many members of the second wave have even fostered this misperception to differentiate themselves from "Communist" mainlanders. Originally, however, this group of immigrants harkens back to mainland China, only moving to Taiwan briefly in the aftermath of China's civil war, long after Taiwan's first Chinese settlers in the 17th century.

Coming from upper class backgrounds, immigrants in the second wave often assumed positions in large institutions, yet rarely made it to senior executive suites. While some topped out at senior engineering levels, many also entered the medical or legal fields, prized for their high status and comfortable salaries which were associated with prestige in both the immigrant and Anglo communities.

Yet another five decades later, the third wave of Chinese immigrating to America arrived in the years before Britain's handover of Hong Kong to mainland control in 1997. Worried that their assets would be seized or devalued by the Communist takeover, a great number of Hong Kong's wealthiest residents speedily moved to the U.S. or Canada, while many others simply obtained foreign passports and remained in Hong Kong. As fears grew greater in the former British colony, even middle class Hong Kongese decided to foot the bill for foreign passports, just in case. Following the lead of Hong Kong's uber-rich, many middle class citizens thus took on dual citizenship while remaining in Hong Kong. Approaching the handover with caution, they now had a get-out-of-Hong Kong card if needed. The husband and children of current Hong Kong Chief Executive Carrie Lam, for example, have taken on British nationality. Others moved outright to the U.S. or Canada.

Similar to those who fled China in the 1950s, the majority of Chinese immigrants in this third wave integrated fairly well into American society. Gaining admittance to America's most selective universities, such as Harvard and Princeton, many third-wavers found employment in large U.S. corporations, became doctors, or rubbed shoulders with white-collar elites working lucrative jobs on Wall Street. A significant percentage also continued operating family businesses, either running factories in southern China or collaborating on deals with mainland and Hong Kong professionals back home. Having leveraged well their linguistic capabilities, several third-wave Chinese became middlemen for Western companies, serving as a bridge between growing opportunities in China and businesses in America.

It is this wave, ironically, who actually benefitted most from China's move to become the factory of the world—most of the factories making mobile phone components or t-shirts were owned not by mainland Chinese, but by Hong Kongese who had taken foreign passports. Others, like Ronnie Chan, who is the Chairman of the Hang Lung Group and member since 1998 of the Committee of 100 (an organization who membership is open only to Americans with Chinese descent), made money in China through real estate.

Finally, the fourth and largest wave of Chinese immigrants—spanning the late 1990s to the present—has been chiefly comprised of mainland Chinese. Yet even within this most recent group of mainland immigrants, there exist clear divides between those arriving prior to 2005 and those immigrating afterward. The first group, which I will call Phase A, constituted mainlanders arriving in the U.S. before 2005, primarily to study abroad and remain in the country for post-graduate employment. Phase B, on the other hand, consisted of mainlanders who made their fortunes in China and brought their wealth to the U.S. after 2005. Appreciating the differences between Phase A and Phase B Chinese immigrants of this latest fourth wave is essential for brands trying to strike the right marketing and sales strategies. In many ways, Phase A and Phase B fourth wave Chinese are as different from one another as are second and third wave immigrants. Having generated wealth through distinct channels and in different environments, Phase A and Phase B differ significantly in their outlook on life and so prioritize different categories when spending.

Before 2005, the goal of most Phase A Chinese immigrants was to study in U.S. academic institutions and then flourish through conventional professional channels upon graduation. High salaries and job opportunities were scarce in China at the time, and Chinese mainlanders had yet to make their fortunes by speculating in real estate or the ever-volatile A-share stock market in Shanghai or the ChiNext (NASDAQ-style) board at the Shenzhen Stock Exchange.

To Phase A, mainland immigrants in the late 1990s and early 2000s, the ideal life was a comfortable one—a job at a Fortune 500 company like Johnson & Johnson, or perhaps a quantitative job on Wall Street; a medium-sized suburban home in New Jersey or Boston; and a Lexus or minivan parked in the driveway. Few Chinese in those days could have predicted the staggering wealth creation that occurred in China only a decade later. Content with the security of an upper middle class American lifestyle, they therefore likened themselves to descendants of second and third wave Chinese immigrants. Prior to China's imminent real estate boom, only the very top of China's richest one percent could have a standalone home, cushioned by a yard and multiple cars.

Mainlanders who immigrated to America in Phase A also tended to be the very best China had to offer academically. Graduating from China's most renowned and competitive undergraduate programs—at Peking, Renmin, and Tsinghua universities—these immigrants represented China's top talent and longed to pursue their graduate studies in the West. Relying on scholarships as their ticket to America, many of China's academically gifted bypassed the Harvards and Stanfords of the world—which offered limited financial support—in favor of any graduate program that granted them money. Zhang Lei, billionaire founder of hedge fund Hillhouse Capital Management, was one of many who faced this predicament. During a ski trip together while we were still graduate students, he revealed to me that he had chosen Yale over Wharton—where he had also gained admittance—largely out of necessity. Only Yale had bestowed him a generous scholarship. Grateful to the university for having granted him the opportunity, Zhang Lei later donated a generous $8,888,888 USD, since 8 is a lucky number in China, to Yale after his rise to wealth.

Billionaire Robin Li (Li Yanhong), founder of Internet search giant Baidu, also falls into this category. Having graduated from Peking University in 1990, Robin Li then attended University at Buffalo, The State University of New York, where he received a master's degree in 1994. Upon his completion of graduate school, he realized the Chinese dream by staying in the U.S., where he worked for IDD Information Services, a New Jersey division of Dow Jones. Following a similar trajectory was Peggy Yu (Yu Yu), now co-founder of Dangdang, China's largest online book seller. Upon graduation from Beijing Foreign Studies University, Peggy Yu subsequently pursued an MBA at New York University where she graduated in 1992. After working a stint on Wall Street, she then moved back to China before the turn of the century and opened Dangdang in 1999.

But Zhang, Li, and Yu were exceptions to the majority of Phase A immigrants. Most mainland Chinese who stayed in the U.S. tended to get solid upper middle class jobs but never reached true wealth status while working in American companies. Feeling they had hit America's glass ceiling after graduate school, the most entrepreneurial members of this generation returned to China in the late 1990s and early 2000s to forge greater wealth. Among this more limited cohort, Robin Li launched Baidu in 2000; Zhang Lei founded Hillhouse after several years of working for Yale's endowment fund and a fund in Washington D.C.; and Peggy Yu established a fortune through Dangdang.

As a result of the above trends, those Phase A immigrants who remained in America to craft their careers typically like their personal and professional lives, but feel they missed out on China's economic growth. Having interviewed over a hundred Phase A Chinese-Americans in the past decade, I have seen this view echoed repeatedly. As one Chinese chemical company executive told me, "The U.S. is great, but I feel I never realized my career potential here. Perhaps I should have moved back to China. But I am too old now." Having moved to Texas for his studies in the mid-1990s, he had worked his way up the corporate ladder for twenty years but hadn't made it big like Zhang Lei or Peggy Yu.

While this batch of Phase A mainland Chinese immigrants have mostly assimilated into Anglo American culture while retaining their Chinese identities, precious few have earned the purchasing power needed to shape entire industries. In most cases, they have put their dreams into their children. Similar to second wave mainland and Taiwanese immigrants of the 1960s, Phase A Chinese parents have largely given rise to the Tiger Mom phenomenon, investing time and ambition in their pre-adolescent and teenage children. Having missed out on China's economic boom despite their prior status as China's best and brightest, these parents pour hours of energy into their children, focusing on piano, math, and other enrichment lessons. One day, their children may achieve their own foregone dreams.

Chinese Phase B immigrants, on the other hand, pose a vastly different ballgame for international businesses. With enormously higher spending power, post-2008 Chinese immigrants bring critically distinct preferences and perspectives to Western markets. If companies are to profit, they would be wise to distinguish between the wallets of Phase A and Phase B consumers. Primarily younger Chinese, Phase B immigrants tend to enter U.S. universities at the undergraduate level or increasingly at the high school level paying for the full ride as opposed to the graduate schools that only Phase A scholarship earners had the privilege to attend.

Backed by the wealth of their parents, many Phase B newcomers are the offspring of Chinese mainlanders who earned their fortunes in China after the turn of the millennium. Now investing their abundant wealth in American real estate or private schooling, this latter category of mainland Phase B immigrants is far wealthier than any of the earlier waves of mainland, Taiwanese, and Hong Kongese immigrants. During China's real estate boom of 2003–2008, few restrictions limited the number of homes you could buy, and deposits could be as low as 0 to 10 percent depending upon city and time. Those who capitalized on the minimal regulations reaped lavish profits.

Now moving to American cities like Arcadia, Phase B Chinese immigrants seek better lifestyles for their families. These parents are therefore much less likely to push their children academically; there is little urgency for their offspring to struggle in pursuit of professional success. On the contrary, many Phase B Chinese parents tend to "spoil" their children, giving rise to modern-day *tuhao*—a Chinese term often used derogatorily to refer to second generation inheritors of wealth, viewed as lazy and entitled by their Chinese contemporaries. Seen by many poorer and middle class Chinese as never having to work hard during their careers, most of these *tuhao* immigrate to America as their parents foot the bill for luxury condominiums and shiny BMWs.

It is certainly critical for brands to distinguish between the preferences and psychology of Chinese immigrants across all four waves. With a keen appreciation of each group's motivations, enterprises will succeed in selling to the Chinese diaspora at large. Most importantly, however, brands will gain most from catering effectively to fourth wave Phase B immigrants—a concentration of spending power rivaled by precious few.

Flight of Wealth

As waves of Chinese immigrants continue to flow and shift, companies must invest in foresight and plan accordingly. To aid in our predictions, we must analyze two fundamental questions regarding the current wave of mainland Chinese immigration to the U.S. and its Anglo neighbors. First, to what extent will the trend continue, and will these Chinese immigrants remain a force capable of changing the landscapes of entire cities and even countries? Second, why are post-2005 Phase B Chinese immigrants moving abroad, predominantly to Australia, America, and Canada, when China's job market is now so good? Despite China's weakening economy in 2016 and 2017, the unemployment rate decreased from 4.02 percent in Q4 of 2016 to 3.97 percent in Q1 of 2017.[vi]

Based on interviews conducted by my firm (CMR) with middle class and wealthy Chinese, it is demonstrably clear that nationals of all socio-economic backgrounds continue to pursue lives abroad. Statistics overwhelmingly support this conclusion. In 2011 alone, over 150,000 Chinese obtained permanent residence outside of China. By 2012, Chinese outnumbered legal Latino immigrants in the United States, and rising figures showed no signs of slowing. As long as Chinese are able to get their money out of the country—which has become increasingly difficult since China's government began efforts in early 2016 to stave off the fleeing funds in excess of $100 billion USD monthly—Chinese will keep emigrating abroad. In CMR's interviews with over 200 Chinese worth $10 million USD or more, over 80 percent told my firm that they had already emigrated abroad or strongly considered doing so. Those in the latter category had made inquiries to law or consulting firms in order to start the process. Among the 500 middle class Chinese consumers we interviewed in 2016 and 2017, the numbers dropped slightly to about 50 percent. But even this figure is shockingly high when considering the economic risks posed by significant brain drain and capital outflow. With such high percentages of wealthy and middle class Chinese wanting to emigrate abroad, deep anxieties abound. How will China retain enough talent and capital to continue sustaining economic growth? Reflecting the panic of Chinese economists and political officials at large, I personally fear for the nation's economy as capital flight and brain drain threaten growth on a colossal scale.[vii]

If China's job market remains so strong, why are so many Chinese determining to move abroad? In speculating on this second question, many western media outlets like CNN have wrongly argued that a large portion of flight results from Chinese opposition to the Communist-led political system. These same media outlets do not draw the same conclusion about political protest towards democracy by the Indians or Taiwanese moving to America. Should we assume Indians are moving to Silicon Valley because they are protesting against democracy in India or is it more likely they move to America for the quality of life? In reality, however, China's capital flight and high immigration figures have more to do with the pursuit of profits and a calmer, cheaper lifestyle. Few have elected to move abroad in the name of political protest or government opposition.[viii]

Based on my firm's interviews, in fact, it is patently not true that Chinese are protesting the government in their move to America and other Anglo nations. With the exception of a handful of dissidents that receive outsized prominence in the U.S.—take Chen Guangcheng, nicknamed, the "barefoot lawyer," for instance—few respondents told us they were leaving out of dislike for the government. Contrary to common American misperception that Chinese nationals are brainwashed by government censorship and propaganda, many of our interviewees were willing to criticize, at times heavily, certain policies of China's political system—much as Americans disparage their own. In fact, Chinese know quite well the strengths and faults of their nation's current political system, often taking both in stride. None of CMR's interviewees, however, listed dislike of the political system among their top 10 reasons for emigrating abroad. Quite the contrary, most generally believed that the central government, for all its limitations, was leading China in the right direction.

Fourth wave Phase B Chinese immigrating in the post-2008 era were typically the political system's greatest beneficiaries. Predominantly insiders—or at least connected to insiders—many of this latest wave were able to buy homes before everyone else, gaining lucrative government concessions in real estate and other ventures.

After casting aside blame of political opposition, a deeper look is required to unearth the real reasons underpinning Chinese immigration to predominantly white nations. Many wealthier Chinese immigrating before 2012 explained that their plans to immigrate and buy houses abroad were largely forged in case they chose to move later on. Typically targeting English-speaking cities such as Sydney and Vancouver, most sought clean air quality, trustworthy medical facilities, and schools of academic excellence. For families focusing chiefly on schools, wives usually moved abroad with their children while husbands either remained in China or commuted back and forth.

Aside from facilitating future prospects abroad, taking on a foreign passport was generally intended to ease everyday lifestyle patterns. Particularly for our wealthiest interviewees, Chinese passports were a thorn in the side of anyone seeking uninhibited, visa-free travel. In fact, a great percentage of our richer interviewees Chinese kept multiple passports in contravention of Chinese law. With a legitimate Chinese passport, they could travel freely within China and, most importantly, buy property. Traveling around the world, however, was much more convenient with one of their fraudulently held foreign documents. In sum, pre-2012 Phase B Chinese immigrants wanted to plant one foot in each camp—retaining their Chinese citizenship and its many accompanying benefits, while keeping doors open abroad.

For post-2012 Chinese, however, two critical shifts occurred. First, as fears of President Xi's corruption crackdown emerged, Chinese citizens circumventing the law began planting both feet abroad. Instead of remaining in China for domestic business purposes while contemplating new horizons, many Chinese now committed wholeheartedly to new lives abroad. Having made clear his resolute position early on, President Xi Jinping followed through with pervasive corruption investigations, appointing Wang Qishan to be in charge of the Central Commission for Discipline Inspection. With no children of his own, Wang Qishan could cut to the bone of China's insidious corruption strains without fear of long-term repercussions for his own kin.

A generally accepted phenomenon of the past, many Chinese businessmen made their fortunes in the 1990s and early 2000s via corrupt practices. Virtually everyone is exposed in some way. In a system that compelled people to bribery, this wealthy cohort saw corruption more as a gray area, a recognized necessity rather than the egregious practice it is now deemed to be—after all, almost no one's hands were clean. By 2016, 120 high-ranking officials were arrested, and 100,000 people indicted for corruption. The tables had turned.

Moving assets abroad to prevent possible arrest, China's post-2012 immigrating businessmen sought to flee the iron fist of Wang Qishan's investigations. Yet their primary means of getting money overseas were no cleaner than their original fortune-making tactics. Many faked the value of invoices; took money out of ATMs; bought expensive products (such as jewelry) in Macau and then returned them for cash minus a commission from the retailer; faked invoices altogether; set up illegal companies overseas; used recently emergent multi-billion dollar underground banks; and asked friends to transfer $50,000 USD worth of currency in their steads. Facing high stakes, China's wealthiest businessmen rushed to secure getaways, and immigration was often their best shot.

The second post-2012 shift prompting wealthy Chinese to move abroad drew links to China's weakening growth rate. Facing a combination of poor air quality, cramped homes and a slowing economy, many Chinese could no longer make the sweeping fortunes of China's bygone go-go days. Furthermore, China's urban centers are often more stressful for everyday residents than those of tranquil European cities—even for China's wealthiest elite. Access to good health care is tough, and simple conveniences like parking spots are often magnified frustrations.

Tired of the hassle, many Chinese have preferred to move abroad where kids and grandkids can live in manicured mansions, driving Porsches and BMWs, at a fraction of China's cost of living. Having already accrued their piles of gold, Phase B immigrants deemed unlikely any further growth at similar scales. Aside from a maturing economy that had reached its peak, President Xi and Wang's corruption crackdowns were only further stressors atop China's pollution and frenzied urban lifestyles.

Implemented in 2012, real estate restrictions in most major cities also made it exceedingly difficult to buy homes. Non-Shanghai *hukou* holders, for example, now had to prove that they were married and had both worked and paid taxes in the city for five years prior to buying a house. Other cities, like Beijing, limited the number of homes one could buy. As a result, Chinese seeking real estate—typically a favorite asset class given its tangible nature—had to buy homes either offshore or in undesirable Chinese cities that had fewer or no limits.

Whether as a result of Xi's crackdowns or an already milked economy, the fourth wave Phase B Chinese have shown destabilizing rates of immigration, not only engendering domestic anxieties but also concerns abroad.

The Impact of Wealthy Immigrants

For many countries receiving fourth wave Chinese, mass immigration from the Eastern superpower is a double-edged sword. Given their own wealthy native populations, the U.S. and its larger cities, like Los Angeles and New York City, are better equipped to absorb large numbers of Chinese, particularly as affordable housing exists in other parts of America. Other nations, however, may experience greater difficulties when attempting to accommodate China's Phase B influx. Australia and Canada, for example, have witnessed disruptive changes within their real estate markets as Chinese buyers run up housing prices to the point at which locals can no longer afford to live in certain neighborhoods. Lacking proper regulatory frameworks, these countries have suffered in part because Chinese homebuyers do not always pay local income tax, unlike in America.

In October 2016, I was invited to keynote a series of events for CPA Australia throughout the country. While in Sydney, I visited my friend Elizabeth at her home. I had heard that spiking housing prices were a cause of tension in the city as more affluent Chinese immigrants continued to drive out local buyers. Many Aussies had started commuting one to two hours from their workplaces in a desperate bid to find affordable housing. I asked Elizabeth about the situation.

"Yes, rising housing prices are becoming a real issue. It's been tough for local Australians to buy homes and we've seen a lot of tension as a result." Similar pressure has become commonplace wherever wealthy Chinese immigrate, from Sydney to Vancouver to Seattle. A former colleague from my Internet technology days, now living in Sydney, had even told me that she'd moved an hour away from work as "everything was being bought up by the Chinese." Prices were simply no longer affordable. Even then, she admitted she felt "lucky." Working a senior position, she enjoyed better prospects than even more inconvenienced colleagues, many commuting four hours each day just to have a yard and a parking spot.

Elizabeth continued by emphasizing an even greater cause of friction—culture change. "Another phenomenon causing tension is that Chinese are now outnumbering locals." She then continued to explain how a friend had switched her kids into a different school when she found that twenty-two of her son's twenty-five kindergarten peers were originally from China. "My friend," Elizabeth reasoned, "loves the Chinese people and welcomes them to Australia. But seemingly none of the kids in her children's classes spoke English or shared any understanding of Australian culture." Her friend's six-year-old son had started to speak better Chinese than English, and she finally felt obliged to move him out.

While cities from Arcadia to Sydney certainly benefit from an influx of Chinese money and talent, local governments must also be prepared for numerous challenges. Given that a multitude of China's fourth wave Phase B immigrants exceed locals in wealth, cities face risks of escalating friction as natives are increasingly pushed out of city centers. Yet if countries add stamp duties as Australia has done, they also run the risk of being perceived as racially discriminatory—singling out and excluding Chinese—and may ultimately sabotage metropolitan efforts to attract consumer wallets.

Countries and cities must therefore craft policies that strike a middle ground, attracting investment without causing tension. In an effort to placate both its locals and immigrant Chinese population, Australia now requires Chinese to buy only new homes, for example. This way, the nation can ensure that resale homes in central locations remain reasonably affordable for locals, at the same time jumpstarting economies farther from urban centers with new real estate developments.

As domestic deterrents and international allure pull China's wealthiest consumers across the globe, Chinese immigrants will continue to provide highly profitable opportunities to small and medium enterprises (SME) catering specifically to the Chinese wallet. For the most part, Chinese immigrants will remain oriented toward English-speaking countries most renowned for their housing and education. Yet within these regions, mainlanders will continue to gravitate towards the locales of earlier Hong Kongese and Taiwanese immigrants, primarily given the prevalence of food and services already adapted to Chinese tastes. Accompanied by large sums of money, the newest wave of Phase B Chinese will establish deepest roots in the communities where they buy real estate. Unlike previous investors, however, mainland immigrants are no longer speculating about the prospects of a life abroad. With feet planted firmly, they now wield purchasing power in a multitude of industries, engaging in the everyday life and developments of neighborhood, municipal, and national economies.

Chinese immigrants can play a positive role in a nation's culture and economy—nations just need to make sure that money from Chinese immigrants does not price locals out of the housing market and totally change the makeup of schools and other public institutions.

******

Dialogue:
Austin Fragomen, Partner and Chairman, Fragomen, Del Rey, Bernsen & Loewy LLP; and Becky Xia, Fragomen Partner based in Shanghai

I first met Austin and Becky in 2016 when I keynoted their annual partner's conference. Finding their knowledge of Chinese immigration deep, I wanted to hear their insights into Chinese immigration as well as how Chinese companies are starting to send more Chinese expatriates abroad.

Rein: To which countries specifically do you see wealthy Chinese immigrating most and why?

Fragomen: The United States remains the most popular destination for HNWI[24] investor immigrants for the third year running. Canada, which has been behind the UK for the last two years, overtook the UK for the first time in 2017, while Australia remains in fourth. Malta, Antigua, and Dominica enter the top ten for the first time, according to the Chinese Immigration Index. Other popular places include, but are not limited to, Europe (e.g., Spain, Portugal), New Zealand, Singapore, Hong Kong, Macau, Malaysia, and Japan.

Education and living environment continue to be the main reasons for emigrating overseas for the fourth consecutive year, accounting for 76% and 64%, respectively; with access to cleaner air, safer food, and better education driving emigration. These immigrants want better options for their children's education; they are distressed about the growing pollution problems, and they are concerned about food safety in China. Among these factors, education for the next generation may be a major one—58% of the investment-based immigrants chose to move for this reason. Other Chinese chose to emigrate because they want to protect their individual assets and properties, to avoid high tax rates in China, to enjoy access to better medical treatment, and to receive stable investment environment and visa-waiver programs.

At the outset, this movement is, generally speaking, still not about migration in the traditional sense, but rather flexibility, ease of mobility, and, in its most basic form, an insurance policy. Where there is an element of settlement involved by some members of the family, it is primarily education driven. This is reflected

---

[24] High Net Worth Individual

in the countries that prove most popular amongst Chinese nationals. Of the top 20 ranked universities globally, 15 are in the United States, and 4 are in the UK (Times Higher Education World University Rankings, 2016–2017).

Cities that are experiencing greater increase in Chinese immigration are mainly in the U.S. and Canada. For example: Los Angeles, Irvine, San Francisco, San Diego, San Jose, New York, Seattle, Portland, Orlando, Boston; and in Canada: Toronto, Vancouver, Markham, Richmond, Calgary, Burnaby; as well as London (UK), and Auckland (New Zealand).

The reasons for such increased immigration flow include: (1) many of these cities have the history of being an immigration center and already had a well-developed Chinese community. This enables "newcomers" to adapt to local society and life more easily and quickly; and (2) those places are considered as a "good place" to live in people's perceptions and seem to meet the requirements of having cleaner air, safer food, good education, and quality healthcare.

It is telling that Antigua and Dominica have entered the top 10 this year as long waiting times are considered the biggest hindrance to overseas immigration by this demographic, followed by language barriers, the difficulty of integrating into mainstream society, and application difficulties. One of the key features of Caribbean programs is their streamlined application processes, designed to facilitate, and of course lower, investment thresholds that are seen elsewhere.

Rein: Do middle class Chinese tend to immigrate to different countries or cities than their wealthier counterparts? If so, to what regions or nations are they moving and for what reasons?

Fragomen: In general, the middle-class Chinese follow the steps of the wealthier Chinese. The current trend is to immigrate to well-developed countries that can provide clean air, safe food, better environment, quality education, and so on. More and more middle-class Chinese choose to establish alternative residence options outside of mainland China, for family if not themselves, because they want to enjoy a slower-paced life and enable their children to be freed from fierce competition in China to explore alternative educational and social environments. They emigrate for better quality of life rather than for better opportunities or political freedom.

Meanwhile, due to the limit of available capital, some choose Southern European countries (e.g., Portugal, Italy, and Greece) that require lower investment criteria compared with tier-1 destination countries like the U.S. and Canada. Currently these options offer long-term routes to other European countries and, currently, the UK through free movement provisions, although that is likely to change after Brexit.

The statistics now add the Caribbean options to this category. In our view, this signals an increased appetite for strategic alternative citizenship solutions, rather than the actual long-term movement of Chinese nationals to these destinations.

Rein: Several analysts argue that Chinese are immigrating because they oppose China's Communist Party and its policies. Do you agree with this view and to what extent?

Xia: Political opinions seem to play a minor role.

It should be acknowledged that compared to political factors, economic factors, purpose and drive to change/improve one's living standards, seem to play a dominant role. We can already see that the access to better education, good environment, medical care, and safe food have become a primary driver for Chinese to emigrate to another country.

Rein: Previously, the wife and children of immigrating Chinese families would move overseas while the father remained in China to generate earnings. Is this trend still the case? Or is it more common to see Chinese families or retiring parents immigrate at once?

Xia: This might still be the case for Chinese immigrant families, especially where the father's job is the main resource of income. Middle class or working class immigrant families may encounter financial problems if the father cannot find jobs with equivalent income in the destination country. On the other hand, although Chinese economics have slowed down, the job markets in the destination countries may not always be welcoming, and there may be more requirements for the immigrant to find a good job there in terms of language and skill sets.

In an immigrant family, if the main reason for immigration is to offer the children better education, normally the mother will accompany the child to study overseas while the father continues to work and live in China to continue to support them financially.

Again, this is not migration in the traditional sense, but rather a strategic alternative residence driven by a desire for flexibility. The growth in popularity of Caribbean programs demonstrates this.

Malta enters the top 10 for the first time in 2017 and is a case in point. Malta's Investor Program requires effective residence to be shown for a main applicant (but not family members). This requirement is fairly nonprohibitive, allowing for the dominant earner to establish their family in a country where they gain free movement rights across the EU.

Rein: Do you consider the Trump administration's anti-immigration policies to be a risk for Chinese immigration to the U.S.? Or are Chinese wealthier and better educated than most immigrants from other nations and therefore still welcomed by America? To what extent do current U.S. policies deter or cause fears amongst immigrating Chinese? Are these fears sufficient to make Chinese immigrants look to other destinations? If so, which countries are benefitting from an increase in Chinese interest?

Fragomen: No, Trump administration policies do not appear to be deterring Chinese immigration to the United States. The biggest deterrent to Chinese immigration continues to be the lack of immigrant visa numbers ("green cards") for mainland Chinese citizens given the per-country limitations imposed by Congress well before the Trump administration.

By way of background, the United States Congress limits the number of employment-based immigrant visa numbers issued per fiscal year. No one country can receive more than 7% of the annual total and if the demand exceeds the supply there is backlog or "retrogression" for applicants and a delay in the ultimate approval of the green card. For instance, in the EB-5 investor category, popular with high net worth Chinese citizens, the government is only looking at applications filed on or before June 15, 2014, given the high number of applicants from mainland China. It is the extreme delays in case processing that deter the immigration to the United States and the need for investors to seek alternative immigration paths—such as non-immigrant entrepreneurial options including the L-1 intracompany transferee visa.

Given the alternative immigration paths available in the United States, demand from China remains strong. However, for that small subsection of high net worth individuals that feel the United States is no longer a welcoming destination for Chinese immigrants, they might consider other immigration countries such as Canada and Australia, or even some new immigration countries such as Southern or Eastern Europe.

Rein: Recently, some countries and their urban locals have grown concerned that wealthy Chinese immigrants are raising housing prices to the point at which locals can no longer afford to live in certain neighborhoods. To what degree do you consider this an issue, and how should countries deal with these concerns without deterring Chinese immigrants and their investment?

Fragomen: In the countries where the immigration program related to real estate purchase is available, their cities can attract the wealthiest individuals from all over the world, including wealthy Chinese. From the top 10 destination list, these countries include Antigua, Dominica, Portugal, and Spain.

However, in a lot of these countries, non-immigrants are also allowed to invest and purchase. It really depends on what countries we are talking about and their specific investment and immigration policies.

The housing market in some of these cities can, however, cause the displacement of the lower-income locals. This very problem contributed to the closure of Singapore's Financial Investor Scheme in 2012, which was replaced by the more stringent Global Investor Program—with no resident property purchase option available. The UK also removed the option to invest 25% of a Tier 1 Investment in real estate in late 2014.

Given the higher housing prices in the city, locals choose to move away from central areas and possibly away from immigrants. This may cause potential social and economic issues, and the party of interest may take this as an opportunity to raise more anti-immigration policies while immigrants may not always be the sole responsible party.

The destination countries should think of a good balance between attracting investment and maintaining a healthy local economy. They may consider limiting foreign investment through restricting purchases and placing higher taxes for non-resident buyers, so that there could be a distinction between the purchases placed by immigrants and non-residents.

Rein: Aside from rising housing prices, what other issues should Chinese immigrant destination countries be concerned about? How should they deal with these problems?

Xia: The locals also often fear that cheaper and illegal foreign labor may take jobs away from them, as well as having too many immigrants will weaken their local culture and solidarity.

A better understanding of the local market demands and suppliers may help both the government and local residents deal with the fear. One way to help immigrants blend in more quickly is to offer solidarity courses or programs so that they can join the mainstream society in the destination country as soon as possible.

Rein: How has Fragomen's business expanded in the realm of helping Chinese companies get work visas for going abroad? Are your clients primarily growing organically or through outbound M&A?

Fragomen: We have been helping more and more Chinese companies with their immigration matters in and outside China and we are becoming more well-known among the Chinese companies as a global immigration firm, which can not only help them in obtaining work visas for different countries but also provide valuable strategic immigration solutions in their globalization. In our view, most Chinese companies are growing organically as they expand their business globally.

As governments move toward more immigration restrictions and compliance provisions, Fragomen is well-positioned to assist Chinese citizens and companies find creative solutions for their personal and business immigration needs. For instance, in the U.S. market, as the more traditional immigration paths have narrowed because of backlogs (e.g., EB-5 category), Fragomen is uniquely positioned in the market given our full-service offering to use a combination of entrepreneurial non-immigrant visa options (e.g., L-1s and H-1Bs) and other employment-based immigrant categories such as the EB-1 extraordinary ability and intra-company transferee visas to successfully assist companies and citizens quickly enter the United States.

Case Study:
Bring Chinese to You and Focus on Integrity and Morality

When I was growing up in New Hampshire in the 1980s, Larry Bird and the Boston Celtics ruled the basketball courts.

Decades later, when my son Tom developed the interest and showed hints of aptitude for basketball, I sent him to Boston Celtics summer camps held at the team's training facility in Waltham, Massachusetts. Thrilled by the sight of its regal banners highlighting all the Celtics Finals wins I'd celebrated in my youth and jerseys of Hall of Famers Bird, Robert Parish, and Kevin McHale, I was likely more excited than Tom was, the first time I was let into the locker room.

It was at Tom's summer camp that I met 78-year-old Joe Amorosino, the General Manager and Supervisor of the Celtics Camps. Having begun his career nearly 60 years earlier at Hopkinton High School, Joe became at the time Massachusetts' youngest ever head of a high school basketball team. Over the decades, dozens of his players went on to play college basketball or went pro in Europe.

A notable member of the Massachusetts Basketball Coaches Hall of Fame, Joe has the compassionate smile of a teacher. When I sat down to talk to Joe about his camp, I was curious to ask him about how it had changed over the years. Looking around the second time I sent my son to the camp, I was surprised at the increasing number of Chinese campers compared to the previous years. When I mentioned the observation, he nodded knowingly. "In 2015 we had 30 kids from

Shenzhen, China. And many more were keen to get in on the program," Joe explained. His camp had been contacted by a for-profit league in Shenzhen that brought the campers in a group, accompanied by coaches. When I inquired whether Joe had continued to collaborate with the Shenzhen firm, he explained that Chinese demand had shifted dramatically from group-based to individual. "We are still in touch and they still send players but we have found more and more players from China are booking directly through our website with us." Even in the previous two years, more and more Chinese parents sought to book trips on their own rather than through a group-organizing agency. As I looked around the waiting room, I found many Chinese parents waiting and watching their kids play.

Savvier consumers with customized demands, Chinese parents by and large now prefer to research specific camps, planning their children's trips individually. Many will even select camp locations to match up with family holiday destinations, touring with their children after summer camp completion.

Nonetheless, Joe's Chinese campers have risen greatly in number over the years, now a group of wealthier youngsters whose families book directly. When I asked Joe about the primary reasons for Chinese demand, his answer was immediate: "They like two things. One, we focus on the fundamentals; and two, we are centered around a mentality of teaching the whole camper, focusing on morality and character rather than the sheer goal of winning."

Joe's words were echoed by one parent I spoke to. One Beijing woman, Julia Yan, whose 11-year-old son attended the camp told me, "I like how the camp focuses not just on basketball skills but also integrity and morality."

Frustrated with Chinese schools' rigidly fervent focus on winning, and only winning, wealthy Chinese parents have sought to counterbalance domestic academic stringency with a more holistic approach to child development. In light of the crushing pressure to get ahead faced by their children, Chinese parents have increasingly jumped on the bandwagon of team-building and moral education. Precisely fitting the bill, one of Joe's trademarks is his "Thought of the Day," in which he praises the virtues of good character and integrity, often focusing on self-discipline, perseverance, and personal responsibility.

That said, one of the benefits of the Celtics camps is they have a good mix of nationalities among campers. By far, Americans make up the vast majority of campers. This is important for Chinese parents—they want their children to learn about American culture and, perhaps most importantly, want them to practice English rather than hang out with other Chinese students. For the Celtics camps, it attracts the very best American youth basketball players as well as international students—which fits Chinese desires.

Key Action Items

1. Cater to Chinese consumers that increasingly book directly rather than through group-based agencies. Apart from seeking cheaper options, Chinese parents prefer doing autonomous research and selecting camps that match their customized demands. Even small and medium enterprises will do well to set up advertising campaigns that target Chinese families on websites like Ctrip, or via social media platforms like WeChat.

2. While all parents are interested in the tangible aspects of a camp (or school)—such as academic quality or the athletic prowess of the coach—it is important that companies emphasize morality and character-building as conveyed through Joe's Thought of the Day. Apprehensive about the "make money at all costs" mentality dominating China's academic and social institutions, many wealthy Chinese intentionally send their children to the U.S. or Europe to nurture character and integrity.

3. Ensure that the number of attending Chinese campers—or that of any non-Western campers for that matter—is well exceeded by the number of American or native English-speaking students. Chinese parents are eager for their children to be ensconced in an American learning environment, both for the purpose of improving their English language skills and for immersion in the culture. Most parents will refuse to send their kids a second time—further criticizing a camp in WeChat groups populated by other potential customers—if the majority of a camp's attendees are Chinese.

Chapter 8
Chinese Tourism: The CMR Chinese Hourglass Shopping Model

Queenstown, New Zealand, March 2016

I was 15,000 feet up in the air, my feet dangled out the open airplane door as wind seared my face. For reasons that escape me, I was about to voluntarily somersault into the air at 200 kilometers an hour toward the hard surface of the earth. Below me stood the snow-capped mountains of Queenstown, New Zealand, looming above the Dart River.

I have no recollection of whether I finally agreed to jump; yet I was suddenly shoved forward and plunged into nothingness. Reflexes swiftly took over, and I screamed "Geronimo!" and Suddenly I flew like a bird above New Zealand's water-dotted terrain.

***

Fifteen thousand feet below, I had entered Queenstown's skydiving shop two hours prior to my jump. Two of the shop's three salespeople were from mainland China and welcomed me in Chinese. At the front of the store sat two piles of registration forms, one in English and one in Chinese. Taken somewhat by surprise, I glanced around at the people queued up—about 80 percent were Chinese.

There was Little Wu, the petite twenty-six-year-old telecom executive from Sichuan province who had brought her parents on vacation. Having spent a year assigned to her company's division in Morocco, Little Wu beamed with pride when she told me she had paid for her parents' trip. She was eager to show them the world, as they had never experienced such opportunities for exposure in their own youth.

There was also the group of fifty-somethings from Shanghai who had come to travel around New Zealand and Australia for a fun-filled nine days. Their apparent leader, Old Zhang, had squat shoulders, short-cropped hair, and smoking lines that contoured the corners of his mouth. He explained to me that his group travelled together every year to a different place. They had not been afforded the chance to travel the world in their 20s and 30s like Little Wu was able to, so they were making up for it now, wandering to far corners of the globe. Last year was

DOI 10.1515/9781501507618-008

Japan, this year was New Zealand, and next year was still in the planning phase—perhaps the Maldives or even continental Africa.

Two couples in their twenties, sitting apart from the other visitors, had marked themselves as newlyweds. They later told me they were from Beijing and Jiangsu, respectively, and had come to New Zealand on their honeymoons. Deciding against the typical European honeymoon, they wanted to try something different. "Everyone goes to Italy," Eric from one of the couples said, as his new wife nodded affirmatively, "but we wanted to try something special. New Zealand is exotic and full of nature. Besides, I like their Manuka honey."

Between the various age groups of touring mainlanders, every Chinese I spoke to told me they had relied almost exclusively on Ctrip—China's leading online retailer in comprehensive travel services. Not only had they used the site to determine where they would travel, but most mainlanders had also booked their entire trip through Ctrip—from plane tickets to hotel reservations to adventure packages, like skydiving or boating.

China's consumers who travel separate from a tour group are often only booking on Ctrip or Qunar, spending hours independently conducting research online. Travel agents play a fairly minor role in China for younger consumers who book online. If not accessing Chinese sites, mainland tourists may look to foreign sites that have localized, such as TripAdvisor. In contrast to most online travel sites in America, however, Chinese tourists tend to look for high-end customization, even in online purchases.

Most of my interviewees also told me they were literally open to anything in the world, from Antarctica to Africa to the Galapagos Islands. They had not begun planning their trips with New Zealand—or anywhere else—in mind. Instead, they had all simply used their mobile phones to search for info and reviews on New Zealand and various other destinations. Primarily accessing the expertise of online communities, most tourists had searched for advice on WeChat messaging groups, both of their school alumni and local neighborhoods—trusted community members. Impressed by New Zealand's glowing reviews, my skydiving companions had then booked via Ctrip or Qunar where you could find cheaper rates for jumping than you could expect at the shop.

Given the sheer volume of Chinese Ctrip users, the travel retailer has been vastly successful in securing better deals for Chinese clients than would be possible by purchasing directly from the seller. Intriguingly, however, while my skydiving cohorts had taken advantage of Ctrip's cheaper rates, most of them had booked the most expensive packages, choosing to jump from the highest altitude allowed and hiring a private cameraman to jump along with them. They assured me I just had to do the same, otherwise I would regret it for the rest of my life. You only have one opportunity to record your first jump, Anita—Eric's new bride—reasoned.

Seeking adventure, and wealthy enough to do so, independent Chinese tourists like Eric and Anita or Old Zhang's friend group increasingly provide an avenue for online travel retailers like Ctrip—catering to countless individual tourists who now research and plan everything themselves. The stereotypical busload of middle-aged Chinese tourists being carted around by a flag-waving tour guide to shopping destinations is fast becoming a thing of the past. While financial and legal limitations formerly restricted wanderlust-prone Chinese—requiring them to travel in regulated tourist groups or not at all—several critical shifts have replaced cookie-cutter travel groups with autonomous sightseers.

A historical appreciation of this shift to today's more liberated Chinese travelers is critical in understanding how Chinese outbound tourists have so suddenly transformed the global tourism industry. With this historical backdrop, we may also have a better handle in determining whether and to what extent China's outward drive will continue, as well as what it means for the travel and leisure sectors.

★★★

Until the late 1990s, it was difficult for most Chinese citizens to secure a passport, let alone the financial means to travel abroad. For anyone who braved the logistical nightmare, aspiring travelers needed the support of their companies simply to file a passport application. But a company's blessing was not easy to come by—you were out of luck if you failed to tread the correct political line or even if your boss disliked you personally. Learning to play the political game was a necessary prerequisite for anyone seeking basic privileges that most Americans take for granted, such as securing a passport.

Around the turn of the millennium, however, China's government began reforming these regulatory frameworks under President Jiang Zemin and Prime Minister Zhu—alongside the SOE reforms we explored in Chapter 4. Resulting from political efforts to get the government out of people's everyday lives, company and government permission was no longer needed to travel abroad, get married, or get divorced. In a swift repeal of tight regulations, the Chinese were granted a whole host of personal freedoms often viewed as givens in the West.

While Chinese personal freedoms still lagged behind those of the democratic world, these post-1990s reforms saw a massive liberation of the populace. To Chinese who had grown up during the dark years of China's Cultural Revolution (1966–1976), their current life seems abundantly punctuated by personal freedoms. Having experienced dramatic improvements within the span of a few decades, many Chinese therefore have little objection to the country's media censorship—a target of much negative criticism by Americans looking in (and perhaps down) on China. With no experience of China's trying times, younger Chinese are often less understanding of the government's restrictions on information and personal liberties, particularly those who have gained international exposure through study abroad. Nonetheless, many still do not bridle enough (yet?) to cause major protests.

Reforms under President Jiang and PM Zhu indeed transformed the landscape of what was possible for everyday Chinese consumers. Yet even with the easing of government restrictions on passport issuance, low salaries and general inability to get visas prevented most Chinese from traveling abroad in the 1990s and at the turn of the millennium. At the time, most foreign countries were still wary of Chinese tourists within their borders—they worried that Chinese visitors would overstay their visas and remain illegally in the country to find work or get involved in prostitution. Despite China's economic boom, a majority of citizens still lived in abject poverty, often making only $50 a month waiting tables or operating factory equipment. Naturally drawn by the alternative, Chinese manual laborers could make twenty times their Chinese salary scrubbing dishes in the dingy kitchen of a Chinese restaurant in Italy. Prettier girls could make similar monthly salaries at establishments of disrepute.

In order to reduce the risk of illegal immigration and prostitution, foreign countries therefore imposed strict precautions when granting visas to Chinese. In the late 1990s and early 2000s, most states typically only granted visas to members of approved large tour groups—these were thought to have better oversight and control over visiting tourists, often holding on to member passports and other documents during the trip. In fewer cases, nations might grant individual visas to China's ultra-rich, required to prove their wealth with bank statements, property ownership deeds, company letters of guarantee, and detailed itineraries (down to hotel reservation numbers).

Smarter tourist destinations, like Bali in Indonesia, Jeju Island in South Korea or Chu Quoc in Vietnam, allowed Chinese tourists to secure visas on arrival. Rewarded for their lenience, these regions experienced massive spikes in tourism. As one twenty-eight-year-old man from Guangdong told me in Bali one day, "I chose to come here because it was easy for all of my family to get a visa to Bali."

Yet even then, most visas restricted Chinese tourists to only the island parts of nations; countries were still not ready to discard concerns about illegal Chinese immigration. Even as late as 2014, two of my employees, both with master's degrees from Ivy League universities in America and letters of reference from my firm's human resources department, were denied tourist visas to Singapore. As a result, Singapore and many other states have lost out on Chinese tourist spending, hampered by the smaller scale of travel destinations, which relegated trips to a mere few days or week at most.

But in 2007, fears of the Chinese tourism began to dissipate slowly. The world increasingly viewed China as a true economic superpower. And newly rich Chinese, who had made enormous profits from the real estate market, started to spend their fortunes abroad as immigrants (as we saw in Chapter 7).

All of the sudden, affluent Chinese spenders carting bags full of money could be seen buying luxury homes and premium goods from Arcadia to Paris to Auckland. Within a few years, China's high-spending tourists captured the world's attention. By 2012, Chinese consumers spent more per capita in the London Olympics than tourists from any other nation, beating second place UAE residents by 10 percent. Since 2012, Chinese have been the biggest spenders of foreign travel globally, surpassing the United States and Germany with $165 billion USD spend in 2014 versus $110.8 billion USD and $92.2 billion USD, respectively. Many of these Chinese had already immigrated abroad, obtaining foreign passports for ease of travel.

Accommodating the onslaught of China's newly minted tourists, foreign countries rushed to revise their visa-granting policies, seeking to ease the process for potential Chinese visitors. Realizing that stringent visa regulations were deterring Chinese tourist wallets, Italy, for example, made it easier for residents of certain Chinese cities to secure visas by allowing applicants to go to the consular office nearest where they live, rather than where their hometown *hukou*, or residence permit, was registered. The United Kingdom granted visas within 24 hours and Japan and Thailand both permitted travel by individual middle class tourists, bringing in record tourist numbers. In 2016, 6.37 million mainlanders visited Japan, spending 1.47 trillion Yen, a 27.6 percent increase year over year. The month Japan eased the restrictions, a 24-year-old young woman from Anhui went there immediately. She told me as she was preparing to go, "I have always wanted to visit Japan myself, not on a tour group. I am so excited."

Nevertheless, visa-granting processes remain far too cumbersome in many countries. I remember that as recently as 2015, I was helping the mother of a Chinese billionaire prepare bank statements to get a mere tourist visa to South Africa. Mounds of paperwork became too much of a burden and the mother decided not to visit. Drawn to an easier passage, her party instead switched to Bali, which allows Chinese to apply for visas on demand.

As countries started to realize that high-spending Chinese tourists far outnumbered illegal immigrants seeking under-the-table jobs, many leapt to capitalize on the trend. Opening the spigot, those that have profited most are home to the easiest visas. And as eager Chinese adventurers continue to travel the globe, those who have yet to relax their policies may find themselves far behind.

★★★

Just as large numbers of Chinese immigrants are changing the housing and education landscapes of the Anglosphere, Chinese tourists are similarly impacting the fortunes of tourist haven states. As competition for China's tourists grows greater, it is essential for countries and companies to understand the demands and shopping habits of this target audience. Vastly different from those of Europeans and Americans, Chinese consumer shopping habits are continuously evolving, having undergone fundamental shifts in recent years. To sell and market successfully, businesses in the tourism industry must therefore grasp these shifts and identify Chinese purchasing patterns.

Perhaps the most fundamental transition recently undergone by Chinese consumers is that from goods to experiences. Having long invested their new capital in luxury products, the modern Chinese consumer has now moved away from physical goods, opting instead for travel and experiences. Instead of buying a Louis Vuitton handbag, for instance, a Chinese millennial will likely settle for Coach to use her savings on a cameraman when skydiving abroad. Now, the real luxury consists of broadcasting your extravagant experiences—going on safari in Botswana, taking a selfie at the North Pole, or sipping wine in Napa. In today's digital age, sharing snapshots with friends on WeChat Moments holds much more allure than a Louis Vuitton handbag.

Chinese consumers will continue to buy luxury products, but for different reasons that the ones that drove sales from 2007–2012. No longer the aspiration purchase bought to show off in public, opulent commodities are now purchased more because they fit the income level and desired lifestyle of their buyers. Women buy Gucci or Chanel bags because they like how they feel toting them, or men buy a Hermes belt for the sense of style. Singles, a group numbering around 200 million, spend money on themselves and self-fulfillment.

Moreover, the desire to shop abroad has lessened among Chinese consumers as they spend more time on experiences and as companies equalize pricing globally and the Chinese government lowers import tariffs. Instead of spending five days in Paris, spending at Galeries Lafayette or on Champs-Élysées, Chinese tourists now gravitate more toward museums and vineyards, where they spend the majority of their stay. Concentrating their city shopping into one or two days, Chinese consumers have also grown fond of duty-free stores in airports like China Duty Free or Shilla Duty Free. Particularly as airlines now charge more for baggage, Chinese tourists have seized the advantages of duty-free shopping, which both grants them more time to visit sites and offers a free passage home for otherwise bulky purchases. At first, the duty-free frenzy may seem disadvantageous to retailers, granting them less time to target China's wallets. But the shift to airport shopping—not to mention online retail—may be helpful indicators for businesses seeking more profitable channels. And shoppers, short of time, often are swayed by impulse at the very last minute.

In terms of *how* Chinese shop, let's start with the refined Chinese skill of bargaining. Trying to get the cheapest deal for even the most expensive packages is a key habit of Chinese tourists and shoppers in general. Relentless negotiators, the Chinese have long held a legacy of bargaining and bartering at roadside stalls and open-air markets, where prices are spoken, not written. Unlike many Americans who shy away from negotiating in stores—afraid of coming off as cheap or stingy, Chinese almost consider it a sin not to attempt to negotiate a better deal, regardless of where they go. Even if they leave unsuccessful, at least they tried.

Chinese consumers have a keen eye for value and have zero qualms about looking frugal. Persistent in fighting for deals on even the priciest of products, Chinese consumers go big on important buys and skimp on the trivial ones. You can witness this trend simply driving down the highway to airports in Beijing or Shanghai, where Bentleys and Rolls-Royces get parked in breakdown lanes on the shoulder of the road. Even the owners of million dollar cars can't bear to spend $1.75 USD in airport parking lots—doing so would be a wasteful extravagance.

Regardless of wealth bracket, Chinese consumers adopt this attitude across the board—splurging requires the greatest indulgence, and everything else must be covered at minimal cost. For air travel and hotels, Chinese will either go for first class cabins and penthouse suites, or scrimp on the cheapest economy flight and standard double. Precious few opt for mid-level rooms or premium economy airline seats. They either have the budget and go decadent, or go cheap on base value. Similarly, this is why so many Chinese carry instant noodles with them on vacations even on trips to pricey locations like the Maldives or Seychelles—it is not because they are not willing to try local food but they often cannot afford to dine in the restaurant of a five-star hotel. They want to try a decadent and luxurious hotel room but need to cut corners on dining and spa treatments.

The divergence between these habits and those of European tourists was especially underscored as I anxiously prepared to skydive with my fellow flyers. As the Queenstown shop's employees called us to board buses headed for the tarmac, Western foreigners all seemed to assemble near one bus, while Chinese gathered near the other.

Perplexed at first, I quickly realized why. Divided by the height at which we were jumping, it soon hit me that almost all of the Chinese tourists were skydiving at the most expensive 15,000 feet, while every other foreigner had elected to jump at 12,000 feet. For an extra fifteen seconds of hurtling through the air, Chinese tourists had willingly paid fifty percent more. But that was not the end of it. About 60 percent of the Chinese skydivers on board had hired a separate cameraman to film their dive, increasing the price of the package by another 50 percent—a frill the other foreigners had chosen to forego.

★★★

In daily life, Chinese consumers' spending criteria translate to shopping patterns within what I call the *CMR Chinese Hourglass Shopping Model*. Chinese consumers will either shop at the top of the hourglass for luxurious brands, items, or travel experiences they deem important or aspirational, or at the bottom of the hourglass for cheaper products. Brands positioned in the middle, which neither confer status nor save money, get passed over by consumers. C&A and Gap, for example, rarely fare well in China. Falling into a no man's land, these brands are considered neither cheap enough nor expensive enough, offering only moderately good quality. A far-reaching phenomenon, the *CMR Chinese Hourglass Shopping Model* holds relevance both to Chinese consumers' purchase of physical products and to their pursuit of experiences and travel.

Similarly, when travelling, Chinese will prefer to either fly business class or first class, or take budget airlines like Air Asia or red-eye flights in order to save one night of hotel accommodation. It is unlikely they will pay for premium economy seating on an airline like United—they either have the money and want to luxuriate in a top-end cabin or save as much as possible by flying budget airlines.

In real world day-to-day spending terms, a young Chinese consumer might shop from the cheapest online food options on Ele.me or Meituan—two of China's leading food delivery apps—or skip lunch altogether to save money. But after months of saving, she might then splurge on a thousand-dollar-a-night hotel room in Paris at the Prince de Galles Hotel or a gourmet food and wine-tasting tour in Tuscany. They want that memorable experience that they can keep in their hearts and which they can share on WeChat Moments with their friends.

Within the realm of hotels, Chinese will likely choose between skimping on a hostel or economy hotel chain, and splurging on a luxury five-star hotel like the Ritz Carlton or Mandarin Oriental—often during the same trip. In interviews with my firm, the China Market Research Group, many consumers have illustrated this very trend. Having booked a two-star motel or hostel for the majority of their vacation, many of those interviewed explained that they often stayed their first and last nights in a luxury hotel to get a taste of extravagance. They might also share a five-star room, say an over-the-water bungalow, with three or four other friends to split the costs of an expensive room. It would be rare for them to stay at a solid three-star hotel, such as a Holiday Inn or Best Western, for the entirety of their trip.

One twenty-four-year-old woman from Changchun—a northeastern Chinese city famed for its coal-belching factories—told me, "I just spent $1000 USD a night for an over-the-water villa in the Maldives." Earning a monthly salary of $1200 USD, she explained that she had lived sparingly for months, saving on everyday necessities, buying the cheapest undergarments, and even sometimes skipping meals to afford the trip.

When analyzing the *CMR Chinese Hourglass Shopping Model*, it becomes clear why solid, middle class brands like Marks & Spencer, and Gap have largely failed in China, missing the mark in their pursuit of Chinese consumer wallets. Awkwardly positioned between mass market and premium, they relinquish any chance of being considered good value. Meeting the criteria of neither camp, these brands are quickly overtaken by expensive counterparts at the top of the hourglass—think Four Seasons Hotels and Resorts, Shangri-La Hotels and Resorts, Rimowa Premium Travel and Carry-on Luggage, Godiva Chocolate—and cheap ones at the bottom, like Samsonite's American Tourister brand, Hong Kong Airlines, Huazhu Hotels Group which has budget brands like Hanting Express and Hi Inn.

One of the key areas that companies selling to Chinese tourists need to understand is that no Chinese truly think of themselves as middle class—as the shoppers at Macy's in the United States would most likely self-identify—they think of themselves on the way to riches. Everyone in China has family members or friends who started off poor who got rich in the past two decades and they assume they or their children will reach that level of wealth. Thus, they never really buy experiences and trips that are too positioned or affiliated with a middle class lifestyle.

The U.S. certainly has its fair share of shoppers who save coupons and only buy on sale. Yet unlike Chinese tourists and buyers, these American consumers rarely go for high-end luxury items and experiences. Purchasing within lower price brackets in all categories, America savers tend to buy cheap brands as well as solidly middle class ones—aspiration purchases might include a pair of Nike Jordan shoes, a diamond pendant from Zale's, or a spring break trip to Disneyland.

But for Chinese consumers, the line separating billionaires from everyday Chinese is much more blurred, even similar in many regards. No matter one's income, the great majority of China's tourists and shoppers adhere to the *CMR Hour Glass Shopping Model*. Just as hoteliers are accustomed to dealing with billionaire guests housed next to China's version of price-sensitive consumers, cufflink-clad butlers may serve top businessmen and former farmers in the same evening. Even the most penny-pinching Chinese want to experience the good life in some way—whether it be staying at the St. Regis or Aman Resorts for a night at the end of a trip, buying a Chanel wallet or money clip, or spending on a diamond from Tiffany & Co. as a souvenir from a trip, or scuba-diving to an exotic location off the coast of the Philippines or Indonesia.

Within the tourism and hospitality industries, businesses have a stake in marketing themselves appropriately—whether promoting luxury at the top of the hourglass or thriftiness at its base. As optimal advertising and retail channels evolve with the preferences and shopping patterns of Chinese consumers, companies and countries must learn how best to capitalize on the trends elaborated above.

★★★

The need to adapt to China's tourists is more important than ever. Thirsting to see the world, China's contemporary consumers are propelling airlines to open new direct routes; Boston luxury shops like Tiffany & Co. to hire Mandarin-speaking staff; and companies as far as New Zealand need to learn how to advertise on Ctrip, sometimes selling directly to consumers through online markets such as Taobao. The reality is that regardless of location or size—whether a Fortune 500 firm or a small salmon fishing shop—businesses around the globe must learn how to target Chinese tourists on their own home turf. As elucidated above, China's travelers conduct all their research and trip planning at home, often booking everything independently via Ctrip and other online travel portals long before they leave the country. Without a prominent presence online, ready to cater to Chinese tourists, companies can be guaranteed a miss.

In the tourism sector, this means offering once-in-a-lifetime experiences that are not easily obtained—this is the major growth area. Chinese consumers like to share their experiences with friends and acquaintances on WeChat Moments. Showing off a trip is the new luxury and way to separate from the masses rather than toting a Louis Vuitton handbag. The pressure to show off one's trips is so serious that photography studios throughout China will now help people create fake trips to show off on WeChat Moments. If you want to pretend to visit Paris, photo shops can create fake visits to the Louvre Museum or a wine tasting at a vineyard in the Loire Valley.

Chinese consumers are increasingly becoming sophisticated, in many ways hyper-sensitive to trends overseas. They now adopt trends faster, and often research them more in-depth than even consumers in the countries where the trends started. You are more likely to see the newest trip or latest show fashion on the streets of Shanghai or Shenzhen than in New York as Chinese try to catch up, and thus overtake, trends in the Western world, whether it be wearing Stan Smith shoes as in the United States or eyeglasses without lenses, a trend that was popular in Japan. They follow influencers on Sina Weibo or on WeChat.

What is critical for brands is to ensure that their products, trips, and services fit the conception of the Chinese dream and lifestyle. It does not work anymore just to show rugged male models and long-legged, blond female models in advertising campaigns. The campaigns need to show models with the same body types and aspirations of Chinese.

Chinese consumers somewhat paradoxically want to see, learn from, and explore the rest of the world; yet at the same time are becoming more and more confident and proud of their own country.

***

Going forward, the trend of outbound travel will continue as Chinese want to see the rest of the world and take a break from the crowds and pollution in China. As Stephen Ho, the CEO of Greater China for Marriott International told me, "There is definitely outbound growth. 130 million Chinese travelled abroad in 2016 and we expect that number to hit 200 million in the next three to five years because middle class incomes are rising. Out of 1.3 billion people, only about 10 percent have a passport. Just imagine the outbound tourism as more people get passports—which I think will happen as more people become middle class."

That is not to say that domestic tourism is not becoming hot—many younger Chinese especially want to visit far flung places within China. Gansu, Qinghau, Yunnan, and Sichuan are becoming hot spots for domestic tourists. The key for companies is to understand the Chinese tourist and general consumer demand to try new things, spend on experiences, and buy either at the top or the bottom of the *CMR Hourglass Shopping Model*.

******

Dialogue:
Jane Jie Sun, CEO of Ctrip

Aside from being the CEO of one of the most successful companies in China, Jane is also very active outdoors. In 2011, she ran a full marathon for 42km with her husband. She hiked up Mt. Kilimanjaro in 2012 and hiked the Himalayas in 2013. She is also enjoys skiing and scuba-diving as well as dancing and aerobics.

Rein: Where do you see the next hotspots for Chinese tourists and why? Do you see the most growth in outbound or domestic tourism?

Sun: Given that China's per capita GDP is rising and many countries are lifting visa restrictions, I think growth will primarily be concentrated in outbound travel. Now that many more Chinese can afford opportunities beyond their own borders, they will likely choose international destinations more than they will domestic ones.

Rein: Historically, Chinese have travelled in tour groups. Do you see a shift toward individuals more independently planning their own trips? Where do they want to visit? What do they want to do when travelling? Is shopping still an important component of travel, or are tourists electing to spend more on experiences like skydiving and scuba diving?

Sun: On the whole, I think the divide between group and individual travel can be determined along the lines of language ability. Travelers who can speak English generally prefer to travel by themselves, while tourists who speak no English seem only to travel in groups.

In terms of choosing a destination, Chinese tourists tend to follow a progression. At first, Chinese travelers normally begin with domestic destinations. But as China's tourists grow wealthier, many use their earnings to visit nearby international destinations like Southeast Asia, Korea, and Japan. Another important factor in determining where Chinese consumers have gone are visa restrictions. When European nations lifted their visa restrictions, for example, many Chinese began traveling to Europe. Similarly, after the U.S. granted a 10-year visa, large numbers of Chinese tourists started visiting America.

With regard to tourist activities, many traveling Chinese females still enjoy shopping during their trips abroad. But as Ctrip has offered various theme tours, we have seen high demand from our customers for these experiences, exploring new opportunities such as diving, skiing, photography, hiking, biking, golfing, etc.

Rein: What are wealthy Chinese consumers looking for in a trip? Are they looking for one-of-a-kind adventures, such as safaris in Africa or cruises to Antarctica? Do they travel to the same place every year, like Americans summering in the Hamptons or the French on the Riviera, or do they try different locations?

Sun: Throughout China's history, Chinese people have been taught to learn through travel. Confucius famously taught: "It is better to travel ten thousand miles than to read ten thousand books." As a result, I think many Chinese are conditioned to be curious and adventurous by virtue of their culture and history.

This means they tend to be less limited, aiming to travel as far and wide as possible—from the North Pole to the Antarctic, from Africa to America, and from Europe to Asia. (In fact, you will typically find more Chinese in the areas you mentioned above than people from other countries).

Rein: How do millennials and younger travelers differ from older consumers? Are they using mobile devices to book their trips, or do they still use call centers?

Sun: Nowadays, young travelers are largely using mobile devices to book their trips. They also prefer to travel by themselves, as opposed to older tourists who often still travel in groups.

Rein: How are terrorism and pollution impacting Chinese tourism?

Sun: While these factors may indirectly affect tourism, the desires of Chinese tourists are fairly intuitive. Just as anyone in the world would, Chinese travelers prefer to visit areas that are peaceful, clean, and safe. If they feel welcomed by the nation's local people, they tend to go back again and again.

With regard to political controls, countries that make it easy for tourists to apply for a visa, facilitating their entry and showing them hospitality, will attract the greatest amount of inbound business.

Rein: Are there any special tours or packages that Ctrip has offered that might surprise analysts? Any other myths on the Chinese tourist or on the sector?

Sun: We offer a number of wide-ranging tours to suit both the needs of high-end and budget customers. Everyone can find a product that suits his or her demands.

To give an idea, our most expensive tour costs more than 200,000 USD per person, and includes an 88-day adventure around the world. And guess how long it took us to sell these packages? Only 17 seconds! We have seen again and again the buying power of Chinese consumers.

Rein: Ctrip has acquired Skyscanner. What are your plans for outbound investment? Do you expect to grow organically or through more acquisitions? When you buy a company abroad, do you take a hands-off approach or do you insert Ctrip executives into key management positions?

Sun: In thinking about the future of Ctrip, we always focus on organic growth. In acquiring Skyscanner at the end of 2016, we have planned to take a collaborative approach and build upon the strengths of the site. Skyscanner has a strong price comparison engine for air tickets, for example, and we hope to work with its team to help them with direct booking facilities.

In general, Ctrip's philosophy is to identify a good team and let it operate independently. Our contribution to their business consists in bringing them our customers as well as sharing both industry knowledge and experience. We aim only to strengthen their operations and help them grow in expertise.

Rein: Any final thoughts?

Sun: I strongly believe that travel can bring people together from all around the globe. Exposure to all that the world offers has the power to foster mutual understanding among people with the most diverse of backgrounds.

As Chinese tourists begin traveling the world, it is my sincere hope that we can bring the best of Chinese culture to the people and cultures we visit when abroad. In a similar spirit, I hope tourists from other nations will also share the best of their culture with us so that we may learn and flourish as an international community.

Through the nurturing of such mutual understanding, not to mention promotion of international exchange, I see travel as a medium for world peace.

Case Study: Localize Sales Staff Globally

Marriott International has been one of the most successful foreign companies selling to Chinese consumers traveling both domestically within China and going abroad. Two keys to their success has been catering to the needs of the Chinese market: (1) not only by scaling products and services for the Chinese consumer specifically, but (2) also by launching new companies, such as a joint venture with Alibaba, to target Chinese consumers.

To capture the share of Chinese consumers traveling abroad, Marriott has focused on creating loyalty by focusing on the needs of consumers, whether American or Chinese, to be "recognized and acknowledged and focusing on great service," as Stephen Ho, the CEO of Greater China for Marriott International tells me.

Marriott did not just cater to Chinese preferences by offering slippers and hot water kettles in rooms, but by creating the "Li Yu Program" in the Asia-Pacific with plans to roll it out globally. In the Li Yu program, Marriott trains Guest Service Officers (GSOs) to understand what the needs and demands are for Chinese consumers specifically. For example, GSOs will know the best Chinese restaurants or activities that mainlanders specifically like. They set up special events for Marriott Rewards and SPG (Starwood Preferred Guest) Rewards Members—their two major loyalty programs—to go backstage to meet famous Chinese pop stars, or go to the pitch at Formula 1 Racing.

For Marriott, they are also seeing the shift for Chinese consumers wanting to spend more on experiences like water sports at properties in Maldives or Thailand, and not just about shopping—their GSOs help customers arrange their trips. As Ho tells me, "In Japan, for example, previously Chinese spent 75 percent of their budget on shopping, that number has dropped more to 40 percent as consumers spend more one lodging, dining out, and entertainment." Marriott trains their staff to understand the shifts in consumer behavior and be ready.

Part of this is by hiring mainland Chinese to work not just in China but in properties around the world. As Ho says, "Not only does this make staff happy that they have a career path and get to see the world, but our guests like to be able to communicate in Mandarin or even local dialects with people from their hometowns."

"Smart move," I thought as Ho told me what Marriott did. I remembered arguments I'd had with luxury brands, as late as 2012, which were hesitant to hire Chinese-speaking staff in their European and American stores. Worried that Chinese-targeted personnel might tarnish their image, these brands were, in fact, sacrificing consequential profits. When considering luxury brands, Chinese consumers are keen to communicate with staff before making a big purchase, particularly when having saved for it. Acutely intent on choosing the right product, the value-oriented Chinese also seek out brands whose staff can teach and guide them about available products, pricing, and quality.

Even more than catering to Chinese consumers, Marriott understood that it had to change business models in order to benefit from China, so they teamed up with internet giant Alibaba to create a joint venture to have a Tmall store that is jointly run and merges Marriott's expertise in hospitality with Alibaba's technology expertise. The joint venture is to create a seamless, one stop experience for Chinese traveling, and create a way for Alibaba's 500 million users, and Marriott's 100 million loyalty customers, to use each other's services better.

They will not just be offering hotel bookings, but also plane tickets and experiences like scuba diving or skydiving that Chinese consumers want. The system will also help Chinese secure visas. Payment is also an issue. As Ho told me, "Many Chinese do not have a credit card. We have already offered Alipay as an option for our guests in mainland China, and we plan to roll out this payment option globally."

Another critical method of catering to Chinese buyers involves offering indigenous payment platforms and channels, such as WeChat pay and Alipay. As most Chinese possess debit cards widely unaccepted by U.S. websites and physical stores alike, it is vital that brands either build indigenous payment channels into their website for product shipping, or sell their products on a localized site already equipped with the proper payment platforms. GNC, for example, has been very successful at selling from their U.S. website directly into China. When accessing the U.S. site from within China, pop up ads in Chinese direct Chinese consumers to special deals and products like Vitamin D preferred more by Chinese than Western consumers that get enough Vitamin D from sunshine. They also allow Chinese consumers to pay via Alibaba's Alipay or Unionpay, a Chinese payment network.

Key Action Items

1. Hire Chinese language staff in brand stores overseas. Chinese like to buy from a salesperson they can communicate with, as Marriott has demonstrated. And this preference—combined with that of increased understanding of a product—trumps most Chinese tourists' desire for an authentic experience of buying from a local. It is therefore advisable to have a mix of local and native Mandarin-speaking salespeople to offer authenticity but also ensure that an expert is on hand to answer questions.

2. Integrate Chinese payment channels, such as Alipay, into online shopping platforms and physical stores overseas, as Marriott has done. These will significantly enhance convenience for mainland-based Chinese online shoppers as well as China's numerous outbound travelers. It is common to find 7-Elevens and other retail stores in Thailand, for example, equipped to receive Chinese forms of payment.

Chapter 9
Conclusion

October, 2017

I received a call from Alyssa Abkowitz, a journalist with the *Wall Street Journal*. She wanted to ask me about the Xi Clapping game (measuring how fast and how many times people clap for Xi)launched by the internet giant Tencent that had debuted during the opening day of the 19th National People's Congress. To kick off the Congress which ultimately would choose who would be China's leaders for the next 5 years, President Xi heralded in an "Era of National Rejuvenation."

Most of the western press like the Guardian reported[i] that President Xi's speech went on for three and a half hours or that former President Jiang Zemin looked at his watch numerous times and had to use a handheld magnifying glass to read Xi's remarks. The Globe and Mail's Nathan VanderKlippe tweeted that he was trying to "I Spy" how many people were asleep at a photo taken of the Congress.[ii]

But in my interviews with Chinese and in scanning social media, I found the opposite was true—it was clear there was pride in President Xi's remarks that China was becoming powerful again and had the leader to carry out that rejuvenation.

I told Alyssa that most of the western media got the story wrong in their analysis of Xi's speech—rather than be bored of his remarks, Chinese were proud.[iii] To show support, they played the Xi clapping game where a clip of Xi talking about national rejuvenation was broadcast. Players could then click on the screen repeatedly to applaud. Within 24 hours, the game had been played nearly 1.5 billion times.

The Xi clapping game shows the intersection of Chinese government power, rallying Chinese consumer nationalism and the role of the business community. To show support for the government, Tencent launch a game that got Chinese excited about the direction of the country. To appease and make the government happy, companies domestically like Tencent have always tried to launch products and services that demonstrate their support. Companies that do this tend to profit more and get regulatory supported when needed.

The War for China's Wallet has shown China's President Xi Jinping is looking to signal to the world that China has reached a level of power that demands respect and equal billing to western nations that have ruled the world political system since the end of World War II. Although President Xi is not looking to replace

DOI 10.1515/9781501507618-009

the world system, he is looking to increase China's role in it and will utilize all economic and political means to achieve that—foreign companies that follow Tencent's playbook will gain the support of both the Chinese government and Chinese consumers.

President's Xi moves to gain power beyond its borders are really an extension of his political predecessors Presidents Hu Jintao and Jiang Zemin policies to regain the power China felt it had before the collapse of the Qing Dynasty in 1911. The difference is that President Xi has systematized his ambitions through direct initiatives like OBOR. More importantly, China has become an economic superpower and President Xi is now willing to use that economic Wallet to coerce other countries to follow its political ambitions and views.

With the power vacuum left by American Presidents Obama and Trump, China has accelerated its plans to increase power by dangling its wallet as a carrot. Countries are being forced to get closer to China economically and politically or else feel China's wrath through its economic cudgel.

At the same time, the whole world is now re-assessing its closeness to America. Other countries now realize that future American presidents might continue what they see as Trump's isolationist policies or the laissez faire policies of the Obama administration. Countries that are in a position to have to make a choice are reverting to back up plans to get closer to China and rely less on America. Regardless of whether Trump or his intellectual cohorts and followers remain in political power, China is presenting itself to be the responsible and, perhaps more importantly, predictable partner which countries, especially those with non-Democracy based political systems, prefer. It is also showing itself as a partner h which can improve your economy and that does not view economic trade as a zero sum game as some of Trump's advisors seem to believe.

Yet at the same time, there is deep unease in getting too close to China. There remains mistrust by many countries, especially those in close proximity in China, about losing political independence. *The War for China's Wallet* has shown that China does not seek allies in the conventional sense, but tries to force countries to follow it through a series of coercive economic techniques to effectively gain what it wants.

The power shift toward the East combined with China's use of money as a tool to achieve power creates great opportunities for companies whose political leaders cozy up to China as Duterte in the Philippines and Trudeau in Canada have done by moving into the *Hot* and *Warm Partner* categories. Real profits are to be made by western companies from President Xi's OBOR and other initiatives, as we have seen from Honeywell's example. The Chinese state and Chinese consumer wallets alike are powering the profits of even the largest companies and industries in the world.

Yet, despite all the profits to be made, there is uneasiness with an ascendant China in many quarters. The country forces countries to bend to its political will and ideology or else it will punish it—Hollywood is a prime example. Any actor or studio that makes China the bad guy in a film will be banned as what happened to Richard Gere for his closeness to the Dalai Lama and for his negative portrayal of China in his 1997 movie *Red Corner*. That is why you see so many movies with Chinese heroes, while the enemies remain North Koreans or Russians. Hollywood is a perfect tale of caution for the world's companies and countries alike--they make huge profits in China as box office sales there eclipsed America's in 2015 for the first time, but to continue, the producers must essentially sell their editorial independence.

If it is difficult for a company or sector to withstand Chinese pressure, it is even harder for a single company to adhere to Chinese requests without alienating its home markets. Even Cambridge University Press, the world's oldest publisher founded in 1534, in August 2017 announced that it had blocked online access to 300 articles that its import agency objected to in its China Quarterly journal. Editors stated that if they had not censored its own catalog, the Chinese government would block access to its entire catalog to Chinese consumers, as it had done to Lexis Nexis previously for not bowing down to censorship requests. Yet protests from the western world hit CUP, with authors and academics like Christopher Balding calling for boycotts until CUP re-posted links to the articles.

It is not known whether CUP will become blocked forever in China or if its journals will remain accessible to the Chinese population after it took its stand. Yet the reality is that CUP cannot stand on its own easily, only governments can push back against China's growing arm as the sticks of the State are too enormous.

Going forward, countries and companies have to understand the thinking process and viewpoints of both China's government and consumers, much as countries had to learn about America when it wielded so much influence in the post- World War II era. The ones that do, will see the Chinese Wallet powering profits for the next two decades. The ones that do not, well, will lose out on the world's greatest growth engine.

Endnotes

Preface

[i] Bloomberg, With Some Countries, China is in the Red, 2017,
http://www.bloomberg.com/news/articles/2017-08-20/with-some-countries-china-is-in-the-red

Chapter 1

[i] USC-US China Institute, President Clinton's Beijing University Speech, 1998,
http://china.usc.edu/president-clintons-beijing-university-speech-1998
[ii] GlobalSecurity.org, South China Sea Oil and Natural Gas,
http://www.globalsecurity.org/military/world/war/spratly-oil.htm
[iii] Global Risk Insights, What China's Aircraft Carrier Means for its Naval Defence Capabilities,
2017, http://globalriskinsights.com/2017/06/chinas-aircraft-carrier-naval-defence/
[iv] BBC News, Chinese jets intercept US aircraft over East China Sea, US says, 2017,
http://www.bbc.com/news/world-asia-china-39971267
[v] CNN World, China installs weapons on contested South China Sea islands, report says, 2016,
http://www.cnn.com/2016/12/14/asia/south-china-sea-artificial-islands-spratlys-weapon-systems/index.html
[vi] CNN World, South China Sea: China building more islands?, 2016,
http://www.cnn.com/2016/09/08/asia/south-china-sea-scarborough-shoal-philippines-china/index.html
[vii] CNN World, China installs weapons on contested South China Sea islands, report says, 2016,
http://www.cnn.com/2016/12/14/asia/south-china-sea-artificial-islands-spratlys-weapon-systems/index.html
[viii] Reuters, Greece blocks EU statement on China human rights at U.N., 2017,
http://www.reuters.com/article/us-eu-un-rights-idUSKBN1990FP?utm_campaign=trueAnthem:+Trending+Content&utm_content=5946737704d3011604316be5&utm_medium=trueAnthem&utm_source=twitter
[ix] The Diplomat, How China Came to Dominate Cambodia, 2016,
http://thediplomat.com/2016/09/how-china-came-to-dominate-cambodia/
[x] NPR, U.S. Demands Cambodia Repay Loan From Vietnam War Era, 2017,
http://www.npr.org/2017/05/30/530683478/u-s-demands-cambodia-repay-loan-from-vietnam-war-era
[xi] South China Morning Post, How Singapore's military vehicles became Beijing's diplomatic
weapon, 2016, http://www.scmp.com/week-asia/politics/article/2051322/how-singapores-military-vehicles-became-beijings-diplomatic
[xii] South China Morning Post, What's really making Beijing angry with Singapore?, 2016,
http://www.scmp.com/week-asia/opinion/article/2024089/whats-really-making-beijing-angry-singapore

DOI 10.1515/9781501507618-010

xiii Bloomberg News, China Frictions May See Singapore Miss Out on Belt-Road Billions, 2017, https://www.bloomberg.com/politics/articles/2017-05-18/singapore-out-in-the-cold-as-southeast-asia-chases-china-cash

xiv Huffington Post, Mango Wars Get Sticky As Chinese Vow To Boycott Filipino Fruit, 2016, http://www.huffingtonpost.com.au/2016/07/14/mango-wars-get-sticky-as-chinese-vow-to-boycott-filipino-fruit_a_21432519/

xv The US-China Business Council, US Exports to China (2006-2016), https://www.uschina.org/reports/us-exports/national

xvi Business Insider, CHART: How America's Trade Deficit With China Exploded From Nothing To $316 Billion In 26 Years, 2013, http://www.businessinsider.com/chart-us-trade-deficit-with-china-2013-4

xvii U.S. Department of Agriculture, U.S., China Finalize Details to Send U.S. Beef to China , 2017, https://www.usda.gov/media/press-releases/2017/06/12/us-china-finalize-details-send-us-beef-china

xviii KSL, What Legacy Will Huntsman Leave in China, 2011, http://www.ksl.com/index.php?nid=148&sid=15337586

xix Twitter, 2017, https://twitter.com/jorge_guajardo/status/885725117958860800

xx UC San Diego, Is China the Next Mexico? Lessons from the One-Party Model, 2014, https://china.ucsd.edu/_files/Jorge_Guajardo_keynote

Global Edge, Mexico: Trade Statistics, https://globaledge.msu.edu/countries/mexico/tradestats

BBC News, Mexico to pay China rail firm for cancelling project, 2015, http://www.bbc.com/news/business-32840712

Chapter 2

i KBS World Radio, N. Korea Criticizes China over Sanctions and Pressure, 2017, http://world.kbs.co.kr/english/news/news_hotissue_detail.htm?No=10070379

ii Global Times, Building up nuclear deterrence best response to THAAD, 2017, http://www.globaltimes.cn/content/1037016.shtml

iii People's Daily Online, China should offer military response to THAAD: expert, 2017, http://en.people.cn/n3/2017/0427/c90000-9208655.html

iv Global Risk Insights, Why China's boycott of South Korea is viral marketing genius, 2017, http://globalriskinsights.com/2017/03/china-south-korea-boycott-viral-marketing-genius/

v Global Risk Insights, Why China's boycott of South Korea is viral marketing genius, 2017, http://globalriskinsights.com/2017/03/china-south-korea-boycott-viral-marketing-genius/

vi Reuters, China reacts with anger, threats after South Korean missile defense decision, 2017, http://www.reuters.com/article/us-southkorea-usa-thaad-china-idUSKBN16709W

vii Reuters, Hyundai flags weaker China sales after missile row; Kia's March China sales halved: source, 2017, http://www.reuters.com/article/us-southkorea-autos-china-idUSKBN17511C

viii Reuters, South Korea, U.S. to deploy THAAD missile defense, drawing China rebuke, 2016, http://www.reuters.com/article/us-southkorea-usa-thaad-idUSKCN0ZO084

[ix] Newsweek, U.S. Military Presence In Asia: Troops Stationed In Japan, South Korea and Beyond, 2017, http://www.newsweek.com/us-military-japan-north-korea-asia-590278 (figure as of late 2016)

[x] USA Today, South Korean President Moon Jae-in suspends further THAAD deployment, 2017, https://www.usatoday.com/story/news/world/2017/06/07/south-korean-president-moon-jae-suspends-thaad-deployment/102582572/
Global Times, South Korean president may follow path of Duterte to maximize benefit, 2017, http://www.globaltimes.cn/content/1047450.shtml

[xi] The Observatory of Economic Complexity, http://atlas.media.mit.edu/en/profile/country/mng/

[xii] The Diplomat, Norway-China Relations 'Unfrozen', 2016, http://thediplomat.com/2016/12/norway-china-relations-unfrozen/
NobelPrize.org, The Norwegian Nobel Committee, https://www.nobelprize.org/nobel_prizes/peace/prize_awarder/committee.html

[xiii] Forbes, Yes, China Has Fully Arrived As A Superpower, 2009, https://www.forbes.com/2009/12/15/china-superpower-status-leadership-citizenship-trends.html

[xiv] Reuters, Forbidden City coffee shop replaces Starbucks, 2007, https://www.reuters.com/article/us-china-starbucks-idUSHAR44723720070924

[xv] CNBC, Starbucks offers to pay health insurance for parents of some China employees, 2017, http://www.cnbc.com/2017/04/13/starbucks-offers-to-pay-health-insurance-for-parents-of-some-china-employees.html

Chapter 3

[i] CNN, Qatar hosts largest US military base in Mideast, 2017, http://edition.cnn.com/2017/06/05/middleeast/qatar-us-largest-base-in-mideast/index.html

[ii] Reuters, China, Saudi Arabia eye $65 billion in deals as king visits, 2017, http://www.reuters.com/article/us-saudi-asia-china-idUSKBN16N0G9

[iii] ValueWalk, OBOR Completely Dwarfs The Marshall Plan, 2017, http://www.valuewalk.com/2017/05/obor-2/

[iv] China Daily, President Xi's Speech at Arab League Headquarters: Full Text, 2016, http://www.chinadaily.com.cn/world/2016xivisitmiddleeast/2016-01/22/content_23191229.htm
Foreign Policy, China's New Grand Strategy for the Middle East, 2016, http://foreignpolicy.com/2016/01/26/chinas-new-middle-east-grand-strategy-iran-saudi-arabia-oil-xi-jinping/
Rand Corporation, China in the Middle East, 2016, http://www.rand.org/content/dam/rand/pubs/research_reports/RR1200/RR1229/RAND_RR1229.pdf

[v] China Daily, Wen: 100m Chinese live in poverty, 2012, http://www.chinadaily.com.cn/china/2012wenvisitla/2012-06/21/content_15516310.htm
Forbes, China Is Just Like A Teenage Boy, 2010, https://www.forbes.com/2010/01/19/china-teenage-google-leadership-citizenship-rein.html

vi Amazon, The End of Copycat China: The Rise of Creativity, Innovation, and Individualism in Asia, 2014, https://www.amazon.com/End-Copycat-China-Creativity-Individualism/dp/1118926765/ref=sr_1_1?ie=UTF8&qid=1421993431&sr=8-1&keywords=shaun+rein
Amazon, The End of Cheap China, Revised and Updated: Economic and Cultural Trends That Will Disrupt the World, 2014, https://www.amazon.com/End-Cheap-China-Revised-Updated/dp/1118926803/ref=pd_sim_14_1?_encoding=UTF8&pd_rd_i=1118926803&pd_rd_r=7TSEFVCF4QSR88TAXZ8M&pd_rd_w=ySTzH&pd_rd_wg=Giu01&psc=1&refRID=7TSEFVCF4QSR88TAXZ8M
vii Radio Free Asia, Xi To Be 'Weak' President, 2012, http://www.rfa.org/english/news/china/xi-jinping-11122012110129.html
viii Darwin Wealth Creation, Foxconn: World's No. 1 contract electronics maker - Washington Post, 2017, https://darwinwealthcreation.com/foxconn-world039s-no-1-contract-electronics-maker-washington-post/

Chapter 4

i AEI, China's SOE sector is bigger than some would have us think, 2016, http://www.aei.org/publication/chinas-soe-sector-is-bigger-than-some-would-have-us-think/
ii Buy Buy China, Bright: Can Bulgarian bacteria save Chinese milk?, 2012, http://www.buybuychina.com/bright-can-bulgarian-bacteria-save-chinese-milk/

Chapter 5

i Reuters, China's Wanda buys Ironman Triathlon owner for $650 million, 2015, http://www.reuters.com/article/us-world-triathlon-m-a-dalian-wanda-idUSKCN0QW04X20150827
Hilton, Hilton Worldwide Closes Sale of the Waldorf Astoria New York and Reaches Agreements to Redeploy Proceeds to Acquire Five Landmark Hotels, 2015, http://newsroom.hilton.com/index.cfm/news/hilton-worldwide-closes-sale-of-the-waldorf-astoria-new-york-and-reaches-agreements-to-redeploy-proceeds-to-acquire-five-landmark-hotels
ii The Telegraph, Alibaba buys half of top Chinese football team for $192m, 2014, http://www.telegraph.co.uk/finance/newsbysector/mediatechnologyandtelecoms/digital-media/10879802/Alibaba-buys-half-of-top-Chinese-football-team-for-192m.html
iii Reuters, China tells workplaces they must have Communist Party units, 2015, http://www.reuters.com/article/us-china-politics-idUSKBN0OF09X20150530
iv CNBC, China's tech giants are pouring billions into US start-ups, 2017, http://www.cnbc.com/2017/03/08/chinas-tech-giants-are-pouring-billions-into-us-start-ups.html
v Reuters, China's XCMG buys majority of Germany's Schwing, 2012, http://www.reuters.com/article/xcmg-schwing-idUSL6E8FJ1U620120419

Chapter 6

[i] National Women's Health Network, 10 Years after HPV Vaccines' Approval, Where Do We Stand?, 2016, https://www.nwhn.org/10-years-hpv-vaccines-approval-stand/

[ii] Quartz, Japanese diaper makers are fighting a new competitor: Chinese diaper pirates, 2013, https://qz.com/160028/japanese-diaper-makers-are-fighting-a-new-competitor-chinese-diaper-pirates/

[iii] Asian Correspondent, China arrests 130 suspects over expired and improperly stored vaccines, 2016, https://asiancorrespondent.com/2016/03/china-arrests-130-suspects-over-expired-and-improperly-stored-vaccines/#trpltpqQTUK8SqCT.97

The Guardian, China's vaccine scandal widens as 37 arrested over illegal sales, 2016, https://www.theguardian.com/world/2016/mar/23/chinas-vaccine-scandal-widens-as-37-arrested-over-illegal-sales

[iv] Financial Times, Okamoto condoms: objects of desire for Chinese tourists in Japan, 2015, https://www.google.co.th/url?sa=t&rct=j&q=&esrc=s&source=web&cd=1&cad=rja&uact=8&ved=0ahUKEwjyo76sm_bUAhWBsY8KHaLUDF4QFggkMAA&url=https%3A%2F%2Fwww.ft.com%2Fcontent%2Fda364b80-4cb8-11e5-9b5d-89a026fda5c9%3Fmhq5j%3De1&usg=AFQjCNHGKCORruliZ-WE6e5TZ75_EZg4Jw

Daily Mail, Protection racket: Millions of TOXIC condoms seized in China after police raid gang who were selling knock-offs that cost 1p each to make, 2015, http://www.dailymail.co.uk/news/peoplesdaily/article-3050283/Millions-toxic-condoms-seized-China-gang-caught-selling-knock-offs-cost-1p-make.html

Bloomberg, Chinese Group Buys James Bond Condom Brand, 2017, https://www.bloomberg.com/news/articles/2017-05-25/the-name-s-bond-jissbon-condom-named-after-007-sold-to-china

[v] Huffington Post, The Confucian Consumer and Chinese Luxury: FAQs, 2010, http://www.huffingtonpost.com/tom-doctoroff/the-confucian-consumer-an_b_547295.html

[vi] Gary King, How Censorship in China Allows Government Criticism but Silences Collective Expression, 2013, https://gking.harvard.edu/publications/how-censorship-china-allows-government-criticism-silences-collective-expression

Palgrave, Governance and Politics of China, 2015, https://he.palgrave.com/page/detail/?sf1=barcode&st1=9781137445278&loc=uk

[vii] The Wall Street Journal, P&G Tripped Up by Its Assumptions About Diapers in China, 2015, https://www.wsj.com/articles/p-g-tripped-up-by-its-assumptions-about-diapers-in-china-1439445897

Quartz, Johnson & Johnson is treating Chinese customers like "second-class" citizens, say the Chinese media, 2013, https://qz.com/94519/johnson-johnson-is-treating-chinese-customers-like-second-class-citizens-say-the-chinese-media/

Chapter 7

[i] Los Angeles Times, How Arcadia is remaking itself as a magnet for Chinese money, 2014, http://www.latimes.com/entertainment/arts/la-et-cm-arcadia-immigration-architecture-20140511-story.html

[ii] Migration Policy Institute, Chinese Immigrants in the United States, 2017, http://www.migrationpolicy.org/article/chinese-immigrants-united-states

[iii] Bloomberg, Why Are Chinese Millionaires Buying Mansions in an L.A. Suburb?, 2014, https://www.bloomberg.com/news/articles/2014-10-15/chinese-home-buying-binge-transforms-california-suburb-arcadia

[iv] PBS, Column: What's really at stake in the EB-5 investor visa overhaul: honesty, 2015, http://www.pbs.org/newshour/making-sense/column-whats-really-at-stake-in-the-eb-5-investor-visa-overhaul-honesty/

[v] OurDocuments.gov, Chinese Exclusion Act (1882), https://www.ourdocuments.gov/doc.php?flash=false&doc=47

[vi] Goggle, https://www.google.com/search?q=china+unemployment+rate&oq=china+unemployment+rate&aqs=chrome.0.0l6.3159j0j9&sourceid=chrome&ie=UTF-8

[vii] PRI, Why Chinese immigrants choose America, 2012, https://www.pri.org/stories/2012-12-21/why-chinese-immigrants-choose-america
Pew Research Center, The Rise of Asian Americans, 2012, http://www.pewsocialtrends.org/2012/06/19/the-rise-of-asian-americans/

[viii] CNN, Why Asians want to move to the U.S., 2012, http://www.cnn.com/2012/07/19/business/asia-u-s-immigrants/index.html

Chapter 9

[i] The Guardian, Xi Jinping tests eyelids – and bladders – with three-and-a-half hour speech, 2017, https://www.theguardian.com/world/2017/oct/18/xi-jinping-tests-eyelids-and-bladders-with-three-and-a-half-hour-speech-congress

[ii] Twitter, 2017, https://twitter.com/nvanderklippe/status/920494394872037383

[iii] The Wall Street Journal, Three Cheers for Xi Jinping! Wait, Make That a Billion, 2017, https://www.wsj.com/articles/tencent-launches-smartphone-game-in-support-of-chinas-president-1508415173

Index